Instructor's Resource Manual

for

Samovar, Porter, and McDaniel's

Intercultural Communication
A Reader

Eleventh Edition

Margaret Bennett Walters
Kennesaw State University

THOMSON
WADSWORTH

Australia • Brazil • Canada • Mexico • Singapore • Spain • United Kingdom • United States

Printed in the United States of America

1 2 3 4 5 6 7 09 08 07 06 05

Printer: Thomson West

ISBN 0-495-00161-9

Thomson Higher Education
10 Davis Drive
Belmont, CA 94002-3098
USA

CONTENTS

INTRODUCTION

This resource manual has been designed to assist instructors in using McDaniel, Samovar, and Porter's *Intercultural Communication: A Reader,* Eleventh Edition. This introduction includes suggestions for organizing the course, a brief description of chapter resources, and suggestions for leading post-exercise class discussions. In addition, instructional aids such as sample course schedules for both quarter and semester systems and a number of film, video, and Internet resources are provided.

ORGANIZING THE COURSE

There are a number of ways to set up a college-level intercultural communication course. Some instructors use a culture-specific approach, where the communicative behavior of one or more specific cultures is studied. Other instructors follow a culture-general approach, where the influence of culture on the communication process is explored as it applies to nearly all cultures. There are also courses that emphasize specifically the psychological, sociological, or linguistic influences on intercultural communication. Some intercultural communication college courses are similar to intercultural training workshops because they emphasize experimental simulation and role-playing activities designed primarily to increase students' cultural sensitivity and intercultural communication competence. *Intercultural Communication: A Reader* provides a set of readings that would complement any one or combination of these approaches. The diversity of the articles provides instructors with enough flexibility to teach a course in intercultural communication based on their own personal teaching style and approach to the subject.

CHAPTER RESOURCES

Each chapter of this manual is divided into six sections: Chapter Synopsis, Chapter Outline, Discussion Questions, Exercises, Popular Film Suggestions, Test Items (Multiple Choice, True/False, and Essay Questions).

Chapter Synopsis

Each chapter synopsis provides a summary of each article included in the text chapter. Special points of interests are identified.

Chapter Outline

The chapter outlines cover the significant points of the essays in each chapter. The outline is organized by essay, yet where appropriate, information is grouped in one area rather than separately by essay.

Popular Film Suggestions

Two to three popular films are suggested for use with each chapter. The films have been chosen because they portray some of the characteristics of intercultural communication discussed in the readings. You might use a whole film, requiring students to view it outside of class or showing it during class if you have time. You could also choose scenes from a movie to show to highlight some intercultural communication. In any event, *you should view any film you plan to preview in class* for its appropriateness to your particular audience of students.

Discussion Questions

Many instructors prefer to incorporate class discussion as a primary mode of instruction. Therefore, each chapter offers discussion questions for each article that will inspire students to talk about the readings.

Exercises

Activities can be particularly engaging for students in an intercultural communication course. They offer a change from the traditional university lecture by allowing students to demonstrate and experience concepts provided by the instructor or the course textbooks. Additionally, using activities in the classroom is a powerful way to engage students in the course and in their own learning. Probably most important in the intercultural communication course is that activities transcend the classroom: "Instructional games, simulations, and role plays can enhance relevance of course material as students apply it in situations often designed to take them beyond the immediate classroom" (Nyquist & Wulff, 1990, p.350).

This manual offers a variety of instructional activities for each chapter of the text. The following is a description of each activity type and accompanying benefits.

Role-Play:

Role-playing is a training activity where two participants (or more though larger numbers are not common) take on characteristics of people other than themselves in order to attain a clearly defined objective. These "other people"—or roles—are usually fictitious although they must be completely believable in the eyes of the training population for the role-play to work. Participants who are not actively involved in the role-play function as observers and look for certain things related to the overall objectives as the role-play unfolds (McCaffery, 1995, p. 19). Benefits include:

- Participants get a clear sense of identifiable skills in interpersonal situations, how they work, and the impact of things done effectively and ineffectively—participants have an opportunity to feel what it is like to try out new or enhanced skills in real situations.
- Participants also get a chance to feel what it is like to be in another role. (McCaffery, 1995, p. 24)

Simulation Games:

Simulation games provide interactive opportunities to practice new behaviors and experiment with new attitudes and points of view in a non-threatening, non-judgmental environment. They are particularly useful in intercultural training, since, in a very short time, they can stimulate cognitive and affective understanding and broaden participants' perspectives (Sisk, 1995, p. 82). Benefits include:

- Promotes critical thinking as participants analyze possible moves and probable consequences of those moves. Participants also must plan rationally and think through countermoves.
- Because chance is introduced, simulation games demonstrate that life is not always affected by logical plans or even intuitive solutions
- Students learn on three levels: information, process, and strategies
- Simulation games teach social values such as competition, cooperation, and empathy
- Simulation games increase participants' knowledge and skills
- Simulation games establish a sense of group dynamics and self awareness among participants.
  (Sisk, 1995, p. 89)

Critical Incidents:

Critical incidents are brief descriptions of situations in which there is a misunderstanding, problem, or conflict arising from cultural differences between interacting parties or where there is a problem of cross-cultural adaptation. Each incident gives only enough information to set the stage, describe what happened, and possibly provide the feelings and reactions of the parties involved. It does not explain the cultural differences that the parties bring to the situation. These are discovered or revealed as a part of the exercise (Wright, 1995, p. 128). Benefits include:

- Increases participants' awareness of their own typical, idiosyncratic, or culturally determined interpretations and explanations of others' behavior and their own attitudes and responses in situations such as the ones described
- Draws out for comparison and analysis of various interpretations and perceptions of participants
- Clarifies the cultural differences in the incidents that might have contributed to the misunderstandings, problems, and conflicts
- Helps students behave more appropriately and effectively in similar situations.
  (Wright, 1995, p. 129)

Culture Assimilator/Intercultural Sensitizer:

"This instrument is specifically constructed to sensitize persons from one cultural group to the assumptions, behaviors, norms, perceptions, interpretations, attitudes, and values—in short, the subjective culture-of persons from another cultural group" (Triandis as cited in Albert, 1995, p. 165). Benefits include:

- Imparts knowledge of the subjective culture of the target group

- Assists participants develop more accurate expectations in intercultural interactions
- Helps participants interact more effectively with persons from the target culture
- Improves knowledge and application of cross-cultural communication concepts
- Increases participants' intercultural sensitivity.
  (Triandis as cited in Albert, 1995, p. 165)

Case Studies:

Case studies are realistic examples of intercultural situations that include "sufficient detail to make it possible for the participants in a training program to analyze the problems involved and to determine possible solutions" (Nadler as cited in Lacey & Trowbridge, 1995, p. 187). Benefits include:

- Reflects the actual complexities of cross-cultural interaction and illustrates that such situations are rarely as simple as they seem
- Encourages participants to question the notion that there is one right way or one correct answer
- Helps participants learn to weigh carefully the many factors that affect cross-cultural interaction and to avoid snap judgments that may have negative consequences for the trainee once on the job or in the field
- Encourages students to learn from each other and to appreciate different opinions and is thus particularly effective in a group representing different cultures.
  (Nadler as cited in Lacey & Trowbridge, 1995, p. 193)

Field Exercises:

Field exercises take the students outside the classroom to examine or experience the specified intercultural communication topic in real life. Benefits include:

- Increases their knowledge and behavior by experiencing the actual event outside the classroom
- Allows students to experience members of other cultures
- Allows students the opportunity to practice the intercultural communication skills that they have learned in the classroom and from the textbook
- Helps students interact more effectively with members of other cultures.

Media Searches:

Media searches take students through all forms of media (the Internet and World Wide Web, papers, films, magazines, television, the arts, and so on) to find examples of specific intercultural concepts. Benefits include:

- Students learn the widespread nature of the cultural phenomenon
- Students come to realize the cultural diversity of the world
- Students realize the inevitability of cultural contact

- Concepts are applied to the larger social setting and globalization.

Test Items

Test items are included at the end of each chapter. Multiple choice, true/false, and essay questions are provided for constructing examinations.

SUGGESTIONS FOR POST-EXERCISE DISCUSSIONS

A helpful tool to use when planning an exercise is Covert's (1978) **EDIT** system. This system suggests that students "**E**xperience" the activity, "**D**escribe" what happened, "**I**nfer" general principles from the activity, and then finally "**T**ransfer" or apply the principles to their own lives. When discussing the exercise experience with students, Bloom's (1956) taxonomy of educational objectives is helpful for developing different types of questions and bringing students to different stages of awareness. The example below illustrates how this taxonomy can be used to lead a class discussion towards greater levels of higher-order thinking after conducting one case study exercise described in Chapter Three:

Exercise 3.5: Conflicting Messages

(1) *Knowledge*: Describe the interaction between Tim and Raj.
(2) *Understanding*: How did Raj react to Tim's behavior?
(3) *Application*: Have you ever been in a situation when someone perceived you as unfriendly even though you did not feel particularly unfriendly or distant?
(4) *Analysis*: What happens when this occurs in an intercultural situation? What other factors are involved that are not necessarily present in an intracultural situation?
(5) *Evaluation*: Did you think Tim was rude? Do you think Raj overreacted?

Whatever method of questioning you use, any activity should always be discussed or debriefed afterwards in some fashion. A carefully considered list of questions is useful in guiding this discussion.

Activities often serve as illustrative catalysts for the more illuminating discussion session that takes place afterwards. It is during these classroom discussions where students come to grips with the concepts illustrated in the activity by verbalizing and sorting through their experience. The post-activity discussion is not merely a quick overview of what happened, with a few substantive comments made only by the teacher. As Nyquist (1979) has stated, an instructional discussion is a developmental process whose "purpose is to move students toward new understanding and appreciation" (p. 7). Students should be talking to each other with the instructor acting as question poser, clarifier, and summarizer.

SAMPLE COURSE SCHEDULES

It is common for instructors to use *Intercultural Communication: A Reader* in conjunction with another intercultural communication textbook. Although the reader can be used alone, undergraduate textbooks in intercultural communication can provide a comprehensive foundation for the study of culture, communication, and intercultural interaction. The course schedules provided on the following pages propose two organizational frameworks for using the *Reader* as the sole reading material in an intercultural communication course. They are intended only as guides and not as completed, ready-to-use course schedules. Your own course objectives, assignments, reading materials, and scheduling preferences must of course be considered when constructing a syllabus and course schedule.

If you are using a textbook in addition to the *Reader,* you will need to modify these frameworks accordingly. Because the course schedules provided include the use of every article in the *Reader,* these schedules will also need to be revised if you plan on using only selected articles. Weekly topic areas and corresponding readings are provided for both a semester and quarter system. The course schedules were developed using the basic organization of the text's eight chapters: (1) Understanding Intercultural Communication, (2) Cultural Identity, (3) International Cultures, (4) Co-Cultures, (5) Intercultural Messages, (6) Cultural Contexts, (7) Communicating Interculturally, and (8) Ethical Considerations.

ORGANIZATION OF A 10-WEEK QUARTER COURSE

Class Period	Content	Weekly Reading
Week 1		
1	Introduction to the Course	
2	Understanding Intercultural Communication	McDaniel/Samovar/Porter
3	Imagining Culture	Cargile
Week 2		
4	Culture and Conflict	Triandis
5	Worldview and Intercultural Communication	Ishii, Klopf, Cooke
6	The Practice of Intercultural Communication	Jensen
Week 3		
7	Cultural Identity	Collier
	Finding My Whiteness	Krizek
8	A Polish Jewish American Story	Drzeweicka/Draznin
9	The Hybrid Identities of Gender Queer	Zimmerman/Geist-Martin
	Ambiguous Insiders	Naber
Week 4		
10	Living Together Vs. Going It Alone	Nesbitt
	The *Wei* (Positioning)—*Ming* (Naming)—*Lianmian* (Face)	Jia
11	India: The Dance of Shiva	Gannon
	Personality and Person Perception in Africa	Peltzer
12	Communication with Egyptians	Begley
Week 5		
13	Unum and Pluribus	Kim
	Does the Worm Live in the Ground	Wilbur
14	Let Me Count the Ways: African/American/ European-American Marriages	Stringer
	Gendered Communication Styles	Wood/Reich
15	Which Is My Good Leg?	Braithwaite
	In Plain Sight: Gay and Lesbian	Eadie
Week 6		
16	The Nexus of Language, Communication, And Culture	Fong
17	German Language: Whose Language, Whose Culture	Kelly-Holmes
18	Dialogue and Cultural Communication Codes Between Israeli Jews and Palestinians	Ellis/Maoz

Week 7		
19	Public Speaking Patterns in Kenya	Miller
20	Mexican *Dichos*: Lessons through Language	Roy
21	Unraveling Cultural Cues: Dimensions of Nonverbal Communication Across Cultures	Andersen/Wang
	Japanese Nonverbal Communication	McDaniel
Week 8		
22	U.S. Americans and Mexicans Working Together: Five Core Concepts	Lindsley/Braithwaite
	Application of American Management Theories and Practices to the Indian Business Environment	Gopalan/Stahl
23	Contrasts in Discussion Behaviors of German and American Managers	Friday
	"Half-Truths" in Argentina, Brazil, and India: An Intercultural Analysis of Physician-Patient Communications	Rao
24	Exploring Culture in Nursing	Mendyka
	Culture and Communication in the Classroom	Gay
	Social Dynamics of the Multicultural Classroom	Le Roux
Week 9		
25	Intercultural Awareness	Chen/Starosta
26	Managing Intercultural Conflicts Effectively	Ting-Toomey
27	The Role of Dialogue in Managing Intergroup Conflict	Roy/Oludaja
	Sojourner Adaptation	Begley
Week 10		
28	Cultural Diversity: A World View	Sowell
	The Limits to Cultural Diversity	Cleveland
29	Intercultural Personhood: An Integration of Eastern and Western Perspectives	Kim
30	Ethical Intercultural Technical Communication	Dragga
	Business Ethics and Intercultural Communication	Brinkmann

ORGANIZATION OF A 15-WEEK SEMESTER COURSE

Class Period	Content	Weekly Reading
Week 1		
1	Introduction to the Course	
2	Understanding Intercultural Communication	McDaniel/Samovar/Porter
3	Imagining Culture	Cargile
Week 2		
4	Culture and Conflict	Triandis
5	Worldview and Intercultural Communication	Ishii,Klopf,Cooke
6	The Practice of Intercultural Communication	Jensen
Week 3		
7	Cultural Identity	Collier
	Finding My Whiteness	Krizek
8	A Polish Jewish American Story	Drzeweicka/Draznin
9	The Hybrid Identities of Gender Queer	Zimmerman/Geist-Martin
Week 4		
10	Ambiguous Insiders	Naber
11	Living Together Vs. Going It Alone	Nesbitt
12	The *Wei* (Positioning)—*Ming* (Naming)—*Lianmian* (Face)	Jia
Week 5		
13	India: The Dance of Shiva	Gannon
14	Personality and Person Perception in Africa	Peltzer
15	Communication with Egyptians	Begley
Week 6		
16	Unum and Pluribus	Kim
17	Does the Worm Live in the Ground	Wilbur
18	Let Me Count the Ways: African/American/ European-American Marriages	Stringer
Week 7		
19	Gendered Communication Styles	Wood/Reich
20	Which Is My Good Leg?	Braithwaite
21	In Plain Sight: Gay and Lesbian	Eadie
Week 8		
22	The Nexus of Language, Communication, And Culture	Fong
23	German Language: Whose Language, Whose Culture	Kelly-Holmes
24	Dialogue and Cultural Communication	

	Codes Between Israeli Jews and Palestinians	Ellis/Maoz
Week 9		
25	Public Speaking Patterns in Kenya	Miller
26	Mexican *Dichos*: Lessons through Language	Roy
27	Unraveling Cultural Cues: Dimensions of Nonverbal Communication Across Cultures	Andersen/Wang
Week 10		
28	Japanese Nonverbal Communication	McDaniel
29	U.S. Americans and Mexicans Working Together: Five Core Concepts	Lindsley/Braithwaite
30	Application of American Management Theories and Practices to the Indian Business Environment	Gopalan/Stahl
Week 11		
31	Contrasts in Discussion Behaviors of German and American Managers	Friday
32	"Half-Truths" in Argentina, Brazil, and India: An Intercultural Analysis of Physician-Patient Communications	Rao
33	Exploring Culture in Nursing	Mendyka
Week 12		
34	Culture and Communication in the Classroom	Gay
35	Social Dynamics of the Multicultural Classroom	Le Roux
36	Intercultural Awareness	Chen/Starosta
Week 13		
37	Managing Intercultural Conflicts Effectively	Ting-Toomey
38	The Role of Dialogue in Managing Intergroup Conflict	Roy/Oludaja
39	Sojourner Adaptation	Begley
Week 14		
40	Cultural Diversity: A World View	Sowell
41	The Limits to Cultural Diversity	Cleveland
42	Intercultural Personhood: An Integration of Eastern and Western Perspectives	Kim
Week 15		
43	Ethical Intercultural Technical Communication	Dragga
44	Business Ethics and Intercultural Communication	Brinkmann
45	Course Summary	

FILM AND VIDEO RESOURCES

This section includes several film and video resources that connect with and complement many of the articles in the *Reader.* With the literally thousands of titles available to instructors throughout the United States, you should be able to find several non-print resources to enhance the reading and lecture material in your course. A short, one-sentence description is given for each title and, when available, the year, publisher, and length of the film or video are provided. You should view those films and videos that you are interested in before showing them in your class. Other titles may be found by checking your own school's library reference section and media collection, or conducting a search on the internet. In addition, several titles of film and video locators are provided to help you in your search for instructional media materials.

You should discuss each film with your students. Students should have an opportunity to talk about what they saw and heard so that concepts and ideas explored in readings, lectures, and exercises may be linked to each film.

Note: Popular films are listed individually in each chapter.

Titles

A Clash of Cultures, 1986, 60 min.: Explores African cultural adaptation to outside forces.

All Under Heaven: Life in a Chinese Village, 1986, 58 min.: Chinese language film (with subtitles) that tells of the history and life of one village in rural China.

American Tongues, 1987, 56 min.: Through interviews with U.S. Americans from many regions of the country, people discuss their attitudes and perceptions of theirs and others' speech.

America—Black and White, NBC, 1981, 75 min.: Through profiles of common citizens, details the serious social and economic situations of African Americans in the U.S.

Asianization of America, 1986, 26 min.: Explores the increasing influence of Asian immigrants to the United States, their influence on the American market, and negative stereotypes which Americans have had toward Asian immigrants.

Being Muslim in India, 1984, 41 min.: A family portrait of a Sunni Muslim and successful businessman in India.

Birthwrite: Growing Up Hispanic, 1989, 60 min.: Through interviews with Latino writers born or raised in the United States of Mexican and Puerto Rican parents, provides insight into the different worlds these writers experienced as children of a minority group.

Black on White, 1986, 58 min.: A film that explores the origins of black English and life in the U.S.

Brazil Hew of South America, 1988, 55 min.: Basic introduction to the people of Brazil, including people of different social, ethnic, and geographic groups.

Christians, Jews and Muslims in Medieval Spain, 1989, 52 min.: Traces the history of Christian, Jewish, and Muslim life in the Iberian peninsula from Roman times through Muslim conquest, through Christian reconquest. Emphasizes unique coexistence.

Communication- The Nonverbal Agenda, 1988, 20 min.: Discusses the influence that nonverbal cues can have on the meanings of our words.

Donahue: Street People, WGN, 1980, 45 min.: Interviews with several homeless people.

Ethnic Notions, 1987, 56 min.: A comprehensive, historical look at cultural stereotypes of African-Americans as portrayed through the U. S. media.

Gefilte Fish, 1984, 15 min.: Cultural changes are represented as three generations of Jewish women prepare Gefilte fish, a traditional holiday dish.

Hard Time, Dave Bell Productions, 1980, 50 min.: Documents life in a maximum security prison.

I'isaw: Hopi Coyote Stories, 1981, 28 Min.: The social group is represented in the Hopi Indians of Arizona who have been relatively successful in maintaining their land base, language, ceremonies, and cultural identity.

Introduction to American Deaf Cultural Rules of Social Interaction, 1985, 60 min.: Provides an introduction to social interaction among people who are deaf.

Introduction to American Deaf Culture- Values, 1986, 60 min.: Provides an introduction to the unique values and traditions of persons who are deaf.

Language,1988, 55 min. (The Mind Series, Part 7): Explores different theories and ideas about the evolution of human language.

Living Africa: A Village Experience, 1983, 34 min.: Portrays the daily experiences and concerns of the people of Wassetake, a small village on the Senegal River in West Africa.

The Five Pillars of Islam, 1988, 30 min.: Explains the major religious principles of Islam.

The Pinks, and the Blues, (Nova), WGBB, 1980, 57 min.: Discusses the socialization process that makes boys "male" and girls "female."

The Primal Mind, 1983, 58 min.: Explores the basic differences between Native American and Western cultures.

Racism 101, 1988, 58 min.: Documents the racial tension that exploded on the University of Michigan campus after racist jokes were aired.

The Rice Ladle—The Changing Role of Women in Japan, 1981, 28 min.: Explores the changing roles of women in Japan.

We're Moving Up: The Hispanic Migration, NBC, 1980, 81 min.: Discusses the population and socioeconomic changes of the Latino people; values, cultural characteristics, and historical information are addressed.

Yo Soy, 1985, 60 min.: Documents the progress that Chicanos have made in politics, education, labor, and economic development in the past two decades.

Film and Video Locators

AID Catalog of Films, Agency for Economic Development's Training Office, USAID Library, 1621 North Kent Street, Rosslyn, VA 22209. (Films on Third World and non-Westem countries only.)

The Educational Film Locator, Consortium of University Film Center. (Available in major libraries.)

Tricontinental Film Center, Third World Cinema, P.O. Box 4430, Berkeley, CA. UNESCO Publications Centre, P.O. Box 433, New York, NY 100 1 6.

The 1986 Video Sourcebook, National Video Clearinghouse, I 00 Lafayette Drive, Syosset, NY 11791.

Helpful Sources for Compiling Film and Video Resources

Directory of selected resources. (1988). Portland, OR: Intercultural Communication Institute.

Educational media collection. (1991). Seattle: Instructional Media Services, University of Washington.

Kohls, L. R., & Tyler, V. L. (1988). Area studies resources, Provo, UT: David M. Kennedy Center for International Studies, Brigham Young University.

Samovar, L. A., & Stefani, L. A. (November, 1995). Teaching the intercultural communication course at the college and university level. A short course conducted for the Speech Communication Association Convention, San Antonio, TX.

Samovar, L. A., & Stefani, L. A. (November, 1994). Teaching the intercultural communication course at the college and university level. Short course conducted for the Speech Communication Association, New Orleans, LA.

Schmidt, W. V., Freeman, J. B., Samovar, L. A., Kim, Y. Y., & Dodd, C. H. (November, 1984). Teaching the college course: Intercultural communication. A workshop presented at the convention of the Speech Communication Association, Chicago.

Stevens, G. 1. (1993). Videos for understanding diversity. Chicago: American Library Association.

INTERNET RESOURCES

The internet has provided new opportunities for students to learn about other cultures. It is itself a place with much cultural diversity and offers teachers and students new resources to study intercultural communication. A search for intercultural resources on the internet can be easily done by using any of the major search engines. This list of resources will only highlight some of the more interesting kinds of Web sites that you can use to help you teach and your students learn intercultural communication. The internet has become so user-friendly that the most effective and efficient way to find information on intercultural communication topics is to do an individual search on a particular country, culture, religion, language, etc. One word of caution, however, if you are asking students do research reports on various cultures. University students have become so accustomed to using *only* the Web to access information for research that they forget about other kinds of information that university libraries typically hold. Remind them of that ancient form of communication called "the book." Books are still the most plentiful source of information available on other cultures.

University Web Sites. Students could learn a great deal about intercultural communication by surveying university Web sites in different countries. For example, B'Not Torah Institute at http://www.bti.org.il/ for orthodox Jewish women provides information not just on university programs but includes essays written by members of the Institute. Such essays can provide valuable insight into the values, beliefs, and ways of communicating in other countries and cultures. A simple search of "Yahoo!" provides an enormous list of countries with university websites: http://dir.yahoo.com/Education/Higher_Education/Colleges_and_Universities/By_Region/Countries/.

Government/Embassy Web Sites. It is common for even the smallest countries to have an official national Web site that includes information for tourists and others interested in finding out more about the country. For one example, Jordan has numerous official government Web sites such as http://www.kinghussein.gov.jo/ (a site dedicated to the memory of the late King Hussein), http://www.noor.gov.jo/index.htm (personal Web site of Queen Noor), and http://www.nic.gov.jo/ (The Hashemite Kingdom of Jordan National Information System).

Regional and Culture-Specific Sites. There are some Web sites that are devoted to providing information on a specific region, culture, religion, or country. For example, Arab Net at http://www.arab.net/ is an excellent first-stop website for finding information about virtually every Islamic country in the world. And Hindu Resources On-line at http://www.hindu.org/ provides countless links to Hindu-related websites.

CIA—World Factbook. *The World Factbook* (http://www.cia.gov/cia/publications/factbook/index.html) provides national-level information on countries, territories, and dependencies, but not subnational administrative units within a country. Though intended for use by government agencies and employees, the site provides much useful information about foreign countries. *The World Factbook* provides information on the administrative divisions of a country as recommended by the United States Board on Geographic Names (BGN). The BGN is a component of the U.S. Government that develops policies, principles, and procedures governing the spelling, use, and application of geographic names—domestic, foreign, Antarctic, and undersea. Its decisions enable all departments and agencies of the US Government to have access to uniform names of geographic features. Also included in the *Factbook* are entries on parts of the world whose status has not yet been resolved (e.g., West Bank, Spratly Islands). Specific regions within a country or areas in dispute among countries are not covered. The Web site also an excellent reference map section.

Intercultural/Cross-cultural Training Organizations. A large group of training organizations can be accessed by doing a search using the search term "intercultural communication." For example, the Intercultural Management Institute at http://www.imi.american.edu/ describes services that include cross-cultural orientation and negotiations, multicultural management, and U.S. business culture training. Consider asking students to do a research project that includes surveying intercultural training and consulting organizations and reporting on common practices and recent trends.

International Chat Rooms. One way to provide students with more experiential learning opportunities is to have them join a chat room focused on a particular language, culture, or country. An "AltaVista" search using the term "international chat rooms" reaped 14,700 sites, including a Japanese-English chat room at http://www.nihongo.org/english/chat/; and Women Online Worldwide at http://www.wowwomen.com/contents.html. Do remind your students, however, that they need to proceed with caution as they enter and begin to converse in an on-line chat room. This kind of intercultural communication doesn't have the benefit of face-to-face interaction and they should exercise good sense and discretion as they chat.

References for Introduction

Albert, R. D. (1995). The intercultural sensitizer/cultural assimilator as a cross-cultural training method. In S. M. Fowler & M. G. Mumford (Eds.), Intercultural sourcebook: Cross-cultural training methods, Vol. 1. Yarmouth, Maine: Intercultural Press.

Bloom, B. S. (1956). Taxonomy of educational objectives: Cognitive domain. New York: David McKay Co.

Covert, A. (1978). Communication: "People speak" instructor's manual. New York: McGraw-Hill.

Lacey, L. & Trowbridge, J. (1995). Using the case study as a training tool. In S. M. Fowler & M. G. Mumford (Eds.), Intercultural sourcebook: Cross-cultural training methods, Vol. I. Yarmouth, Maine: Intercultural Press.

McCaffery, J. A. (1995). The role play: A powerful but difficult training tool. In S. M. Fowler & M. G. Mumford (Eds.), Intercultural sourcebook: Cross-cultural training methods, Vol. I. Yarmouth, Maine: Intercultural Press.

Nyquist, J. L. (1979). The instructional discussion method. Seattle: University of Washington.

Nyquist L., & Wulff, D. H. (1990). Selected active learning strategies. In J. Daly, G. Friedrich, & A. Vangelisti (Eds.), Teaching communication: Methods, research, and theory, Hillsdale, NJ: Lawrence Erlbaum.

Sisk, D. A. (I 995). Simulation games as training tools. In S. M. Fowler & M. G. Mumford (Eds.), Intercultural sourcebook: Cross-cultural training methods, Vol. I, Yarmouth, Maine: Intercultural Press.

Wright, A. R. (I 995). The critical incident as a training tool. In S. M. Fowler & M. G. Mumford (Eds.), Intercultural sourcebook: Cross-cultural training methods, Vol. I, Yarmouth, Maine: Intercultural Press.

CHAPTER RESOURCES

This section of the manual provides suggestions for using each chapter of the *Reader*. Each chapter includes: chapter synopsis, chapter outline, class discussion questions, popular film suggestions, exercises, and test questions. Each chapter synopsis identifies primary concepts or questions that your students should be able to identify and answer after reading the articles in the chapter. The chapter outline covers major concepts discussed in the chapter readings. The discussion questions provide ways to engage your students in an in-depth, thought-provoking discussion on issues related to ideas expressed in each chapter. Each discussion question is focused on central ideas from one article. The films suggested for classroom use have been chosen because they portray some of the characteristics of intercultural communication discussed in the chapter readings.

The exercises provided are of three primary types: reflective, experiential, and case studies. The reflective exercises often ask students to work alone or in groups and consider their own feelings about a particular topic related to intercultural communication. These exercises can also be used as take-home assignments. The experiential exercises ask students to "do" intercultural communication in either simulated or authentic situations. And finally, the case studies provided for each chapter ask students to consider examples of intercultural communication and identify the primary issues, problems, and solutions for each one. All exercises include questions to facilitate small group and/or whole class discussion. Finally, each chapter ends with multiple choice, true/false, and essay test items for each article.

Chapter 1 Approaches to Understanding Intercultural Communication

Chapter Synopsis

This chapter introduces the topic of intercultural communication and provides a spectrum of approaches to culture, communication, and interactions between cultures. Your students should be able to answer four broad questions about intercultural communication after reading the articles in this chapter:

- What is intercultural communication?
- How do cultures differ communicatively?
- What influences and/or impedes intercultural understanding?
- What contributes to one's worldview?

In "Understanding Intercultural Communication: An Overview of the Basics," McDaniel, Samovar, and Porter stress the importance of intercultural communication both at home and abroad. Their essay introduces students to the specific subjects and issues associated with intercultural communication; discusses the different purposes of communication and culture; and looks closely at the major variables that are a factor in communication between people of diverse cultures.

Cargile's essay, "Imagining Culture with a Little Help from the Pushmi-Pullyu," examines the definition of culture through the lens of dialectics, arguing that culture exists as part of a larger whole in a dynamic push-pull relationship, which he demonstrates using the "pushmi-pullyu" metaphor.

Triandis, in "Culture and Conflict," reviews two ways in which culture is related to conflict: cultural distance and cultural syndromes. He introduces ten cultural syndromes that he then relates to the situation, communication and conflict.

In "Our Locus in the Universe: Worldview and Intercultural Communication," Ishii, Klopf, and Cooke discuss how the concept of worldview shapes culture. Elements of worldview are provided as well as types of worldviews. They argue that religion plays a fundamental role in shaping one's worldview and provide numerous examples that allow students to examine various religious worldviews.

Jensen's argues, in "The Practice of Intercultural Communication: Reflections for Professionals in Cultural Meetings," that globalization has created an increased need for the practice intercultural communication, especially given the emergence of professional practitioners in multiethnic societies. He contends that simple answers to cultural differences do not aid these practitioners in doing intercultural communication. Jensen posits four analytical tools for intercultural communication, drawn from recent research in the field and a poststructuralist perspective of cultural identity.

Chapter Outline

History and development of Intercultural Communication:

- Increased contact between peoples of different cultures
- War and commerce broaden cultural exchange
- Spread of world's three largest religions—Islam, Buddhism, Christianity
- Language, arts, technology expanded across cultures
- Alliances and treaties
- Rise of nation states
- New world political and economic order after WWII
- Fall of Berlin Wall in 1989 opens door to multipolar political order
- Globalization
- Changes to U.S. domestic population
- Issues at stake in today's world

Eight Major Structural Components of Communication

3. Sender
4. Message
5. Channel
6. Receiver
7. Response
8. Feedback
9. Environment
10. Noise—physical, psychological, physiological, and semantic

The Purpose of Culture

11. To provide a framework for imparting meaning to events, objects, and people
12. To instill an identity, or sense of self

The Characteristics of Culture

- Culture Is Learned—often called enculturation
- Culture Is Transmitted Intergenerationally
- Culture Is Symbolic
- Culture Is Dynamic
- Culture Is Ethnocentric

Patterns of Cognition

Northeast Asians	*Westerners*
• Employ holistic thinking pattern	• Use linear, cause-and-effect model—value logical reasoning and rationality
• See problems as much more complex and interrelated, requiring greater understanding of, and emphasis on, collective rather than individual parts	• Problems can best be solved by systematic, in-depth analysis of individual components, progressing from simple to more complex
• In Japanese-U.S. business negotiations, Japanese tend to revisit or reopen issues that U.S. side considers concluded	• U.S. negotiators find practice frustrating and time-consuming, believing that once a point has been agreed to, it is completed

Verbal Behavior—Role of Language

Nonverbal Behavior

- Includes gestures, facial expressions, eye contact and gaze, posture and movement, touch, dress, silence, use of space and time, objects and artifacts, and paralanguage

Culture Defined

- Five accepted common characteristics: culture is symbolic, learned, transmitted, changing, ethnocentric
- Proposed sixth characteristic (Cargile): culture is dialectical in nature

A Dialectic Perspective

- Basic notion of dialectics is one of opposition
- People reconcile oppositions through synthesis of contradictory positions
- Dialectics defined not only by opposition, but equally by *time* and *transformation*; dialectics are never *static*

Dialectical Characteristics of Culture

- Living collectively creates tension between pushes of individualism and pulls of collectivism
- Tension builds as result of divergent resolutions of any issue fundamental to group life
- Dialectics helps reveal our capacity for action
- Contradiction inherent to group life can never by irrevocably resolved

West versus East

- Western individualist cultures sample mostly the ***content*** of communications
- Eastern collectivist cultures sample mostly the ***context*** of communications

- *Cultural distance*: Conflict is greater when two cultures are very different than when they're similar; cultural distance is greater when people:
  - Speak different languages
  - Have different religions
  - Experience differing standards of living
  - Have different values, which are related to cultural syndromes

Collectivist versus Individualist Cultures

Collectivist cultures (traditional, most Asian and Latin American cultures)	**Individualist cultures** (North and Western Europe; North America, except Mexico; Australia; New Zealand)
• More likely to sample collective self • To think of themselves as interdependent with their groups (family, coworkers, tribe, coreligionists, country) • To value group goals over personal goals • To use group norms to shape their behavior • Use of "we" preferred; ambivalent about "me"	• More likely to sample individual self • To see themselves as autonomous individuals independent of their groups • To value personal goals over group goals; to use personal attitudes to shape behavior • To abandon personal relationships not seen as optimally beneficial to them • To require use of "I" and "you" in languages

Cultural Syndromes

- **Complexity:** cultures either simple or complex
- **Tightness:** tight cultures vs. loose cultures
- **Individualism and Collectivism:** individualism emerges in societies that are both complex and loose; collectivism emerges in societies that are both simple and tight
- **Vertical and Horizontal Cultures:** hierarchy is natural order in vertical cultures
- **Active-Passive Cultures:** generally individualist cultures are more active than collectivist cultures
- **Universalism-Particularism:** generally, individualists are universalists and collectivists are particularists
- **Diffuse-Specific:** diffuse cultures respond to environment in holistic manner; specific cultures discriminate different aspects of stimulus complex
- **Instrumental-Expressive:** generally, individualists more instrumental (*get the job done*) and collectivists more expressive (*enjoy the social relationship*)
- **Emotional Expression or Suppression:** collectivists tend to control free expression of negative emotions (other-focus); individualists often high in emotional expression (self-focus)

Four Stages of Communication

- **Unconscious incompetence:** people are unaware of their miscommunications
- **Conscious incompetence:** people realize they're miscommunicating but don't know why
- **Conscious competence:** people get to know more about a culture and make an effort to communicate in a different way
- **Unconscious competence:** people develop habits of correct communication with members of other cultures

Sources of Miscommunication Result from Differences in:

- Perception of causes of behavior (*attributions*)
- Interpretation of paralinguistic cues
- Way people use time (monochromic time vs. polychromic time)
- Structure of messages (linear vs. non-linear)
- *Pragmatism* (what works best for each situation) vs. *collectivism* (ideal for all)
- Interpersonal difficulties between universalist and particularist
- Communication *associative* in some cultures, *abstractive* in others (West)

Worldview

Worldview shapes cultures and plays a large role in defining reality and explaining the purpose of human life.

Elements of worldview:

- Redfield (1953): anthropological analysis with 12 general conceptions (see page 33)
- Pennington (1985): 10 salient characteristics (see page 33)
- Gilgen and Cho (1979): psychological analysis showing East-West dichotomy (see page 33)
- Dodd (1987): nine groupings, some of which contrast East and West (see pages 33-34)

Formation of Worldviews:

- Is implicit, not verbally expressed.
- Develops in early childhood
- Shaped by social community, shared images and constructions of social group or class
- Influenced by religion

Types of Worldview: Helve (1991) classifies worldview as three types:

- **Scientific:** based on rules of exact science
- **Metaphysical:** based on abstract general reasoning without empirical base (such as beliefs in Santa Claus, ghosts, witches, fairies, elves)
- **Religious:** serves as foundation of worldview

Eastern and Western Religions: Religious Similarities

- Sacred writings
- Authority figure
- Rituals

- Speculation about life's mysteries
- Religious ethic, set of moral principles

Eastern: (Eastern and Southern Asia—Korea, China, Japan, India, and others)
- Religious traditions feature harmony as ultimate good (Hinduism, Shintoism, Buddhism, Confucianism, and Taoism)
- Everything is benign, nothing is worth worrying about
- Deity in every place and in every form (in rocks, animals, and humans)
- Polytheistic
- Everything relative to situation—no absolute right

Western: (Jewish, Islamic, Christian)
- Ultimate good is transformation—divine grace is desired end
- Monotheistic
- Everything is headed somewhere, to Kingdom of God, to heaven, to an end
- At end of life, there will be an accounting or payoff (life, death, resurrection of body)
- Felicity important beyond earthly life

Intercultural Communication in a Global Context
- Globalization process: cultures moving closer through consumerism, ideology, knowledge about each other
- Localization process: intense focus on our local nation or local ethnic groups
- Globalization has caused new polarization in societies, dividing people into two groups (Bauman):
  - Tourists—can travel freely with few restrictions
  - Vagabonds—forced to travel because of war, poverty, or hunger

"Classic" Intercultural Communication Research
Functionalist approach:
- Tries to predict how culture would influence communication
- Culture seen as barrier to effective communication
- Offers tools to describe expectations of intercultural communication
- Includes competence research
- Hofstede's four dimensions:
  - Power/distance (small/large)
  - Uncertainty avoidance/anxiety
  - Individualism/collectivism
  - Masculinity/femininity

Post-structural Approach:
- Point of departure lies in the actor rather than in the culture
- Interpretations of participant determine what culture person belongs to
- Yoshikawa's "double swing model" (see graph, page 41)

Intercultural Communication Model

Jensen's model develops from a poststructuralist approach using four analytical tools:

- Positions of Experiences
- Cultural Presuppositions
- Cultural Self-Perception
- Cultural Fix Points

Cultural Identity in Intercultural Communication

- Appadurai's categorization of global "scapes":
  - Ethno-scapes—about integration
  - Media-scapes—dominated by mass media
  - Techno-scapes—refer to global technological development
  - Finance-scapes—draw attention to autonomous cycle of finances
  - Ideo-scapes—illustrate how ideologies develop across national borders
- Different meanings of cultural identity:
  - Functionalist perspective
  - Constructivist perspective
- Cultural identity as an analytical tool

Chapter Discussion Ideas

This question is best asked at the first class meeting, as a way to segue into discussing the purpose of the course.

Why should we study intercultural communication?

Ask students to list spontaneously their reasons for taking an intercultural communication course. What do they hope to get out of the course? What are the benefits? Why even have such a course? List student responses on the chalkboard.

Ask students to give their answers aloud. Play the "devil's advocate" and encourage students to elaborate on their reasons. For example, a common response to why we should study intercultural communication is that it will increase intercultural understanding among peoples of the world and help people get along. One response to this answer is that not everyone wants to communicate with people who are culturally dissimilar and what really are the benefits of such interactions? Hasn't communication been known to strain rather than improve intercultural relations? Why can't we just stay in our own communities and communicate with the people who are like us? Such a response can spark further dialogue on the inevitability of intercultural contact, as well as force students to challenge the assumption that communication always and necessarily improves understanding.

Finally, ask students to give one way that their lives could change as a result of taking an intercultural communication course. How will they have changed their lives or ways of thinking and communicating with culturally dissimilar individuals after the course has ended? Encourage students to be specific about these changes and have them write the changes down on paper, so they can refer back to them at the end of the term.

2. Is perception strictly a physiological process? To what degree is perception influenced by one's culture? Is all perception really culturally and individually based? Isn't there such a thing as "fact" or "objective reality"? Can't we agree that many things about the world just are? Given all this, how are we to understand perception? This question encourages students to think of perception as a series of complex and sometimes contradictory processes, rather than an automatic function of being human.
3. Discuss how a dialectical approach helps us understand the presence of both individualism and collectivism in a culture. Have students identify some of the oppositions that they see in U.S. American life. What are some characteristics of collectivist cultures? What are some characteristics of individualist cultures? How do these characteristics differ? Have students identify whether they belong to individualist cultures or collectivist cultures. What cultures do they believe to be individualist? Collectivist?
4. With which worldview do students most identify? Why? This can provide a discussion to determine why some students believe in certain things while others have different beliefs, values, etc. Are these beliefs based in their worldview? Is their identification with this worldview related to their own culture? How does their worldview contribute to their culture?
5. What has been the impact of globalization on cultural identity? In what ways does cultural identity influence intercultural communication?

Chapter Exercises

Exercise 1.1: Intercultural Communication Model

This exercise asks students to construct their own model of the intercultural communication process based on those elements they feel most influences an intercultural interaction. Students will apply the knowledge they have learned in Chapter 1 to their own experiences as intercultural communicators. Briefly review the elements of intercultural communication as outlined in the article by McDaniel, Samovar, and Porter. Then divide the class into groups of 4-5 students. Ask students to illustrate intercultural communication by constructing a model of the process. Each group should decide which elements of intercultural communication they will include in their model. Suggest to the students that they use their own interactions with culturally different peoples as frameworks for choosing their model's components. For example, some students may have experienced an intercultural situation where language was a barrier in the interaction. Others may have noticed particular nonverbal behaviors that were markedly different than their own. Also stress to students that they should think of the basic process of communication as discussed in other courses they've taken in communication.

Ask each group to present its model using a hypothetical intercultural interaction as an example that shows how the model works in "real life." If students are given enough time, some groups may choose to develop a skit to illustrate their model. Each group should state the respective cultures of the interactants, the scene (in a restaurant, on a date, in a classroom, etc.), and the affiliation level of the dyad (strangers, acquaintances, friends, lovers, etc.). The following questions are offered to stimulate discussion: How did you come up with these components? Which components do you feel most impact intercultural communication? Why? Which components do you feel pose the biggest challenge for interactants? The least challenge? How are the components of the communication process affected by the added variable of culture? Can any component of the communication process escape culture's influence?

Exercise 1.2: How Others Perceive Us

This exercise asks students to imagine how others might perceive them culturally and individually in an intercultural interaction. The objective of this activity is to make students aware of how others might perceive them in an intercultural setting and how closely these perceptions match students' own perceptions of their cultural and personal characteristics. Have students answer the following two questions individually. Impress upon them that they are to imagine, as much as possible, how others would perceive them, not how they perceive themselves. It might be helpful for students if they would imagine an intercultural encounter that they have had previously.

List *10 cultural predictions* that you think others would use to describe you in an intercultural interaction.
List *10 individual predictions* that you think others would use to describe you in an intercultural interaction.

Afterwards, the class may either be separated into small discussion groups or a large class discussion may follow. Have students share some of their answers. Possible questions for discussion might be: Where might people get these cultural and individual characteristics? How accurate would their impressions of you be if these were the only predictions they could make about you? What errors would they make? Do you think that their impression is the "real" you? How similar are their cultural and individual predictions? How different are they? Where are the contradictions? In what situations do you think it would be useful to make strictly cultural predictions? Only individual predictions? When are both most useful? Should people only assess others based on perceived individual characteristics?

Exercise 1.3: Interactional Rules

This exercise includes aspects from all the articles in Chapter 1. Specifically, it illustrates how communication is so strongly rule-governed and yet we follow these rules unconsciously. By taking part in a cross-cultural simulation activity, students will gain insight into the difficulty that arises when two culture-specific rule systems are used in an intercultural interaction. Divide the class into two groups, the ***Sopa culture*** and the ***Epa culture***. Each group should receive handouts with culture-specific rules that will govern its behavior when it interacts with the other (rules are provided as handouts on the next two pages). Give students the rules one class period before the day that the game is to be played. This will ensure that each student will be adequately prepared to take part in the simulation. Tell students not to share their group's rules with any member of the other group. The success of this game hinges on each team not being explicitly aware of the rules that govern the other group's behavior.

After students have been given adequate preparation time to learn the rules of their assigned cultures, have the two groups take part in a twenty-minute interaction session. You may set up a scene where the two groups will negotiate a business transaction or a party where there are both social and business conversations taking place. You could even provide some refreshments to make a party scene more realistic. Some students from the same culture may wish to pair up as friends, lovers, students, siblings, a married couple, or business partners. After the two cultures have interacted, have the students write for five minutes on the following questions: What specific behaviors of the other culture did you notice? What social rules do you think were governing these behaviors?

As with all cross-cultural simulations, a class discussion should follow. Students should come away from this discussion with an understanding of some of the cultural rules that guide their own daily interactions and the impact that interactional rules have on intercultural communication. Each of the articles in Chapter 1 is relevant to this exercise. Some possible questions to stimulate discussion: What were some of the difficulties you experienced in preparing for this interaction? Which rules of your "adopted culture" conflicted with the rules of your "true" culture? When did you begin to catch on to some of their social rules? What was one of the first things you noticed about how the other culture behaved? What was your initial internal reaction? What was your external reaction to this behavior? How did you (or why didn't you) modify your behavior to compensate for the other culture's rules? What were some of the most difficult moments during your interactions? What were some of the most enjoyable? Did successful communication take place? What information about the other culture do you wish you had been given before your interaction? What information about your own culture could be given to other cultures to aid them in their interactions with you?

Exercise 1.3: Interactional Rules

Rules for the Sopa Culture

Sopas are extremely social, but their socializing is dictated by the women. Men can speak freely with other men, but must be restrained in contact with women. This matriarchal society is also highly materialistic. A major source of conversation is derived from discussing each other's material assets.

Example of greeting: Hi, Derek! How's your new radial tire?

Keep in mind the following social rules:

A. **Initiating Conversation**. Always begin social contact with a materialistic statement. Inquiries into each other's financial situation are considered proper etiquette.

B. **Degree of Verbalization**. Constant verbalizing is a sign of successful communication. Perpetual chitchat is critical both in social and business interactions.

C. **Sex Roles**. Women must remember to protect their males from strangers. If a stranger stands too close to a male member, intercept without speaking.

D. **Nonverbal Behavior**

<u>Touching:</u> Each touches the other, except handshaking is considered an insult. Men must wait to be touched by women before they can reciprocate.

<u>Gestures:</u> The right hand is considered an evil and disgusting part of the human anatomy. It must never contact a human or be used in giving something to another. Right palm facing a person is an obscene gesture.

<u>Eye Contact:</u> Women engage in sustained eye contact. Men lower their eyes when speaking to women or strangers.

<u>Facial Gestures</u>: Wetting one's lips with the tongue is considered a very provocative or complimentary gesture to be used ONLY when one wishes to "charm" the opposite sex. Tongue rolling is a definite attempt at hustling. (Gestures can be used by both sexes.)

E. **Business**. This highly materialistic society thinks of business as merely an extension of their social life, only more aggressive. Although men can initiate a sale, ONLY WOMEN CAN BARTER and complete the transaction.

Exercise 1.3: Interactional Rules

Rules for the Epa Culture

Epas believe in the separateness of the self from others. If possible, they would live in isolated cells, but since they form a group, they make all attempts to cooperate while minimizing self-revelation. Epas are themselves only part of the natural cycle and, therefore, hold nature as sacred as humans. They speak *through* nature so all communication is a metaphor.

Example: This rose is wilting. (*I am tired.*)
Does the cow sit at your table? (*Do you eat meat?*)
How are the saplings in your forest? (*How is your family?*)

Keep in mind the following social rules:

A. **Initiating Conversation**. Always begin social contact with reference to the weather or other natural phenomena.

B. **Degree of Verbalization**. The ability to use metaphorical language is an art form that establishes a type of caste system. Clear, moderately slow speech production punctuated with intermittent silence to enable aesthetic appreciation is a sign of articulate communication.

C. **Sex Roles**. Within the culture an asexual attitude prevails. Members tend to find other cultures very exciting but strangers sometimes misunderstand the treatment of sex and "nature's function."

D **Nonverbal Behavior**

Touching: Epas are essentially aphysical and, therefore, avoid touching one another. An interesting feature in this culture is that individuals seem to touch and hold themselves (i.e., arm folding, face touching, etc.) a lot. Positive sentiment is expressed in flowery metaphorical language.

Gestures: **Yes/agreement/happiness**—signified by touching chin to chest (rapid chin touching = great excitement/vigorous agreement). **No/disagreement/disgust**—rolling the shoulders. "Say again" or "repeat" is indicated by touching your fist to your forehead.

Facial Gestures: The human tongue is considered a disgusting part of the human anatomy. Showing your tongue or pointing a finger is considered a GRAVE insult.

E. **Business**. The following only relate to business negotiations:

All trading is done standing.
Women cannot touch money.

Exercise 1.4: Collectivist and Individualist Cultures

This exercise will help students understand the characteristics of both collectivist and individualist cultures. Divide the class into two groups. Ask students in one group to identify characteristics of collectivist cultures. Ask students in the second group to identify characteristics of individualist cultures. Then have students list which characteristics they can identify as part of their own culture. Are these characteristics those identified as being part of a collectivist or an individualist culture?

Exercise 1.5: East vs. West

This exercise will allow students to clearly differentiate between the East/West Dichotomy as outlined by Gilgen and Cho (1979) in Ishii, Klopf, and Cooke. More importantly students will be provided an opportunity to understand both dichotomies.

Divide the class in two groups. Designate one group to represent the East and the other to represent the West. Using the East/West dichotomy outlined on page 33 of the textbook, have students provide an example of each of the characteristics. Then ask all students to explain which worldview they can relate to and why. Specifically, have them articulate why they could live under the beliefs of one worldview versus another.

Exercise 1.6: Cultural Self-Perception

Using numerous and diverse popular magazines, select advertisements for products and services and bring them to class for students to analyze. Divide the class into small groups of three to four students. Pass out the magazine ads and ask students to construct a narrative based on their ads and the magazine they're found in. Then have students try to identify their own narratives from the narrative they've constructed about the "others" in the ads. What cultural presuppositions can they identify that they brought to the task of constructing narratives of "others." Are there factors of ethnocentrism influencing their narratives? Which cultural communities do the students identify with? Do the students identify themselves as distinct from other cultural communities? Do the students idealize their own cultural community?

Chapter 1 Popular Film Suggestions

The following film suggestions can be used to illustrate some of the cultural issues and perspectives discussed in this chapter. If you do not have time to show an entire film in class, students can be urged to rent and watch the film at home. Another way to use the films is to show pertinent scenes in class and then discuss them in light of the chapter 1 readings. Each of these films has been chosen because its tone is light, even when dealing with serious subject matter, and thus a good introduction for students new to the issues of intercultural communication, in particular cultural identity, worldview, cultural differences, individualism versus collectivism, East-West cultural differences, and cultural conflict.

- ***Eat Drink Man Woman*** (Taiwan, 1994; writer/director: Ang Lee; 2 hr 4 min; Chinese with English subtitles). This film examines the intergenerational conflicts faced by a family—a Chinese master chef and his three daughters. The eldest daughter works in a professional office and is the most Westernized of the three; the second daughter is a school teacher; the third works in a fast-food restaurant. The film illustrates the changes occurring within the Taiwanese culture through the escapades in love and work of the three daughters. Most instructive are the ways in which the daughters interact with their father during their traditional Sunday dinners at which he prepares and serves their favorite foods, often quite elaborate productions. The film also handily illustrates the concepts of the fuzziness of culture as described by Cargile, as the daughters' increasing individualism rubs up against the father's collectivism.

  Web References:

  Berardinelli, J. *Eat Drink Man Woman*: A film review. http://movie-reviews.collossus.net/movies/e/eat_drink.html

  Maslin, J. "Film review: Avoiding basic human desires, or trying to." The New York Times Online. August 3, 1994. http://movies2.nytimes/mem/movies/review.html?oref=login&title1=&title2=EAT%..

- ***Bend It Like Beckham*** (U.S./United Kingdom/Germany, 2002; director: Gurinder Chadha; screenplay: Gurinder Chadha, Paul Mayeda Berges, Guljit Bindra; length: 1 hr 52 min). This film deals with the issue of cultural assimilation and illustrates what can happen when worldviews collide (East-West). In this film, a young teenager, the British-born daughter of Sikh parents, dreams of playing soccer, but her parents have different ideas and want her to begin preparing for a grown-up life, learning to cook traditional dishes and planning to marry. She meets a young British female who plays soccer and who convinces her to try out for the all-female soccer team. This movie, like *Eat Drink Man Woman*, nicely illustrates the intergenerational conflict inherent in families who immigrate from one culture into another.

  Web Reference:

  Berardinelli, J. *Bend It Like Beckham*: A film review. http://movie-reviews.colossus.net/b/bend_it.html

Chapter Test Items

Multiple Choice

1. According to McDaniel, Samovar, and Porter, which of the following are NOT among the events that have led to the development of the global village?
   a. globalization of the economy
   b. changes in immigration patterns
   c. developments in communication technology
   d. increased intercultural understanding *

2. Improvements in communication technology have produced many effects worldwide. Which of the following effects is among the most significant to intercultural communication?
   a. immediacy of mass communication *
   b. increased television watching and decreased interpersonal interactions
   c. tendency to objectify people
   d. stronger value of materialism worldwide

3. What is the basic function of culture?
   a. To help people deal with problems
   b. To describe a predictable world in which the individual is firmly rooted
   c. To make sense of surroundings and ease transitions
   d. All of the above *

4. Culture is
   a. static.
   b. innate
   c. random.
   d. learned. *

5. Which of the following are "teachers" of American culture?
   a. The saying, "the squeaky wheel gets the grease."
   b. A mother telling her son, "Dress up is for girls, honey."
   c. both a and b *
   d. none of the above

6. According to McDaniel, Samovar, and Porter, cultures are
   a. highly adaptive and, therefore, undergo complete change with every generation.
   b. dynamic and, therefore, do not retain any particular characteristics over time.
   c. highly adaptive, yet possess a deep structure that resists major alterations.*
   d. do not exist in a vacuum, yet remain static over time.

7. *"Nearly always the folklore of a people includes myths of origin which give priority to themselves, and place the stamp of supernatural approval upon their particular customs"* (10). This statement by Keesing (1965) best illustrates which of the following characteristics of culture?
   a. culture is learned
   b. culture is transmitted from generation to generation
   c. culture is based on symbols
   d. culture is ethnocentric *

8. Which characteristic of culture would be especially detrimental to intercultural communication according to McDaniel, Samovar, and Porter?
   a. culture is symbolic
   b. culture is ethnocentric *
   c. culture is dynamic
   d. culture is learned

9. What are the two dominant social organizations found in a culture?
   a. political affiliation and club memberships
   b. workplace and peer group
   c. school and family *
   d. ethnicity and community identification

10. Silence, eye contact, and handshakes are all forms of what kind of communication?
   a. nonverbal *
   b. paralinguistic
   c. conscious
   d. intentional

11. Cargile argues that culture has a sixth characteristic:
   a. culture is like a plant
   b. culture is dialectical in nature *
   c. culture has no discernible patterns
   d. culture has a simple structure

12. Which of the following are examples of collectivism in U.S. history?
   a. social security
   b. victory gardens
   c. fireside chats
   d. all of the above *

13. From the beginning, U.S. American individualism has been intertwined with two important collectivist traditions
   a. politics and wealth
   b. religion and civic republicanism *
   c. volunteerism and habitat protection
   d. none of the above

14. In collectivist cultures people are more likely
   a. to sample the collective self rather than to sample the individual self
   b. to give more priority to the goals of their in-group than to their personal goals
   c. to use in-group norms to shape their behavior more than personal attitudes
   d. all of the above *

15. Which of the following is not considered an individualist culture?
   a. North American
   b. Australia
   c. New Zealand
   d. Latin American *

16. Which of the following is not characteristic of those in an individualist culture?
   a. sample the individual self
   b. use norms much more than attitudes as determinants of their social behavior *
   c. pay attention to their own needs only and abandon interpersonal relationships
   d. give priority to personal goals

17. Which of the following assumes, "When people come into contact with members of other cultures, they are often not aware of their miscommunications, because they think that the others are more or less like they are"?
   a. conscious incompetence
   b. unconscious incompetence *
   c. conscious competence
   d. unconscious competence

18. Which of the following assumes, "After some interpersonal difficulties people realize that they are miscommunicating, but they do not know exactly what is wrong"?
   a. conscious incompetence *
   b. unconscious incompetence
   c. conscious competence
   d. unconscious competence

19. In the West communication is typically
   a. abstractive *
   b. associative
   c. neither a or b
   d. none of the above

20. Factors that have been found to increase aggression include
   a. biological factors
   b. social structural factors
   c. modeling
   d. all of the above *

21. The rejection of out-groups is especially likely to occur in
   a. collectivist cultures *
   b. individualist cultures
   c. both a and b
   d. none of the above

22. Which of the following is not a belief of the West's worldview?
   a. Humans are separate from nature and overshadowed by a personal God
   b. Humans consist of mind, body, and soul.
   c. Humans are one with nature, they should feel comfortable with anyone. *
   d. Humans have to manipulate and control nature to survive.

23. Which researcher(s) places stress on religion in developing worldview?
   a. Helve
   b. Rubin and Peplau
   c. Samovar and Porter
   d. Emerson *

24. Which of the following does Helve (1991) not consider a part of worldview?
   a. scientific
   b. metaphysical
   c. religious
   d. educational *

25. Which of the following is not a belief of the East's worldview?
   a. Mind and body are one.
   b. Humans have to manipulate and control nature to survive. *
   c. Life is birth, life, death, and rebirth.
   d. Saving face is essential.

26. Eastern and Western religions possess similarities; of the following, which is the most important, according to Samovar, Porter, and Stefani (1998)?
   a. speculations
   b. sacred writings *
   c. rituals
   d. principles

27. Bauman (1999) argues that globalization has caused a new polarization in societies that divides people into two groups:
   a. Creoles and "others"
   b. tourists and vagabonds *
   c. multiethnic and multicultural
   d. none of the above

28. In describing Yoshikawa's "double swing model" of intercultural dialogue, which of the following does not describe the model:
   a. the goal in communication is to eliminate differences *
   b. both partners in communication play both roles as addresser and addressee
   c. communication is seen as an infinite process
   d. the two participants will both change in the meeting

29. The concept of *positions of experience,* seen as an analytical tool,

a. reflects that people in intercultural communication always have different opportunities to give different positions of themselves
b. gives an awareness of how people's different positions are crucial to the interpretation of the communication
c. both a and b *
d. none of the above

30. The intention of the concept of cultural presuppositions is

a. to create awareness about the ordinary process whereby people outside our own social community are often characterized (negatively) on the basis of our own values
b. to increase awareness of the discourses and discursive formations in everyday life
c. both a and b *
d. none of the above

31. Cultural fix points

a. identify some patterns in the conflicts that are characteristic of given periods *
b. are characteristic of emotional statements
c. are not related to societal structures
d. none of the above

32. Appadurai (1991) argues that within the global we have developed a number of "scapes" with greater identity-caring significance than the national communities; which of the following is not a "scape" he identifies

a. finance-scapes
b. ethno-scapes
c. media-scapes
d. identity-scapes *

True/False

F 1. The globalization of the economy has had little impact on intercultural communication among the world's people.

T 2. Intercultural communication occurs whenever a message produced in one culture must be processed in another culture.

T 3. A basic function of culture is to help us make sense of our surroundings.

T 4. The deep structure of a culture (i.e., values, morals, religious practices) rarely changes because it is able to resist major alterations.

F 5. Culture is the internal process by which we select, evaluate, and organize stimuli from the external environment.

T 6. Values are like rules that proscribe behaviors expected of a culture's members.

F 7. More than anything else, differences in language isolate cultures and cause them to regard each other as strange.

T 8. The basic notion of dialectics is one of opposition.

T 9. Contradiction is a defining feature of culture.

F 10. Dialectics are always static.

T 11. Western individualist cultures sample mostly the *content* of communications.

F 12. Conflict is greater when two cultures are very similar than when they are very different.

T 13. A cultural syndrome is a shared pattern of beliefs, attitudes, self-definitions, norms, roles, and values organized around a theme.

T 14. In collectivist cultures people pay attention to the needs of others and stay in relationships even when that is not maximally beneficial to them.

F 15. The four aspects of collectivists cultures are not interrelated.

T 16. Collectivists use action verbs rather than state verbs.

T 17. Conformity is high in tight cultures.

T 18. Hollywood stars live in a culture that is both complex and loose.

F 19. In the West conformity is seen as something that is desirable.

T 20. Vertical cultures accept hierarchy as a given.

T 21. Worldview distinguishes one culture from another.

T 22. Worldview consists of the most general and comprehensive concepts and unstated assumptions about life.

F 23. An Easterner bringing shame to a group is quickly forgiven.

T 24. According to Bukhdal (1967), all understanding is a matter of presuppositions.

F 25. Ethnocentrism requires that we acknowledge the sovereignty of others' culture.

T 26. According to Hall, the self is fragmented and does not contain one identity but several, often contradictory identities.

T 27. Jensen argues that the actualized identity depends on the topic—what the participants are talking about in an intercultural communication.

F 28. Cultural differences can be seen as the only differentiation to interpretation.

T 29. The interpretations of the participant determine what culture the person belongs to.

F 30. In Bauman's dichotomy, vagabonds can travel freely with few restrictions.

Chapter Essay Questions

1. Describe an intercultural communication interaction that you have experienced using the five characteristics of communication as identified by McDaniel, Samovar, and Porter.
2. Describe how the mechanisms of invention and diffusion produce change in a culture.
3. Identify, define, and give an example of each of the six characteristics of culture as explained by McDaniel, Samovar, and Porter. Would you add a characteristic that they do not include?
4. Describe how beliefs, values, and attitudes are interrelated and their relation to communication.

5. How are cultural and intercultural competence different? How are they related?
6. Explain how the following proverb relates the link between family and how we communicate with other people: "The apple does not fall far from the tree."
7. Explain what Cargile means by his claim that culture is "dialectical in nature." Define dialectics.
8. Consider what Nuckolls means by the statement that culture is " 'a problem that cannot be solved' " (as cited in Cargile, p. 18).
9. Of the ten cultural syndromes outlined in Triandis' article, "Culture and Conflict," which of the syndromes most closely relate to a culture of which you are a member? Identify the culture syndrome and provide an example of specifically how the culture you belong to corresponds with the syndrome.
10. Differentiate between "tight" and "loose" cultures.
11. When people come into contact with members of other cultures they communicate through various stages. Briefly review these stages and how they are important in the communication process.
12. Explain the statement, "All humans are ethnocentric."
13. Identify Redfield's (1953) general conceptions of the elements of worldview.
14. Ten characteristics can be generated from Pennington's (1985) conception of worldview elements. Identify and explain five of those characteristics.
15. Explain the East-West dichotomy worldview as described by psychologists Gilgen and Cho (1979).
16. Explain Dodd's (1987) worldview elements.
17. Differentiate between Helve's (1991) three types of worldviews: scientific, metaphysical and religious.
18. Rudyard Kipling's famous words, "Oh, East is East, and West is West, and never the twain shall meet" can be used to describe the colliding worldviews of the East and the West. Compare and contrast these two views.
19. Samovar, Porter, and Stefani (1998) identify five similarities of Eastern and Western religions. Identify, define, and give an example of each of the similarities.
20. Explain the importance of Bauman's claim that globalization has caused a new polarizing dichotomy in societies in which people are either tourists or vagabonds. How does he characterize each of these two groups?
21. According to Jensen, how does the functionalist approach differ from the poststructuralist approach? How can each be used to analyze an intercultural communication?
22. Describe Jensen's poststructuralist model of intercultural communication.
23. Define cultural fix points. Identify your own cultural fix points. Consider how your cultural fix points might play out in a communication situation with someone whose cultural fix points are different. Select a specific communication situation for your discussion. For example, consider this scenario: as you are walking across campus, you notice a small group of students gathered around a man speaking through a megaphone; as you come close enough to overhear what he's saying, he points to you and yells, "Sinner, repent!" Given your cultural fix points, how do you react? Feel? What would you say to him, if you decided to respond?
24. Stuart Hall contends that each of us has multiple, contradictory identities at different points of time. How would you describe your "multiple identities"? Is there one culture to which you feel particularly connected more than the others? Which one? How might your cultural identities influence you in an intercultural communication in a multiethnic society?

Chapter 2 Cultural Identity: Issues of Belonging

Chapter Synopsis

Chapter 2 is concerned with the sources and formation of self-identity. The editors emphasize, as do the readings in this chapter, that one common trait in identity formation is culture. Through the process of enculturation, our identities are formed by and within our first in-groups, which we later expand as we interact with other cultural groups. In today's globalized society, students need to understand the impact of multicultural interactions, since they are increasingly unavoidable. The five essays in this chapter discuss different aspects of culture and identity formation.

Mary Jane Collier, in "Cultural Identity and Intercultural Communication," examines cultural identification and what influences how individuals form their cultural identities, from national and ethnic considerations to gender, profession, geographic location, and so on.

In "Finding My Whiteness: A Narrative of Cultural Identification," Robert Krizek shows how students, can, through a process of self-reflection, get a sense of how their cultural identity has been formed.

In another narrative, the essay "A Polish Jewish American Story: Collective Memories and Intergroup Relations," co-authors Jolanta A. Drzawiecka and Nancy Draznin, examine the influences of family history and collective memory in the development of cultural identity.

A. L. Zimmerman and Patricia Geist-Martin's essay "The Hybrid Identities of Gender Queer: Claiming Neither/Nor, Both/And" addresses the issues of how gender can affect the development of cultural identity through a narrative essay about Amber, a person who was born into a female body but identifies more with being male.

Nadine Naber, in "Ambiguous Insiders: An Investigation of Arab American Invisibility," considers what it means to be an Arab American, and how this identity is a product of anti-Arab racism.

Chapter Outline

Cultural Identity and Intercultural Communication

- Culture is systemic and comprises many complex elements:
  - Symbols and Meanings
  - Norms
  - History
- Types of Cultures
  - National and Ethnic Cultures
  - Gender

    - Profession
    - Geographical Area
    - Organization
    - Physical Ability or Disability
- Cultural Identification as a Process
    - Each individual has a range of cultures to which he or she belongs
    - Cultures affected not only by changing socioeconomic and environmental conditions, but also by other cultures
- Cultural Identity

  Identities are *emergent*: they come to be in communication contexts
- Properties of Cultural Identity
    - Self-perception

      Avowal—the self an individual portrays

      Ascription—the process by which others attribute identities to an individual

      Amae—in Japan, signifies a group-orientation
    - Modes of Expression: Core Symbols, Labels, & Norms
        - Symbols point to central ideas, concepts, & everyday behaviors that characterize membership in a group
        - Labels are a category of core symbols
        - Norms for conduct are based upon core symbols and how they are interpreted—defining who you are tells you how you should behave
- Individual, Relational, and Communal Forms of Identity
    - Cultural membership shown by public communication, rituals, rites of passage, and holiday celebrations
- Enduring and Changing Property of Identity

  Cultural identities change over time because of economic, political, social, psychological, and contextual factors, as well as from influence of other cultural identities
- Affective, Cognitive, and Behavioral Components of Identity
    - Affective component of identity relates to the emotions and feelings people attach to their avowed identities
    - Cognitive component of identity relates to beliefs persons have about the identity they have with each cultural group to which they belong
    - Behavioral component of cultural identity focuses on the verbal and nonverbal actions taken by group members
- Content and Relationship

  People may use in-group language to reinforce their in-group status and establish distance from out-group, or they may use language of the out-group to align themselves with the out-group
- Salience and Intensity Differences
    - Identities differ in salience and intensity in particular contexts
- Cultural Identity and Communication Competence

  Cultural competence is the demonstrated ability to enact a cultural identity in a mutually appropriate and effective manner.

Intercultural competence is the reinforcement of culturally different identities that are salient in a particular situation.

Finding My Whiteness: A Narrative of Cultural Identification

- Aims of author's personal narrative:
  To provide local understanding of his identification as a white male
  To de-normalize whiteness by exposing its power and providing insight into its everyday cultural manifestations
  To encourage readers of all ethnic, racial, and social backgrounds to excavate their own narratives of cultural identity
- Research about whiteness—not a literature review but a listing of published research into the topic of whiteness
- Narrative of cultural identification—follows author's growing sense of disconnectedness from what he blames as his assimilation into the white male American culture and his journey to recapturing a sense of belonging
- Moral of the story
  "[B]ecause of the power of whiteness, it is particularly important for those of us at the center of the center, white males, to expose, name, and narrate how we experience the center" (69).

A Polish Jewish American Story: Collective Memories and Intergroup Relations

- Relation of Nancy's story of her Jewish grandfather's immigration from Poland to America in 1924 and how her grandfather hated the Poles for the anti-Semitism he claimed to have suffered in Poland
- History and Collective Memory
  - History—a reconstruction and a representation of the past, focused on uncovering and (re)interpreting past events
  - Collective memory—an ongoing process of public and collective engagement with the past, interpreting "public offerings" consisting of presences (memories passed down from generation to generation or from written or other media accounts) and absences (information not available in books and popular media)
  - Past selectively made to matter to satisfy particular goals, needs, and emotions of group
- Relations of Jolanta's story of her own Polish-Jewish family background and its different memories of Polish life

The Hybrid Identities of Gender Queer: Claiming Neither/Nor, Both/And

- Author's narrative of what it feels like to be in a female body when she identifies more with being a male, but which is neither male nor female but a third, alternative identity, which she refers to as "my gender queer body"
- Hybridity of gender—the coming together of two or more cultural identities to offer a third identity or alternate identity that is often outside of language

Ambiguous Insiders: An Investigation of Arab American Invisibility

- Early Immigrants (1880-1945)
  - Although most Arabs are Muslims, Arabs who immigrated to U.S. during first period were predominantly Christians—central motive for immigration was economic opportunity
  - By 1916, 100,000 Arabs had immigrated to U.S.
  - By 1924, number of Arabs in U.S. estimated at 200,000 (195,000 Christian and 5,000 divided between Muslims and Druze)
  - Though early immigrants primarily identify themselves according to family, kinship, village affiliation, and/or religious sect:
    - 1882, U.S. officials classified them as Turks because they migrated from an Ottoman province (Syria)
    - 1899, immigration officials begin to classify them as separate "Syrian" ethnic group
    - 1910 U.S. census classified them as "Syrians" under category "Turkey in Asia" (Syrians addressed as Arabians, Armenians, Assyrians, and/or Turks)
    - 1914 debate on racial category of Syrians determines that though they may be Caucasian, privilege of U.S. citizenship reserved for Caucasians of European descent
    - 1914 court decision reversed but discrimination continues
  - By mid-century, Arab Americans the best acculturated ethnic groups in America—a majority identified as white/Caucasian, anglicized their names, replaced Arabic with English, and restricted ethnic identity to private sphere
- Second wave of Arab immigrants (post-1945)
  - Brought new & specific forms of Arab nationalism to U.S. and began to self-identify as "Arab" more than first wave of immigrants had
  - Larger number of Muslims
  - Other differences: new wave included refugees displaced by 1948 Palestine War, others driven by particular political events, and many professionals and university students, unlike previous immigrants
- Third wave of Arab immigrants (post-1960s)
  - Rapid influx of Arab immigrants due to relaxed immigration laws and as result from heightened war and upheaval in Arab world
  - Post-1965 immigrants are more religiously and geographically diverse than previous groups and include more Muslims than Christians
  - Distinguished from predecessors by their much stronger sense of Arab nationalism, heightened criticism of U.S. policy, and weaker sense of civic identification
  - Intensified political consciousness forged by opposition to U.S. policies as well as hostility and marginalization Arab immigrants experience in North America
  - Label "Arab American" a form of resistance to anti-Arab racism in post-1960s era has meant rising tensions between Arab Americans and majority U.S. culture
  - Confused identity from differing waves of Arab immigration and acculturation vs. non-acculturation

    - Their religion also makes it harder for new immigrants to acculturate: Islam, religiously and culturally, generally conflicts with white mainstream "American" culture more than Christianity
- Paradoxical identity faced by immigrants:
    - Classification as "Arab"
    - Racial classification: white-but-not-quite racial/ethnic status
    - Religion
    - Intersection of religion and race

Chapter Discussion Ideas

1. Collier discusses types of cultures. Using her discussion as a basis for consideration, list the names of various cultural groups with which you identify. Do you find conflict between any of these identities?
2. What does Collier mean when she asserts that cultural identities are both enduring and changing?
3. What does Krizek mean when he refers to assimilation as having a normalizing effect on white Americans as well as people of color?
4. What does Krizek mean by a sense of disconnection? What may result from such a sense of disconnection?
5. What are some of the dangers of relying on collective memory as a source for defining cultural identity?
6. In what ways do collective memories contribute to the building of stereotypes?
7. Hybridity is defined as the coming together of two or more cultural identities. Specify a number of situations beyond gender where hybridity enters into the definition of cultural identity.
8. What does Naber mean when she speaks of Arab invisibility?
9. Why does the paradox of Arabs being defined as a monolithic category persist in the minds of many Americans?

Chapter Exercises

Exercise 2.1: Self-Narrative of Cultural Identity

As an out-of-class assignment, have students write a narrative of their own cultural identification, as Robert Krizek does. With what cultural group did they most identify with when young? As they grew up? With what cultural groups do they most identify with now? How would they describe each cultural identity they claim? Which of their cultural identities would they say is the primary one?

Have students bring their essays to class and share their narratives with each other in small groups. In what ways can they identify how their cultural identifications are socially constructed? What might these socially constructed definitions of identity say about identity itself, how it is formed?

Exercise 2.2: Stereotyping

This exercise can be done in two ways—one in which you pick a stereotype represented in the class and discuss the effects of stereotyping on identity, the second in which you choose a stereotyped group not represented in the class and discuss the effects of stereotyping.

Select a stereotyped group represented in the class (women, men, teachers, blonds, mothers, singles, and so on). Have the students generate a list of stereotypes for this group. Then discuss the effects of stereotyping based on this list. Have students discuss someone they know personally who seems to fit in one of these groups but does not fit the stereotype?

Select a stereotyped group not represented in the class (Japanese, Arabs, CEO's of Fortune 500 companies, homeless people, and so on). Have students generate a list of stereotyped for this group. Then discuss why the stereotypes may or may not fit the group. What evidence is there, drawn from students' personal knowledge of someone in one of these groups, if possible, that the stereotype if oversimplified or dangerous? Discuss the effects of stereotyping.

Exercise 2.3: What Is Truly American? Uncovering Stereotypes

Have students get into small groups and read the two accounts of attending a baseball game that follow. The first is written by an Englishman, the second by an American. Each, however, shows stereotypical thinking about other culture(s). Have students identify the stereotyping going on in the two write-ups and explain how such stereotypes are fair or unfair.

(1) From **Dr. Neil's Adventure (http://drneil.blogspot.com/2004/07/truly-american-experience.html): A truly American experience** (Dr. Neil is English born but travels extensively in Europe, Australia, & U.S.)

I went to a baseball game last night! I went to see the Seattle Mariners play against the Anaheim Angels. The Mariners lost 8 - 2. It made no difference to me who won, the event itself was the fascination for me.

It seems the main reason most people go is to have somewhere they can drink and eat for a solid three hour stretch. I have to say most of them didn't look like they should be quite so hungry.

I had a vege-dog, after all I couldn't miss out on the full experience.

All I can say is it's certainly not cricket :)

(2) **Truly America's pastime** by Donald J. Ankney, Daily Staff *(The Online Daily of the University of Washington: Sports,* *http://archives.thedaily.washington.edu/1997/100797/past100797.html*), 10/07/1997.

I seldom go to baseball games.

It's not that I don't like baseball. I actually really enjoy going to games — the sound of the crowd, the crack of the bat and the personalities of the players. Who doesn't love rooting for the home team?

But I always feel guilty about going. Baseball has always just been fun. It hasn't challenged me as an audience member in the same way that something like opera does; in most art, the audience has to work to try and glean the meaning from an intentionally vague production.

That changed last Wednesday at the opening of the Mariners/Orioles series in the Kingdome. Maybe it was the excitement of the playoffs. Or maybe it was the detachment of being in the very back row of the Kingdome.

Whatever it was, baseball took on a new, deeper meaning for me that night.

Most sports are very European. Two groups of people — be they political states, ethnic groups or athletic teams — are battling one another, invading each other's territory attempting to dominate.

Soccer is nothing more than a summary of European history.

Even football and basketball, two sports of United States origin, are homage to European cultural dominance.

But baseball is a truly American sport.

There are no territories, no half-court line separating two peoples. There are no invaders and no defenders.

In baseball, the two teams share the field. One team doesn't actually try to stop the other from running the bases. The goal of the fielder is to get the ball to the base before the runner gets there, not to stop him from getting there.

Can you imagine the Serbs and the Croats living together like that, accepting each other's presence in Sarajevo, simply trying to live and work as best they can without interfering with the other?

The most distinctly American thing about the game is the field. It isn't a box full of carefully designed boundaries and borders. There are only two lines extending from the plate, with the space in between extending forever without limits.

Baseball doesn't try to limit how far you can hit the ball — nothing is stopping you from sending it into orbit. The only limit on the batter's accomplishment is the batter himself.

Is this an overly idealistic view of America? Perhaps.

But is it an overly idealistic view of what baseball really stands for? I don't think so.

Like much great art, baseball is about things as we would like them to be, rather than what they currently are. In baseball — in art — we place our hopes and our dreams: what we strive for.

A home run isn't just a point on a scoreboard. It's somebody who accomplished the impossible. It's the American dream.

Perhaps it's no coincidence that fireworks also celebrate Independence Day.

Exercise 2.4: Analyzing Arab American Web Sites

Divide students into small groups and have each group conduct Web research into one of the following Web sites. Have them gather the following information and report it to the class in a general discussion session.

1. Is the Web site credible? Who sponsors the site? Does the site have a mission statement (may be located on the "About Us" page)?
2. What is the site's main message or emphasis?
3. Do you agree with what is said or presented at the site? If yes, why? If not, why not?
4. What stereotypes about Arab Americans do you think the Web site seeks to counter or address? Is the site successful in this endeavor?

Web Sites:

- American Arab Institute: http://www.aaiusa.org/
- American-Arab Anti Discrimination Committee: http://www.adc.org/
- Arab American Action Network: http://www.aaan.org/
- Arab American Affairs: http://www.arab-american-affairs.net/
- Network of Arab American Professionals: http://www.naaponline.org/
- Arab Americans, Allied Media Corporation: http://www.allied-media.com/Arab-American/Arab%20american%20Demographics.htm

Have students tie their discussion of these Web sites and their messages to the Naber article they've read. For instance, have students list and discuss some of the social issues that work against the recognition and acceptance of Arab Americans as fully recognized members of U.S. society.

Chapter Film Suggestions

- ***Tales from Arab Detroit*** (Documentary, 1995; director/writer: Joan Mandell; VHS 45 min.) Summary Online (http://www.viewingrace.org/browse_sub.php?film_id=262&subject_id=9): "Detroit, home to 200,000 Arab Americans, is the largest Arab community in North America. This revealing documentary was filmed during the 1993 Detroit visit of renowned Egyptian storyteller Sheikh Ghanim Mansour, one of the last people to recite from memory the 1000-year-old 100-hour epic tale of the Bani Hilal tribe. The purpose of his two-week stay was, in the words of narrator Bushra Karamen, to make us think again about who we are and where we came from. Older Arab Americans of Palestinian, Lebanese, Yemeni and Syrian backgrounds relate the saga of family migrations and discuss the gulf between generations. Young people, including a rapper, members of the Warren Street Gang and a girl's basketball team, demonstrate how cultural constants - family, music, poetry - have been transformed through exposure to American society. Director Joan Mandell interweaves the performances of Sheikh Mansour with scenes at a local high school, hotel ballroom and downtown shopping mall to form a tapestry of Arab America's myriad experiences."

  Web References:

  Films on the Subject of Arab-American Identity: *Tales from Arab Detroit.* http://www.viewingrace.org/browse_sub.php?film_id=262&subject_id=9

  New Day Films: *Tales from Arab Detroit.* http://www.newday.com/films/Tales_from_Arab_Detroit.html

- ***Shtetl: A Journey Home*** (PBS Documentary; 1996; director, Marian Marzynski; 180 min.) "The film starts when Marian Marzynski, the filmmaker accompanies Nathan Kaplan, a 70 year-old Jewish man from Chicago to Bransk, a small Polish shtetl in Eastern Poland. It is here where their confrontation with the past begins. Throughout the film, several Holocaust survivors will make their way back to Bransk and share with us their stories. *Shtetl* takes a bold and illuminating look at Jewish/Polish relationships in both the past and the present. Shot in Poland, Israel, and the United States, *Shtetl* is a universal tale about Jews and those who live around them. However, unlike *Shoah*, which tells the story of these who died, Marzynski's *Shtetl* is a film about those who survived. Its moral is about civil rights for a minority living in a multi-ethnic society" (http://www.logtv.com/films/shtetl/default.html).

  Web References:

  Shtetl: A Journey Home, http://www.logtv.com/films/shtetl/default.html.

  Cohen Center for Holocaust Studies, Keene College, *Shtetl*, http://www.keene.edu/cchs/videos.cfm?category_id=7.

Chapter Test Items

Multiple Choice

1. According to Collier, culture is
    a. systemic
    b. what groups of people say and do and think and feel
    c. the communication that links people together
    d. all of the above *

2. To create a culture, groups must
    a. join a club
    b. define themselves as a group *
    c. be made up entirely of friends
    d. none of the above

3. The following are gender cultures:
    a. mothers and fathers
    b. chauvinists
    c. gays and lesbians
    d. all of the above *

4. Cultures are affected by which of the following
    a. changing socioeconomic and environmental conditions
    b. other cultures
    c. a and b *
    d. none of the above

5. Ascription is
    a. the process by which others attribute identities to an individual
    b. stereotypes
    c. attributions
    d. all of the above *

6. To the Japanese culture, *amae*
    a. is the Confucian term for harmony
    b. signifies a group orientation *
    c. means "friend"
    d. none of the above

7. The following terms are labels or core symbols for a culture
    a. American
    b. Hispanic
    c. people
    d. a and b *

8. The behavioral component of cultural identity focuses on
    a. on how members of a group interact
    b. the verbal and nonverbal actions taken by a group
    c. on how members of a group react to one another
    d. all of the above *

9. According to Krizek,
    a. the process of self-identification has been handed over to the media
    b. whites assume that theirs is a universal experience
    c. all cultures share some similarities
    d. all of the above *

10. Whiteness is
    a. a socially constructed racial classification *
    b. applicable only to those with certain chromosomes
    c. an inclusive paradigm
    d. not a valid label for a culture

11. According to Drzewiecka and Draznin, history is
    a. objective
    b. a reconstruction and a representation of the past
    c. focused on uncovering and (re)interpreting past events
    d. b and c *

12. The concept of collective memory is
    a. a creative and purposeful process
    b. selectively made to matter to satisfy particular goals
    c. one that presumes "multiple conflicting accounts of the past"
    d. all of the above *

13. Hybridity can be defined as
    a. revolutionary self-assertiveness
    b. the coming together of two or more cultural identities to offer a third or alternate identity
    c. a and b *
    d. none of the above

14. The concept of a "queer gender body"
    a. refers to a female trapped in a male body
    b. refers to a male trapped in a female body
    c. disrupts the binary of all male or all female *
    d. none of the above

15. The first wave of Arab Americans occurred in
    a. 1820-1850
    b. 1880-1945
    c. 1890-1900
    d. 1890-1925

16. U.S. officials classified the first wave of Arab immigrants as
    a. Syrians
    b. Turks *
    c. Arabs
    d. none of the above

17. Although most early Arab immigrants intended to acquire wealth and return to their country of origin,
    a. they could not make enough money as peddlers to buy their return home passage
    b. the majority eventually became permanent U.S. residents *
    c. they could not return home without facing a firing squad
    d. none of the above

18. In 1914, a South Carolina judge ruled that
    a. Syrians were to be classified as Caucasians
    b. the 1790 Act of Congress did not extend to Syrians the same rights as were intended for persons of European descent *
    c. Syrians were a serious threat to North America
    d. Syrians would henceforth be classified as Arab Americans

19. By the mid-19th century Arab Americans were
    a. treated to the same sort of racism faced by the Chinese, blacks, Jews, and Italians
    b. one of the best acculturated ethnic groups in America *
    c. practicing separatism
    d. still speaking Arabic

20. The third wave of Arab immigrants during the post-1960s can be characterized by
    a. a result of relaxed immigration laws
    b. heightened war and upheaval in the Arab world
    c. including more Muslims than Christians
    d. all of the above *

21. The label "Arab American" developed as
    a. more Arabs immigrated to the U.S. during the post-World War II period
    b. a confusion of identity made a label necessary
    c. an antidote to being labeled Syrians
    d. a form of resistance to anti-Arab racism in the post-1960s era *

22. In TV shows, films, and the news media, the concept of Arab
    a. persists as a monolithic category
    b. has no bearing on reality, for Arabs belong to a multiplicity of religious affiliations and emigrate from diverse regions
    c. is a paradox that means violence, racism, and discrimination against Arab, Middle Eastern, and Muslim individuals are acceptable behaviors
    d. all of the above *

23. Naber argues that conflations of the categories Arab, Middle Eastern, and Muslim
    a. are based on ignorance
    b. are random and irrational
    c. are products of a systematic process of neocolonialism *
    d. none of the above

24. According to Naber, anti-Arab media images perpetuate the idea of
    a. a generic Arab/Middle Eastern/Muslim enemy
    b. Arabs as corrupt and backward
    c. Arabs as a threat to U.S. security
    d. all of the above *

25. In the films *Not Without My Daughter* and *Protocol*, the corrupt men are portrayed as barbaric, primarily because they are
    a. Arab
    b. Muslim *
    c. Arab Americans
    d. none of the above

True/False

T 1. Culture is not the people but the communication that links them together.
F 2. Traffic lights in England are called "robots."
T 3. U.S. Americans define themselves as a group based on the use of English as a shared code.
T 4. If we compare Japanese to Germans, the Japanese, as a group, are more group oriented and emphasize status hierarchies more than do Germans as an overall group.
T 5. National and ethnic cultures are the communication systems created by people who share the same nationality or ethnicity.
F 6. Few subcategories of gender cultures exist.
T 7. Each individual has a range of cultures to which he or she belongs in a constantly changing environment.
F 8. Avowal is the process by which others attribute identities to an individual.
F 9. Many Americans practice *amae*.
T 10. Core symbols tell us about the place of humans in the universe.
F 11. Core symbols are difficult to perceive.
T 12. Cultural identities are both enduring and changing.

T	13.	Krizek attributes his lack of connectness to his culture as the cost of being white and male and raised in the 1950s.
F	14.	According to Krizek, whites' self-definition comes from within each person's unique culture.
T	15.	While participating in the Lakota rituals, Krizek felt he reacquired his perspective on the places and events that have constituted his life because of the distance and difference he experienced.
T	16.	Collective memories can turn into ideological dogma when we totalize our own experiences or those of our family members as definitive.
F	17.	Jews living in Poland prior to World War II were seen as contributors to that country's survival during its myriad occupations by foreign invaders.
T	18.	The Holocaust reduced Poland's population of 3 million Polish Jews to between 350,000 and 500,000.
F	19.	Gender can never be characterized as a hybrid—one either is female or male.
T	20.	Though the Syrians' non-European origin received national attention, they were not targeted by racism and discrimination to the same extent as other communities.
T	21.	Arab Americans have been forced into the binary classification "either white or nonwhite."
T	22.	Many Americans assume that Islam is a cruel, backward, and uncivilized religion.
F	23.	The U.S. Census Bureau classifies Arab Americans as nonwhites.
T	24.	Many Arab immigrants bring a social structure to the U.S. that organizes differences between social groups according to religious categories.
F	25.	Naber contends that the Disney movie Aladdin (1992) portrays Arab women in real-life roles.
F	26.	Most Arabs are not Muslim.
T	27.	Edward Corsi, the U.S. Commissioner of Immigration and Naturalization, stated that the Syrian is a "doubtful element" of "Mongolian plasma" attempting to contaminate the pure American stock.
F	28.	After the Arab-Israeli War of 1967, few Arab Americans identified themselves as of Arab descent.

Chapter Essay Questions

1. How does viewing intercultural communication from a cultural identity perspective increase your competence as a communicator?
2. What are some of the benefits of using the cultural identity approach to intercultural communication situations?
3. What social dynamics are unique to whiteness as a cultural identity?
4. How does narrative play a role in the development of cultural identity?
5. What is collective memory? How does collective memory contribute to the construction of a cultural identity?
6. In what ways do collective memories contribute to the building of stereotypes?

7. What is meant by the idea of negotiating a "self," and how does communication enter into that process?
8. List and discuss some of the social issues that work against the recognition and acceptance of Arab Americans as fully recognized members of U.S. society.
9. Explain how the various social factors such as racialization affect the individual development of an American Arab identity.

Chapter 3 International Cultures: Understanding Diversity

Chapter Synopsis

Chapter 3 focuses on cultures around the world and how their worldviews and belief and value systems influence their communication. Students will be challenged with the following four questions about intercultural communication after reading this chapter:

- What cultural differences exist between Eastern and Western peoples?
- How do these differences influence their ways of communicating?
- What are the different modes and methods of persuasion valued and practiced by different cultures?
- How do you learn to interact with and understand people who come from very different cultures around the globe?

Nisbett, in "Living Together vs. Going It Alone," contrasts the cultural characteristics of individualism/independence (as the principal tendency of North Americans) and collectivism/interdependence (the primary characteristic of East Asians), noting that "Asians are more accurately aware of the feelings and attitudes of others than are Westerners" (106). He also examines the differences between Western *erabi* (active, agentic) style, based on the attitude that people can control their environment and thus make it fit them, and the Japanese *awase* (harmonious, fitting-in) style, which rejects the notion that the environment can be manipulated by people; rather people must accommodate their environment.

Jia's article, "The *Wei* (Positioning)—*Ming* (Naming)—*Lianmian* (Face) Continuum in Contemporary Chinese Culture," examines the Chinese concept of this continuum as it applies to government, education, and especially business. He suggests ways in which students can learn how to adapt their communication behavior by understanding the Chinese concept of face.

In "India: The Dance of Shiva," Gannon examines Hindu traditions, which he contends is an integral part of the Indian culture. In order for students to grasp the Indian culture, they must learn about Hinduism. He explores the "Dance of Shiva" as a means to understand Hindu religion. This dance symbolizes the five main activities of the Supreme Being.

Peltzer's article, "Personality and Person Perception in Africa," compares three distinctive components of the people inhabiting present-day sub-Saharan Africa: (1) *traditional* persons whose worldview has been little affected by the modern world; (2) *transitional* persons, who mediate the two cultures—the traditional and the modern; and (3) *modern* persons, who have rejected the traditional worldview and participate fully in the modern world.

Begley, in "Communication with Egyptians," focuses on Egyptian worldview and Islamic religion, values, and language because she understands these to be the most influential cultural characteristics in communication situations between Egyptians and non-Egyptians. Her article anticipates and challenges some of the preconceptions American students might have about Egyptian culture.

These articles will help students understand that members from different cultures bring different histories and worldviews to a communication event and these differences impact and influence interaction.

<u>Chapter Outline</u>

To Relate Effectively with People from Diverse International Cultures:

- You must have knowledge about the people from other cultures
- You must have respect for their diversity.

Individualism-Collectivism Continuum

- Individualism is prevalent in northern Europe, present and former British Commonwealth, United States
  - Value personal distinctiveness
  - Individual choices and personal preferences are characteristic
  - Tend to seek goals of personal accomplishment
  - Feelings of self-worth derive from individual success
- Collectivism is prevalent in most Asian cultures, particularly in East Asia
  - Value sameness and blending in with others
  - Seek group accomplishment
  - Feelings of self-worth usually aligned with feelings of being in harmony with one's group

Independent versus Interdependent Aspects of Western and Asian Cultures

Western Cultures—Independence	**Asian Cultures—Interdependence**
• Training for independence begins very early: Common for children to sleep in their own beds—quite often in separate rooms—promoting independence	• Training for interdependence also begins very early: More common for children to sleep in the same bed as their parents—and perhaps other siblings—promoting interdependence
• Insistence on freedom of individual action, desires for distinctiveness, preference for egalitarianism and achieved status, and belief in universal rules of proper behavior	• Preference for collective action, blending harmoniously with the group, acceptance of hierarchy and ascribed status, and variable rules of behavior, taking into account context and nature of relationships involved

Styles of Conflict Reduction and Negotiation

- Western *erabi* style—the environment can be manipulated for individual goals; "debate" leads to conflict resolution
- Asian *awase* style—the environments cannot be manipulated—people must adjust themselves to it; negotiations do not involve debate but are based on mutual trust and cooperation—goal is mutually satisfying outcome

Chinese Culture

Importance of China as a leading player on the world stage:

- As china's economy grows, so will the interpersonal contact between Chinese and Americans will increase
- Business relationships and joint ventures will increase
- Influence of nongovernmental persons and agencies will become more evident
- To interact successfully with Chinese will require that the deep underlying value dynamics of its culture be grasped; one of those is concept of face

Dynamic of face (in China and other Asian cultures):

- Tied to how Chinese feel and communicate with one another
- Extends far beyond idea of mere personal embarrassment and incorporates emotional, communicative, hierarchal, and personhood dimensions that govern interaction among Chinese

Wei **(Positioning)—*Ming*** **(naming)—*Lianmian*** **(Face):**

- *Wei*—a philosophical construct reflecting Chinese concepts of ontology and axiology
- *Ming*—a linguistic/rhetorical construct that reflects a uniquely Chinese way of social interaction, communication, thinking, and feeling
  - From emotive perspective, affect and human feelings are fundamental aspects of face; face is dynamic and fluid aspect that requires management throughout interaction
  - From personhood perspective, face is a sacred object to be seen by community
- *Lianmian*—understanding Chinese concepts and practices of face can generate important discoveries of Chinese people and Chinese culture

Indian Culture

Religion (Hinduism) forms central theme of culture:

- "Hindu philosophy is the key to understanding India" (Gannon, p. 133).
- Overwhelming majority of Indians are tradition-oriented even though for past millennium, Indian culture has been synthesis of racial, religious, and linguistic influences; changes in that culture and society cannot be understood without reference to Hindu tradition

Hindu Religion:

- Numerous deities, each being different manifestations of one Supreme Being
- Most important gods are Brahma (the Creator), Vishnu (the Preserver), and Shiva (the Destroyer)

Shiva:

- Among greatest names and appearances of Shiva if Nataraja, Lord of the Dancers—the first dancer, a deity who dances as an expression of his exuberant personality
- Dance of Shiva described as the " 'clearest image of the activity of God which any art or religion can boast of' " (Coomaraswamy, cited in Gannon, p. 122); it also reflects cyclical nature of Hindu philosophy

Dance of Shiva a Metaphor for Indian Culture and Society:

- Dancing among Hindus regarded as most ancient and important of the arts
- Every aspect of nature displays dance pattern, called the Daily Dance, but nature inert and cannot dance until Shiva wills it—Shiva dances out the creations and existence of the world
- Shiva lapses periodically into inactivity—cosmos becomes chaos, and destruction follow period of creativity
- Dance symbolizes the five main activities of the Supreme Being: creation and development (*srishti*); preservation and support (*sthiti*); change and destruction (*samhara*); shrouding, symbolism, illusion, and giving rest (*tirobhava*); and release, salvation, and grace (*anugraha*)
- India's history reflects cycles of chaos and harmony epitomized by the Dance of Shiva

Cyclical Hindu Philosophy:

- Philosophy tends to overlap with religion; is regarded as key to life itself—clarifying its meaning and way to attain spiritual goals
- World is considered illusory
- Only happiness worth seeking is permanent spiritual happiness as distinguished from fleeting pleasures or wealth or material possessions
- Life is journey in search of salvation (*mukti*); if the seeker withstands all the perils of the journey, is rewarded by exultation beyond human experience or perception (*moksha*)
- Hindu philosophy directs each individual along a path
- Four paths or ways lead to the ideal state: intense devotion or love of God (*bhakti yoga*); selfless work or service (*karma yoga*); philosophy or knowledge of self (*nana yoga*); and meditation or psychological exercise (*raja yoga*)

Reincarnation:

- Reincarnation or cycle of lives: individual souls (*jivas*) enter world as souls of simplest forms of life but do not vanish with death of original bodies; rather they move to new body or form
- Transmigration of souls takes individual *jiva* through series of complex bodies until a human one is achieved; at this point, the ascent of physical forms ends and the soul begins its path to *mukti*
- Birth of a person into a particular niche in life is determined by the balance of right and wrong actions of his or her soul through its previous cycle—endless cycle of birth, life, and death, the soul's karma, depends on deeds and decisions made in each lifetime

The Four Stages of the Cycle of Life

- First stage is that of a student; primary responsibility in life during this stage is to learn; supposed to develop strong character and good habits to emerge equipped to produce a good and effective life
- Second stage, beginning with marriage, is that of a householder; wants of pleasure satisfied through the family, wants of duty through exercising responsibilities of citizenship, and wants of success through employment
- Third stage is retirement, signifying withdrawal from social obligations, the time for a person to begin true education—to discover who one is and what life's all about
- Final stage is one of *sannyasin* at which person achieves *mukti*; when person finally departs from this world, freedom from cycle of life and death is attained

The Family Cycle

- Preference for a son, for he guarantees continuation of generations and will perform the last rites after his parents' death; word for son, *putra*, literally means "he who protects from going to hell" (p. 125)
- Daughter has negligible ritual significance; she's normally considered an unmitigated expense—someone who will never contribute to family income and who, upon marriage, will take away a considerable part of her family's fortune as her dowry
- Love of family seen as a way to the final goal of life, *mukti*
- Children in India considered sacred—high degree of infant indulgence in richer areas
- In poorer areas, children taken for granted except for firstborn son; reinforced by belief in rebirth—because an individual is not born once and once only, he or she cannot be regarded as a unique event
- Cultural importance of children derived from need to carry on the cycle of life

Father-son bonds:

- Indian father is frequently remote, aloof, and much-feared disciplinary figure
- Son must obey him unquestioningly, pay him respect, and offer complete support in every need both in life and after death
- Father owes his son support, good education, best possible marital arrangement, and inheritance of property

Hindu marriage emphasizes identity, not equality:

- Girls trained to be submissive and docile
- Ideal of womanhood in Indian tradition is one of chastity, purity, gentle tenderness, self-effacement, self-sacrifice, and singular faithfulness
- Problems long faced by women in India: female infanticide, child marriage, purdah (feminine modesty and seclusion), marital mistreatment, and low status of widows
- However, the lower down the economic hierarchy, the more equal are relations between sexes
- Arranged marriage still the norm in India—the concept of life as an illusion makes idea of loveless marriage easier to understand

- Marriages are usually for a lifetime; divorce considered socially disgraceful

The Cycle of Social Interaction

- Sense of duty (dharma) is social cement in India—includes totality of social, ethical, and spiritual harmony
- Dharma consists of three categories: universal principles of harmony (*sanatana dharma*), relative ethical systems varying by social class (*varnashrama dharma*), and personal moral conduct (*svadharma*)
- Prime traditional virtues: leading a generous and selfless life, restraint from greed, respect for one's elders

Social conflict, oppression, and unrest:

- Originate in non-adherence to dharma by those in positions of power, whose actions have created a cycle of disharmony
- Hindus see a quarrel as a drama with three actors—two contestants and a peacemaker, who is seen as the victor in the dispute for restoring harmony
- Because all worldly acts are transient, part of illusion of life, they have no decisive moral significance; but violence not condoned—those acts committed by people aware of their responsibilities are counted against them in their seeking of *mukti*

Caste system (*verna*):

- Though officially outlawed, still a source of constant tension

  Four main castes:
  - Brahmans, seers or religious people
  - Administrators
  - Producers such as skilled craftspeople and farmers
  - Followers or unskilled laborers
- Fifth group below the system: **the untouchables**; its members are engaged in work considered socially undesirable and unclean

  Subcastes, or *jati*:
  - Influence immediacy of all daily social relations, including work; about 3,000 *jati* exist, further divisible into about 30,000 sub-*jati*, with unwritten codes governing the relationships between *jatis*
  - A person's name provides information not only about his or her own jati but also about the region of the country from which the person's family background originated
  - The *jati's* values, beliefs, and prejudices are internalized and thus define the right actions, or dharma, for an individual
  - Ordering of social behavior extends to every institution in Indian life, including the workplace

The Work and Recreation (Rejuvenation) Cycle

- Work enables, prepares, and progresses the individual through the cycle of life toward ultimate aim of achieving *mukti*
- Indians have only partially internalized Western work values

- Work performance is more relationship-oriented than contractual in nature: a competent person may be respected but not included in a group unless he or she possesses the group characteristics
- Family, relatives, caste members, and people speaking same language or belonging to same religion may form in-groups
- Indians tend to work with lifelong friends and colleagues and minimize risk-taking behavior, consistent with Hindu philosophy of life as an illusion
- Importance of honoring family and *jati* bonds leads to nepotism, dishonesty, and corruption in commercial world
- Guilt and anxiety aroused only when individual actions go against the principle of primacy of relationships, not when foreign standards of ethics and efficiency are breached
- American managers must act more authoritatively in India than in the United States

African Socialization and Personhood

- Sub-Saharan Africa seen as region of similar cultures
- Differ from other regions in world because of high illiteracy rate, subsistence economies, and highly permissive child-rearing practices
- Though large degree of diversity found among African cultures, Peltzer identifies three distinctive components of sub-Saharan people:
- **Traditional** people—those who still live within tribal village societies; little affected by modernization
- **Transitional** people—those who live in and shuttle between the traditional and modern cultures
- **Modern** individuals—those who participate fully in the activities of contemporary industrial or postindustrial world

Egyptian Culture

- Three elements must be considered (Begley):
- Egyptian worldview and religion, Islam
- Egyptian values of tradition, social relationships, and hierarchical structure:
  - Because culture is 4,000 to 5,000 years old, Egyptian traditions important
  - Social relationships very important because part of culture if fear of loneliness
  - Hierarchies according to age, gender, and experience are crucial
- Arabic language

Egyptian Worldview and Religion:

- Began as culmination of various African civilizations and beliefs
- Ancient Egypt (*Kemet*, Blackland, to the native peoples) could focus on nation building, art, science, and philosophy because of geographic advantage because vast deserts protected people from invasion on both sides
- A.D. 619, nomadic Arabs invaded Egypt, and eventually Islam replaced other religious beliefs to become prevailing worldview of Egypt

Islamic History:

- Religions influences every part of everyday life

- Islamic beliefs dominate every moment from birth to death and beyond
- About 85% to 90% of Egypt's population, and more than 1 billion people worldwide, are followers of Islam

Islamic Principles:

- Four tenets central to understanding Islam:
  - It is a monotheistic religion
  - God created the world
  - Humans are fundamentally good from birth because they are God's creation and without "original sin"
  - There will be a day of judgment for each Muslim when God decides whether each person will go to heaven or be condemned to hell
- Five pillars for Muslims:
  - First, *shahada* (creed) is the confession of faith
  - Second, salad (prayer); Muslims are required to stop for prayer five times a day, facing in the direction of the holy city of Mecca
  - Third, *zakat* (giving alms) to the poor is expected of each person
  - Fourth, *sawm* (fasting) during month of Ramadan is required
  - Pilgrimage (*hajj*) to Mecca is requisite for those who can make the journey

Islam possesses universal allure:

- Islam is a religion of action, not of contemplation
- Muslims from all cultural and ethnic groups are recognized as equal members within the religion
- Islam does not require complicated rituals or sacrifices

Islam and Politics:

- Each political group publicly supports the *Shari-a* (religious laws), advocates that religious principles should be taught in schools, and allows family concerns to be decided by Islamic ideologies
- Constitution declares Islam the state religion
- Egyptian dilemma: trying to balance Islamic religious laws with attempts to modernize industry and business
- Rise of factions of religious fundamentalism from increasing number of secular laws, technological advance, outside influence, population explosion, and rising unemployment
- Sojourners should be aware of Islamic religious beliefs when conducting business or traveling in Egypt:
  - The Koran exhorts everyone, especially women, to cover themselves modestly
  - Travelers or business people who display knowledge of and respect for Islamic beliefs are more likely to establish friendships and profitable business relations

Egyptian Values:

- Three fundamental values: tradition, relationships, and hierarchical devotion
- Tradition: Religious beliefs play pivotal role in family, politics, business, and education

- Relationships:
  - People fear loneliness; wish to be always surrounded by network of relatives and friends
  - In Egyptian collectivism, family, social, and business taken seriously and give Egyptians great pleasure
- Hierarchical Structure:
  - According to age, gender, and experience
  - In Islam, people submit to God's will in all matters; Muslims do not questions their fate because God alone knows their destiny
  - In Muslim families, oldest male wields authority and power and is responsible for safety and well-being of family members

Egyptian Language and Culture:

- Arabic is one of the oldest living languages in the world
- Arabic used to convey unity, worldview, and artistic impressions

Arabic and Unity:

Egyptian children learn only in Arabic and are taught to memorize and recite lengthy verses of the Koran

Promotes unity within a region

Arabic and Worldview:

Classical Arabic still widely spoken among Muslims of every region

Public prayers and ceremonies worldwide are conducted in Arabic even if the Muslim adherents are not Middle Eastern Arabs

Term *jihad* incorrectly translated as "holy war"' literally means " 'utmost effort' in promotion and defense of Islam, which might or might not include armed conflict with unbelievers" (Lippman, cited in Begley, p. 147)

- Writing as art—Arabic now used as an art form in Egypt.

Chapter Discussion Ideas

1. What are some of the dynamics that lead to the development of the interdependent person? The independent person?

2. How can the Westerner use the concepts of the *awase* and *erabi* styles of conflict and negotiation when dealing with Easterners?

3. How would relationship development differ among people who value *independence* versus *interdependence?* Ask students to describe a person who values an independent perspective of life and one who values a group perspective. Are such persons so different that they could not form a satisfying interpersonal relationship or communicate effectively?

4. What are some of the differences between discourse in the West and discourse in China? How would such differences affect communication?

5. How would the Hindu view of life, the world, and salvation influence communication between Hindus and non-Hindus?

a. Ask students to first describe in their own words the various beliefs of the Hindu religion. Record their responses on the board by labeling separate columns as *Life*, *World*, and *Salvation*.

b. Next, ask them to take another culture that they have read about (the Chinese, for example) and describe how people from these cultures would view these same three topics.

c. With the two sets of cultural beliefs on the board, ask students to reflect on how two people from these two cultures might communicate differently.

6. How does the religion of Islam differ from Hinduism? Are there reasons beyond geographical location for grouping both religions under the rubric of "Eastern." What religion(s) are considered "Western"? How does this binary construction for dividing our world, cultures, religions, peoples, etc., frame our understanding of ourselves as "Westerners" and others as "Easterners"?

7. Could the categories of personhood developed by Peltzer be used to understand social psychological development in other parts of the world? Would they apply to indigenous people in Central or South America? In Australia? If yes, why; if no, why not?

8. How has the West's understanding and definition of *jihad* influenced its attitude towards Muslims? Looking at Begley's alternative definition of the term, do you think Westerners are right in their attitudes? How might such differences account for Westerner's attitudes towards the religion of Islam? Is there a middle ground?

Chapter Exercises

Exercise 3.1: Success Across Nations

Part I. This exercise ties into all the readings in Chapter 3 by having the students expand their definition of what it means to be successful. Having read about the values and culture of people from China, India, Africa, and Egypt, it asks the students to do two things. First, to identify what success means to them. After evaluating their own definition of success, they will attempt to define what it means to be successful if you are a member of one of the cultures examined in Chapter 3. So what is a successful Chinese, Indian, African, or Egyptian man? Woman? Child?

Part II. The second part of this exercise will give students experience interacting with people who may come from different cultural backgrounds than their own. As a basis of comparison between their own definition of success and the definitions of success based on the cultures examined, ask the students to contact one to three people who did not grow up in the U.S. Students should interview each person and determine how each defines success and how each would describe himself or herself as a successful person. Some of the questions below will help students come up with their own definition, analyze the definitions of the cultures, and conduct interviews with others:

Some questions for discussion.

1. How would you define a successful person?
2. How would you define the typical or "traditional" notion of a successful person?
3. Would you say that you are a successful person? Why or why not?
4. How does your success differ from the "traditional" notion of success?
5. How have the people in your life (family, friends, coworkers, spouse or partner, and so on) influenced your success?
6. What problems have arisen for you in your work? What barriers have you had to overcome in order to be a successful person?
7. Have there been any problems relating or interacting with people that have influenced you negatively or positively as you became a successful person?
8. Has interacting with people from different countries and cultures had an impact on your success?

Ask students to write up their findings and compare them with other members of the class.

Exercise 3.2: Guest Speaker

This exercise encourages you to invite members of the Chinese community into your classroom. Two options are suggested for this exercise.

Option 1: If you are in a community with a significant Chinese and/or Chinese American population, invite someone to come in and speak to the students about Jia's article.

Assign Jia's article at least one class period ahead of the day the speaker is scheduled to come. Divide students into small groups and have them generate questions for the speaker. After the groups have generated a list of questions, have them choose their best two questions to turn in. Prepare a list of the students' questions for the guest speaker so that he or she will have some idea of how class discussion might go. It might also be helpful to give the speaker a copy of your course syllabus so that he or she has a better understanding of the context within which the students are reading the Jia article.

It is up to you and the guest speaker to decide how the class will be run on the day of the visit. One idea is to co-lead a discussion based on the questions prepared by the students. A second option is to give the speaker some time to lecture on *an aspect* of intercultural communication between Americans and Chinese, or Jia's article, before leading a class discussion.

Option 2: Adapt option 1 into a series of short presentations of student-conducted interviews with Chinese/Chinese Americans and/or short presentations by Chinese American students about their experience and their family's experience with the ideas found in Jia's article.

Exercise 3.3: Values that Conflict and Correspond

This exercise can be used in conjunction with the Gannon article, "India: The Dance of Shiva." This activity asks the students to consider what they value in their life and make value comparisons between people from India as presented in the chapter, themselves, and a friend or acquaintance from a different cultural background. After reading the article, students can rank cultural values by using the value inventory scale on the following page, using a scale of 1 (most valued) to 10 (least valued). After ranking the values for the Indian culture from the reading and then ranking themselves, students are to ask a person from another country to rank the items.

Have the students report their findings to the class. Use the following questions to discuss students' responses.

1. What were the five top values of the Indian culture?
2. The top values that you ranked and the five top values of your friend?
3. What differences and similarities are there?
4. How do these rankings reflect the values of your cultures?
5. What are some examples of how the Indian culture as well as you and your friend's culture have "taught" you to value certain things in life?
6. What values, if any, were not on the list that you and/or your friend and/or a member of the Indian culture believe should have been included?
7. How might differences in cultural values influence interpersonal interactions?
8. How might such differences lead to interpersonal conflict?
9. How much do similarities and differences in values enhance intercultural communication?
10. What value differences might be insurmountable? Which would be incidental?

Exercise 3.3: Values that Conflict and Correspond

Value Inventory

Rank the following list of values from 1 (most valued) to 10 (least valued). Use Column A to record your prediction of Indian responses. Use Column B to record your responses to the values. Then ask a person from another country or culture to rank the items and record them in Column C. The definitions provided after each value are not meant to be definitive meanings. They are to allow you and your friend to complete this inventory using the same definitions for each value.

Value	A	B	C
1. Happiness (contentedness)			
2. Freedom (independence, free choice)			
3. Salvation (being saved, eternal life)			
4. Family security (taking care of loved ones)			
5. Self-respect (self-esteem)			
6. Equality (sister- /brotherhood, equal opportunity)			
7. Sense of accomplishment (making a lasting contribution)			
8. A world at peace (free of war and international conflict)			
9. Wisdom (a mature understanding of life)			
10. A comfortable life (a prosperous life)			

Value Comparison		
Predicted Top Values of India	**My Top Values**	**My Friend's Top Values**

Exercise 3.4: Showing Our Emotions

In some cultures, the expression of anger by yelling and cursing may be acceptable. In others, it would be considered quite inappropriate. The extent to which we reveal ourselves through laughter, tears, anger, anxiousness, and jealousy depends in large part on how our families and communities displayed emotions and when we were chastised or rewarded as children for emoting inappropriately or appropriately. We learned from culture how to show and not show our feelings.

This exercise focuses on how often and intensely we show our emotions and how we feel when others express their emotions. This exercise is designed to help students understand more about their own emotional responses so that they might be in a better position to begin to understand how and why other cultures use emotion during interpersonal conversations.

Ask students to respond to the list of emotions provided as a handout on the following page by indicating from 1 to 6 how often they express these emotions and how comfortable they feel when others express them. Use the scales provided to rate each emotion. The blank fine at the end of the list is for you or your students to fill in if you or they wish to add any emotions to the list.

After asking students to complete this list, ask them to consider the following questions.

1. Which emotions do you have the least/most difficulty expressing and why?
2. Which emotions do you have the least/most difficulty watching others express and why?
3. Which discrepancies, if any, are there between the extent to which you are willing to show certain emotions and your feelings of comfort watching others express the same emotion?
4. How do you think your expression of emotions and your responses to others' emotions have been influenced by cultural beliefs and attitudes?
5. What differences and similarities are there in the displaying of emotions among your friends or classmates who come from different cultural backgrounds?
6. How might intercultural communication be influenced by such differences?

Exercise 3.4: Showing Our Emotions Worksheet

Displaying Your Emotions		**Watching Others' Emotions**	
1	very frequently	1	very comfortable
2	frequently	2	comfortable
3	occasionally	3	somewhat comfortable
4	not very often	4	not very comfortable
5	rarely	5	uncomfortable
6	never	6	very uncomfortable

____________	angry	____________
____________	loving	____________
____________	concerned	____________
____________	anxious	____________
____________	confident	____________
____________	sad	____________
____________	depressed	____________
____________	jealous	____________
____________	insecure	____________
____________	silly	____________
____________	violent	____________
____________	argumentative	____________
____________	proud	____________
____________	friendly	____________
____________	playful	____________
____________	envious	____________
____________	belligerent	____________
____________	flirtatious	____________
____________	hostile	____________
____________	guilty	____________
____________	unsure	____________
____________	impatient	____________
____________	arrogant	____________
____________	______	____________

Exercise 3.5: Conflicting Messages

A common perception of people from the U.S. held by other cultures is that Americans tend to be friendly yet distant and rather insincere. A Kenyan described people in the U.S. in the following way:

> Americans appear to us rather distant. They are not really as close to other people—even fellow Americans—as Americans overseas tend to portray. It's almost as if an American says, "I won't let you get too close to me"; it's like building a wall. (Feig & Blair, 1975)

While U.S. Americans may feel that by smiling and being informal they are communicating friendliness and openness with people from other cultures, they may also be sending other messages that communicate closed-mindedness and shallowness. How are these other messages sent and how might people from other cultures respond to perceived insincerity?

The following case study of Raj and Tim from Artman (1976) includes some of these mixed messages that we often don't know we are sending. As students read the story, ask them to consider what messages are being sent by both Raj and Tim, and how each is perceiving and responding to the messages. What cultural factors are influencing these messages and responses?

> Tim, an American student, struck up a conversation one day with Raj, an international student from Iran in his class. They had lunch together and talked about their studies, professors they had taken, and the differences between U.S. football and Middle Eastern football (soccer). Tim enjoyed their conversation, especially in finding common interests with an international student. When they parted he suggested that they have lunch together again sometime. The next day he saw Raj on campus and waved and said hello to him. After class the following day, Raj came up and invited Tim to have lunch with him. Tim, preferring to eat lunch by himself that day, declined (however, when he was in the cafeteria a friend came over and sat down with him).
>
> Tim talked with Raj for a few minutes at another class meeting and said hello to him on campus a few times, but then found that Raj avoided looking at him and hurried away after class before Tim had a chance to approach him. After that semester, they saw each other only rarely and on those occasions, even when their eyes met, Raj seemed not to know Tim. Tim responded in kind, but never could figure out what had happened. (Artman, 1976)

After students have read the case study individually or in groups, discuss the scenario in groups using some of the following questions:

1. How did Raj perceive his relationship with Tim after they had lunch together?
2. What messages did he receive from Tim that helped shape this perception?
3. How did Tim perceive his relationship with Raj after they had lunch together?

4. What messages might Tim have sent to Raj that led him to ignore Tim on campus?
5. How do you think Tim was perceiving his own behavior?
6. What might Raj have learned from his culture and Tim from his about "appropriate" friendly behavior among acquaintances?
7. What Iranian and U.S. American values and attitudes are evident from this scenario?
8. How might the miscommunication between Raj and Tim have been alleviated?
9. Think of what could have been done before, during, and after they met to prevent the breakdown of their friendship.

Chapter Popular Film Suggestions

- ***Monsoon Wedding*** (New Delhi, 2001; writer/director: Mira Nair, with writer Sabrina Dhawan; 1 hr 54 min)
  This film covers many of the points found in Gannon's essay, "India: The Dance of Shiva," including the concepts of class/caste, arranged marriage, collectivism, attitudes toward children and family life; the importance of dance to the culture; and the influence of Hinduism in every aspect of the characters' lives. As an online review tells us, "Mira Nair and the writer, Sabrina Dhawan, interweave the ancient and the modern, the old-fashioned and the irreverent, the innocent and the sexual in today's globalized Delhi. The intimate, handheld camera welcomes the viewer into the characters' lives and into Nair's own beloved Punjabi culture - robust, earthy and full of life. The audience is swept into the bacchanalian revelry of kebabs, whisky and Bollywood music that is a Punjabi wedding." (*Monsoon Wedding, A New Film by Mira Nair*. 1/16/2005. http://www.mirabaifilms.com/monsoon.html)
  Web References:
  Monsoon Wedding, A New Film by Mira Nair. http://www.mirabaifilms.com/monsoon.html
  Planet Bollywood: Review of *Monsoon Wedding*. http://planetbollywood.com/Film/MonsoonWedding/

- ***Hotel Rwanda: A True Story*** (Rwanda, 2005; director/writer: Terry George, with co-writer K. Perason). Covers the bloody Rwandan conflict of the 1990s, when a million people were killed in a genocidal civil war between the warring Hutus and Tutsis. The film covers the actions of one man, hotel manager Paul Rusesabagina, who did something to help while the world community stood by. This film offers an opportunity to explore the idea of individual and collective responsibility. Can the actions of one person have an appreciable effect on the world stage? What is our collective responsibility in situations where so many lives are at stake? What other kinds of conflict resolution should have been possible?
  Web References:
  United Artist Official Site: *Hotel Rwanda* http://www.hotelrwanda.com/main.html
  Hotel Rwanda Teacher's Guide http://www.hotelrwanda.com/main.html

- **The Story of Qiu Ju** (China, 1993; director Zhang Yimou; 1 hr 40 min)

  Set in contemporary China, this film examines rural life in China. According to the Amazon.com review, in this "remarkable film about a woman obsessed with exacting an apology from the chief of her small village, director Zhang Yimou (*Red Sorghum*, *Raise the Red Lantern*) tells a deceptively simple story with incredible art. When Wang Shantang (Lei Laosheng), the chief, kicks a chili farmer, Quinglai (Liu Peiqi), between the legs, all the farmer's wife, Qiu Ju (Gong Li), wants is an apology. The chief's reticence sends Qiu Ju on a misguided journey through the legal system in search of satisfaction. What she gets, however, is a harsh lesson in 'be careful of what you ask for.' In the end she finds that life can frustrate our attempts at harmony in the simplest, cruelest ways" (James McGrath. Amazon.com: Review of *The Story of Qiu Ju* (1993). 1/16/2005. http://www.amazon.com/exec/obidos/tg/detail/-/6303023037/ref=cm_rev_editorial_dp/103-5604910-7559814?v=glance&s=video&vi=reviews)

  This film could be used to explore the concepts of face found in Jia's article, especially the interconnection of *wei/ming/lianmian*, as well as the Asian worldview discussed in Nisbett's essay. (English subtitles; 100 minutes)

  Web Reference:

  The New York Times: Movies. Review of *The Story of Qiu Ju* (a k a Qiu Ju Da Guan Si). 1/16/2005. http://movies2.nytimes.com/gst/movies/movie.html?v_id=121848.

Chapter Test Items

Multiple Choice

1. An Asian asked to "tell me about yourself" would be likely to say:
   a. "I work for a company that makes microchips."
   b. "I am fun-loving with my friends." *
   c. "I go camping a lot."
   d. none of the above

2. Japanese schoolchildren are taught how to practice self-criticism in order to
   a. improve their relations with others
   b. to become more skilled in solving problems
   c. to become better at their jobs
   d. all of the above *

3. Western parents:
   a. require their children to do things on their own
   b. make the decision for the child on the assumption that the parent knows best what is good for the child
   c. concentrate attention on objects
   d. both a and c *

4. Which of the following is a component of the Chinese face concept?
   a. positioning
   b. naming
   c. *junzi*
   d. both a and b *

5. The Chinese Confucian, normative view of humans is that they are beings with inherent moral responsibility to cultivate oneself into a
   a. junzi or a shengren*
   b. junzi or mianzi
   c. junzi or lianmian
   d. junzi or wei

6. The term w*ei* could de defined as
   a. a central theme in *Zhouyi*, an ancient Chinese classic
   b. status consciousness
   c. something that can be bought
   d. all of the above *

7. Contrary to the modern Western view of humans largely as free and equal individuals, the concept of *wei* suggests
   a. that humans always live in a hierarchy of social and moral positions and this are "naturally" unequal
   b. the worth, dignity, power, influence, and access to resources of each and every human being should vary according to varying *weis*
   c. that *wei* is a static process
   d. both a and b *

8. The term *ming*
   a. connects *wei* and *lianmian*
   b. is a Chinese word for language/rhetoric/communication
   c. refers to the proper naming of each wei
   d. all of the above *

9. The Hindu god *Shiva* is known as
   a. The Creator
   b. The Preserver
   c. The Destroyer *
   d. None of the above

10. Action or activity is the definition of the Hindu term
   a. nirvana
   b. dharma
   c. karma *
   d. Brahman

11. According to Hinduism, the ultimate aim in life is to
    a. help those who remain in the lower levels of existence.
    b. remain pure of heart and soul.
    c. realize the most profound level of existence. *
    d. experience interconnectedness among all other Hindus.

12. Which of the following statements would people who follow *raja yoga*, the fourth Hindu path to salvation, be most likely to say?
    a. Love lies at the base of every heart.
    b. Work can be a vehicle for self-transcendence.
    c. Ignorance can be overcome through intense study.
    d. We must experience our bodies, our minds, and our spirits to their fullest potential. *

13. Which of the following statements would people who follow *karma yoga,* the third Hindu path to salvation, be most likely to say?
    a. Love lies at the base of every heart.
    b. Work can be a vehicle for self-transcendence. *
    c. Ignorance can be overcome through intense study.
    d. We must experience our bodies, our minds, and our spirits to their fullest potential.

14. According to Hindu Philosophy, during which stage of life is it the individual's prime responsibility to learn?
    a. student *
    b. householder
    c. retirement
    d. all of the above

15. In Peltzer's argument, the outlook of the traditional time concept
    a. describes the life cycle as the process by which the person passes from the present to the past
    b. is cyclic and death is not regarded as final
    c. does not emphasize future, past, or present
    d. both b and c

16. In the development of *traditional personhood*,
    a. the individual is taken over by the group
    b. the individual has no intrinsic value outside the group
    c. females are socialized into female secrets and males into male secrets
    d. all of the above *

17. Which of the following is NOT a central tenet of Islam?
    a. There is only one God.
    b. God created the world.
    c. Humans must struggle to overcome their sinful nature.*
    d. Every Muslim will go to heaven or hell.

18. How old is Egyptian culture?
    a. 4000-5000 years old *
    b. 2000-3000 years old
    c. 7 centuries old
    d. 5 centuries old

19. Which of the following is NOT fundamental to Egyptian culture?
    a. tradition
    b. relationships
    c. hierarchical devotion
    d. privacy *

20. Which of the following does the Koran encourage?
    a. Females who have reached puberty must cover themselves modestly.
    b. Only women over the age of 20 must cover themselves.
    c. Everyone must cover themselves modestly.
    d. c and a, but especially a *

21. Arabs have used the Arabic language to convey which of the following?
    a. unity
    b. worldview
    c. artistic impressions
    d. all of the above *

22. Muslims are required to stop for prayer
    a. once a day facing in the direction of the holy city of Mecca
    b. twice a day facing in the direction of the holy city of Mecca
    c. four times a day facing in the direction of the holy city of Mecca
    d. five times a day facing in the direction of the holy city of Mecca *

True/False

F 1. East Asians find individual distinctiveness desirable.

T 2. In Chinese, there is no word for "individualism."

F 3. When surveyed about their attributes and preferences, North Americans characteristically underestimate their distinctiveness.

T 4. In the Western view, once a contract has been agreed to, it is binding regardless of circumstances that might make it less attractive to one of the parties than it was initially.

T 5. Communication is a fundamental part of face.

T 6. Face is not a static concept but a dynamic and fluid one.

T 7. The higher one's *wei* is, the more truth and knowledge one is assumed to possess.

F 8. Chinese scholars and students studying overseas are considered higher in rank than those in Chinese institutions.

T 9. There are growing cracks of change in the Chinese culture of authority.

T 10. Among Hindus, dancing is regarded as the most ancient and important of the arts.

T 11. Shiva is a deity that dances simply as an expression of his exuberant personality.

T 12. According to Hindu philosophy, a person can pass through the four stages of life in a single lifetime or stay at each stage for many lifetimes.

T 13. In India the lower down the economic hierarchy, the more equal are the relations between the sexes.

T 14. In the traditional view of the life cycle in sub-Saharan Africa, birth signifies the return of a dead person.

F 15. In the traditional treatment of males and females in sub-Saharan Africa, education is unequal between the sexes and weak members are not tolerated, but are thrown out of the group.

T 16. Four tenets are central to understanding Islam.

T 17. Islam possesses a universal allure, which appeals to Egyptians.

T 18. Good Muslims follow the five pillars.

Chapter Essay Questions

1. Discuss the differences between Western and Eastern orientations toward the following view: "Becoming successful and respected is a matter of hard work. It is important for a manager to be older than his subordinates. Older people should be more respected than younger people."
2. Describe the concept of *amae*, a particular type of social relationship unique to the Japanese.
3. Why is debate uncommon in modern Asia?
4. Describe the differences in the Western *erabi* negotiation style and the Eastern *awase* negotiation style.
5. How do *wei* , *ming*, and *lianmian* help maintain a culture of authoritative-relational communication in China?
6. What does *wei* convey about the Chinese worldview?
7. How does the act of bribery relate to *wei* in China?
8. In what ways do both Communism and capitalism in China challenge the traditional ideal and cultural pattern of *lainmian*?
9. What does the Dance of Shiva symbolize?
10. Discuss how the Dance of Shiva relates to Hindu Philosophy.
11. Explain the four stages of life that an individual passes through, according to Hindu Philosophy.
12. Describe the different facets or types of *dharma* that guide a person through his or her life.
13. How does the caste system in India influence communication among its people?
14. Describe the Hindu concept of *Karma*.
15. Discuss the Indian proverb, "A son should be treated as a prince for five years; as a slave for ten years; but from his sixteenth birthday, as a friend."
16. Discuss the role of women in the Indian culture.

17. Describe the differences between the traditional, transitional, and modern individual in sub-Saharan Africa as outlined by Peltzer.
18. Peltzer uses the term *personhood.* What does he mean by this term?
19. Identify and review the four tenets which are central to understanding Islam.
20. Explain the importance of tradition to Egyptian culture.
21. Why is Islam considered a religion of practices? What are the five pillars outlined for Muslims by the religion of Islam? What does each suggest about Islamic values?
22. What attitude do Egyptians usually take to the hierarchical structure of their society?
23. What does the religion of Islam say about hierarchical social positions? Could these be examples of how cultures tend to be self-justifying? Consider Protestantism and the American call to "pull yourself up by your own bootstraps."
24. Explain the connection between language and cultural unity using the example of Arabic in 7th century Egyptian society.
25. Explain the importance of relationships to Egyptian culture.
26. Explain the idea of *Insha'allah* ("If God wills it") as part of Muslim beliefs.
27. After reading the articles in Chapter 3, can you describe an Eastern way of communicating and a Western way of communicating?

Chapter References

Artman, R. (1976). The Miami intercultural communication workshop. In David S. Hoopes (Ed.), *Readings in intercultural communication: Vol. V--Intercultural programming* (pp. 68-106). Pittsburgh, PA: The Intercultural Communication Network.

Feig, J. P., and Blair, J. G. (1975). *There IS a difference: Seventeen intercultural perspectives*, Washington, DC: Meridian House International.

Chapter 4 Co-Cultures: Living in Two Cultures

Chapter Synopsis

This chapter examines the cultural patterns that influence the communication of certain cultural groups in the United States. Five distinct questions form the foundation of this chapter:

- What does it mean and feel like to be "the other" in U.S. society?
- How do power, dominance, and nondominance manifest themselves in intracultural U.S. communication?
- What are some cultural characteristics of nondominant cultures in the U.S. and how do these differ from those of "mainstream" U.S. culture?
- How do members of these cultures communicate intra- and interculturally?
- With what challenges must members of these U.S. cultures contend as they live and communicate in the U.S.?

Kim, in her essay "*Unum* and *Pluribus*: Ideological Underpinnings of Interethnic Communication in the United States," reveals four types of interethnic communication messages: assimilationism, pluralism, reconciliation, and extremism. Examples are provided for each type of message.

In their essay, "Does the Worm Live in the Ground? Reflections on Native American Spirituality," Garrett and Wilbur explore some of the basic cultural elements contributing to what is known as Native American spirituality. Four concepts which are central to the Native American spirituality are discussed: Medicine, Relation, Harmony, and Vision.

Stringer, in "Let Me Count the Ways: African-American/European-American Marriages," explores biracial relationships and the cultural dynamics that can cause conflict and misunderstanding. As she outlines the areas in which misperceptions or cultural conflicts can occur, she suggests ways to improve communication and reduce the potential for misunderstandings.

In "Gendered Communication Styles," co-authors Wood and Reich clearly explain the difference between sex and gender. They posit that sex is genetically determined, whereas gender is socially constructed. They discuss ways in which communication between males and females might be improved.

Braithwaite and Braithwaite, "'Which Is My Good Leg?': Cultural Communication of Persons with Disabilities," interviewed 100 persons with disabilities for an in-depth look into their experiences communicating with members of what they call the "temporarily able-bodied" community.

In his essay "In Plain Sight: Gay and Lesbian," Eadie recognizes that there are a variety of mindsets, ranging from hostile to accepting, regarding the gay and lesbian culture. His essay will introduce students to the unique cultural characteristics and communication styles of the gay and lesbian members of society.

Chapter Outline

Ideological Underpinnings of Interethnic Communication in the U.S.

Four Types of Interethnic Communication Messages:

- Assimilationism
- Pluralism
- Reconciliation
- Extremism

Assimilationism:

- Three core principles of classical liberalism shape arguments of assimilationism:
    - Individualism
    - Universalism
    - Procedural equality
- Messages project societal vision:
    - Immigrants and indigenous ethnic minorities are mainstreamed into normative culture and institutions
    - In turn, they are expected to assimilate themselves socially and culturally
- Messages celebrate personal achievement and self-reliance
    - Place individual identity over and above group identity
    - Question validity and morality of categorical thought
- Primacy of individual hinges on value of equality
- A fair society grants equal rights and equal opportunity for all; equality = "fair play"

Messages of Pluralism, or Multiculturalism:

- Challenge assimilationist messages
    - Deems traditional liberal notions of individual identity and universal application of laws, rules, rights, and responsibilities as false ideology
    - Social and cultural distinctiveness now a rallying point to combat "institutional racism"
    - Demand suppression of "hate speech"
- Emphasize sanctity of group
- Replace old "melting pot" metaphor with new ones—mosaic, quilt, salad bowl—emphasizing distinctiveness of ethnic groups
- Predicted on persistent reality of racial and ethnic prejudice
- Advocate status equality (in place of procedural equality)

Messages of Ideological Reconciliation:

- Occupy "vital center"—the "middle" America
- Reflect struggle of Americans seeking moderation, tolerance, accommodation, integration, and balance

- Indicate ambivalence and contradiction in way Americans think about race, ethnicity, and interethnic relations
  - May support multiculturism but only to extent that ethnic identity is subsumed under common "American identity"
  - May support affirmative action programs based on group identity, but consider quota systems unfair, divisive, and counterproductive
- Can be traced to mainstream, integrationist civil rights movement led by martin Luther King, Jr.

Messages of Extremism:

- Includes marginal voices of separatism
- Preference for maximum in-group/out-group separation
  - Examples: Ku Klux Klan, neo-Nazis, Skinheads, so-called Patriot movements
  - Known for commitment to racial purism, supremacy of white race, even arms training and preparation for race war
- Also come from extreme left as well,
- Examples: New Black Panthers and the Nation of Islam
- Leonard Jefferies' description of white Americans as "ice people"
- Louis Farrakhan's call for black nationalism and economic reparations, assertion of black racial superiority, and his condemnation of Jews as "bloodsuckers"; he's also reported to have called the U.S. "the Great Satan" during visit to Iran
- Separatist messages of extreme left and extreme right converge in:
  - Rigid in-group/out-group distinction
  - Characterization of in-group as "victims"
  - Full-blown confrontational rhetorical posturing
  - Fortification of mutually intransigent moral claims

Native American Spirituality

Fundamental Aspects of Native American Spirituality:

- **Walking in step**—refers to coming together or connecting with the essence of spirituality
  - Walking in step with the Greater Circle
  - Essence of spirituality is about "feeling"
  - Basic Native American spiritual and traditional beliefs (Locust, 1988):
    - Single higher power known as Creator, Great Creator, Great Spirit, or Great One; lesser beings known as spirit beings or spirit helpers
    - Plants and animals, like humans, are part of the spirit world
    - Human beings made up of a spirit, mind, and body that are interconnected
    - Wellness is harmony in body, mind, and spirit; unwellness is lack of harmony
    - Natural wellness—caused by violation of sacred social or natural law of creation
    - Unnatural unwellness—caused by conjuring
    - Each person is responsible for his or her own wellness
- **Medicine**—is everywhere, the very essence of one's inner being, a power that connects everyone to every living being through the heart

- **Harmony**—living in harmony and balance with natural environment central belief; life seen as a gift from the Creator
  - Acceptance very important—emphasizes that everyone and everything has a reason for being; trying to control people or things considered a waste of energy because everything is as it should be at any given time
  - Emphasis on numbers four and seven:
    - Four represents the spirit of each directions—east, south, west, and north—usually depicted in circle
    - Seven represents same four directions as well as the upper world (Sky), lower world (Earth), and center (the heart) to symbolize universal harmony and balance (visualized as sphere)
- **Relation**—refers to all things being connected and respect for this interrelationship
  - Concept of family extends to animal world, plant world, and mineral world, as well as Mother Earth and Father Sky
  - Power of relation symbolized by the Circle of Life (Web of Life), consisting of basic elements of life—fire/sunlight, earth, water, and wind
  - Circle reflects not only the interrelationship of all living things but the natural progression of growth of life itself
- **Vision**—involves knowing what to do with the gift of life, an inner knowledge of one's purpose in the greater meaning of life
- Many different ceremonies across tribal nations; for example, sweat lodge, vision quest, clearing-way ceremony, blessing-way ceremony, pipe ceremony, sunrise ceremony, sun dance, and so on
- Ceremonial practice reaffirms one's connection with that which is sacred

In **American mainstream ideology**, the purpose of life consists of "life, liberty, and the pursuit of happiness..."	From a **traditional Native American perspective**, a corollary would be "life, love, and learning..."

African-American/European-American Marriages

- In 1967 in the U.S., anti-miscegenation laws found to be unconstitutional
- According to U.S. Census, 1993, number of biracial marriages more than doubled between 1970 and 1990
- Such relationships taxed by dynamics of cultural diversity and diverse cultural backgrounds impose additional challenges over and above those which usually face married couples
- Key to successful long term relationship is sharing of at least some core values:
  - Terminal values—the goals or core values
  - Instrumental values—behaviors used to obtain the desired goal or core value
  - Partners must identify both terminal and instrumental values, as well as identify values along critical dimensions, in order to reduce misperceptions and conflict
  - Values can be represented as a series of *value continua* or *dimensions* that describe two opposite poles (e.g., individualism-collectivism)

- Five value dimensions that illustrate potential for conflict:
  - **Terminal goal: completing a job or activity; instrumental behavior: task vs. relationship**
    - Women and African Americans tend to be more relationship oriented
    - Men and European Americans tend to be more task oriented
  - **Terminal goal: Maintaining a harmonious relationship; instrumental behavior: avoiding vs. confronting issues**
    - Both women and European Americans tend to be more conflict avoidant
    - African Americans and men tend toward confronting issues
  - **Terminal goal: achievement of success; instrumental behaviors: individualism vs. collectivism**
    - Both European Americans and men have a tendency to demonstrate individualism
    - Women and African Americans more likely to lean toward collectivism
  - **Terminal goal: independence vs. dependence; instrumental behaviors: maintenance of rules for behavior vs. flexibility of behaviors**
    - In child-rearing practices, European American culture typically encourages independence and flexible rules
    - African American community stresses dependency in children and far less flexible rules for behavior
  - **Terminal goal: respect for authority; instrumental behaviors: formality and strong power distance vs. informality and weak power distance**
    - African American culture tends toward more formality and power distance
    - European American culture tends toward more informality and weaker power distance

Direct and Indirect Communication Styles: Difference likely to create tension

- African American and European American cultures tend to communicate in more direct manner (except in conflict, when European Americans tend to be far less direct)—direct communication style one of time and task, to save time and achieve task as quickly as possible
- Women tend to be less direct than men; indirect communication style intended to build relationship and save face
- Solution: for each partner to understand and genuinely value other person's approach

High- and Low-Context Systems:

- High context: communication system about things that aren't fully explained because everyone in culture "understands them"
- Marrying into a family, new spouse doesn't have high-context so can feel excluded and attribute this to race or ethnicity
- Solution: each partner should provide context or history for events or stories being shared

Detached versus Attached Communication Styles:

- Detached communicator discusses issues calmly and "objectively"
- Attached communicator discusses issues with patience, conveying person feelings

- Detached style is normed more highly for both European Americans and men; the attached normed for both African Americans and women
- Primary solution: identify each partner's styles, gain an understanding of each person's intentions conveyed by individual style, so interpretation can be more accurate

Nonverbal Perspective:

- Eye contact: European Americans tend to look more while listening than speaking; African Americans look more while speaking
- Smiles: European American women encouraged to smile far more often than African American women
- Time orientations: monochronic (ability to track one thing at a time) vs. polychronic (ability to do multiple things at once) can affect communication

Gendered Communication Styles

- Women identified as co-culture
- Differences between feminine and masculine communicative behaviors can complicate interactions and relationships
- Sex—determined by genetic codes that program biological features
- Gender—the cultural meaning of sex
- "Sex is innate, whereas gender is learned and, therefore, changeable."
- People become gendered through influence of many factors

Two Most Important Factors in Learning What Masculine and Feminine Mean:

- Social expectations for males and females
- Interaction in sex-segregated children's play groups
- Girls learn to be cooperative, not to criticize, to pay attention
- Boys learn to be assertive, to focus on outcomes, to be competitive

Gender Gaps in Communication:

- What counts as support: feminine culture sees communication as way to connect; masculine culture sees it as an instrument to do things
- Feedback: feminine culture learns to give lots of response cues—verbal expressions—to build relationships with others; masculine culture focuses on outcomes more than processes, so uses feedback to signal specific agreement and disagreement
- Expressing care: for feminine culture, talking is primary way to express and expand closeness; for masculine culture, doing a concrete favor more likely to express caring
- Independence: masculine culture emphasizes independence and self-sufficiency more than feminine culture
- Talking about the relationship: favored communication style by feminine culture; in masculine culture, talk tends to be perceived as instrument for accomplishing things

Six Ways to Improve Communication between Males and Females:

- Suspend judgment
- Recognize validity of different communication styles
- Provide translation cues

- Seek translation cues
- Enlarge one's own communication style
- Suspend judgment—the first and last principle of effective communication

Cultural Communication of Persons with Disabilities

- Approximately 14 million disabled Americans between ages of 16 and 64
- Passage of the Americans with Disabilities Act (ADA) creates "bill of rights" for persons with disabilities
- Five "key-life functions" affected by disability: mobility, employment, self-care, social relationships, and communication

Challenges to Relationships of People with Disabilities:

- For nondisabled people, lack of experience interacting with disabled people can lead to high uncertainty about how to interact:
    - May feel overly self-conscious and their actions may be constrained, self-controlled, and rigid
    - Behaviors may appear uninterested or unaccepting to the person who is disabled
    - Becomes easier to avoid the disabled
    - Nonverbal behavior may convey rejection and avoidance—keeping greater distance, avoiding eye contact, avoiding mentioning the disability, or cutting conversation short
- Stereotypes nondisabled people may have of disabled persons:
    - Perceive them as: dependent, socially introverted, emotionally unstable, depressed, hypersensitive, easily offended
    - Perceive them as: differing in moral character, social skills, and political orientation

Process of Redefinition (based on interviews with disabled persons):

- Redefining the self as part of a "new" culture—three phases:
    - Stigma isolation
    - Stigma recognition
    - Stigma incorporation
- Redefining disability
    - See disability as one of many characteristics of a person—disability is context-specific; we're all disabled in some way
    - Emphasize person first
    - Sensitize oneself to commonly used labels for being disabled ("polio victim," or "arthritis sufferer")—how people are labeled affects how others see them and how they perceive themselves
    - TAB = "temporarily able-bodied"
    - Redefine "assisting devices" such as wheelchairs (a wheelchair becomes a seat and wheels) and canes (a cane becomes portable railing)
    - Assisting device seen as part of person, not something to be played with
- Redefining disability for the dominant culture
    - To be seen and treated as a person first

Gay and Lesbian Communication of Culture

- Being open about sexual orientation is a political statement
- Lesbian and gay culture must deal with tensions about how open to be about one's sexuality
- Although culture is driven by sexual attraction and desire, being lesbian or gay is not only about sex
- Social proscriptions and dynamics that affect communication
- Media portrayals of lesbians and gays have both perpetuated stereotypes and promoted tolerance and acceptance
- Gay male portrayals in newsmagazine stories—four classic stereotypes (Smyth 2004):
  - Gay males are effeminate
  - Gay males are "sick" or mentally ill
  - Gay males are sexual predators
  - Gay males are "violent, libido-driven monsters"
- From 1969 to 1980, media coverage focused on emerging Gay Liberation movement and reactions to that movement
- American Psychiatric Association removed homosexuality from its list of mental illnesses
- From 1980 to 2002, increasing number of articles about gay men—portrayals as effeminate dropped but newsmagazines still interested in gay serial killers and unusual sexual practices
- Despite dissipation in media coverage, stereotypes still persist in many people's thinking
  - Products of heterosexism—behavior of heterosexual individuals assumed to be "normal," that of homosexual individuals as "deviant"
  - Knowing someone who is gay or lesbian leads to more favorable attitudes: "watching" a gay television show (such as *Will and Grace*) shown to have same result
- Six "interactive stages" in developing non-heterosexual identity (D'Augelli 1994):
  - Recognizing one's attractions and feelings are not heterosexual; telling others that one is not heterosexual
  - Summarizing self-concepts, emotions, and desires into personal identity as gay/lesbian/bisexual
  - Developing non-heterosexual social identity
  - Disclosing one's identity to parents and redefining familial relationships afterward
  - Developing capabilities to have intimate gay/lesbian/bisexual relationships
  - Becoming a member of a gay/lesbian/bisexual community
  - Stages are interactive because they rely on communication with others to occur

Chapter Discussion Ideas

1. Ask students to engage in a class discussion on the following Orwellian quote: "All men are created equal—some are just more equal than others."
    a. Begin by inviting students to look closely at the terms in the sentence. Who is not included? What does "equal" mean? What does it mean to be "created equal"?
    b. Next, ask students to consider U.S. society. Who are the "some" that are more equal in the United States? Why are these people more equal than others? What do they have, what privileges do they have that others don't? Who are those that are not "as equal" as those who are "more equal"? What prevents them from being as equal as the others?
    c. Finally, ask students why, if we know that some people are more equal than others, does this situation persist in society today? Why hasn't it been changed? What will have to happen to make all people equal to each other? Is this possible? Are hierarchically structured, class-based societies inevitable? Will there always be those on the bottom and those on top?

2. What do Garrett and Wilbur refer to when they write about "walking in step"? What feelings would generally be associated with walking in step? Does one have to be Native American to benefit from walking in step?

3. The sharing of at least some core values is considered to be one of the keys to successful long-term relationships. Ask students what they believe to be essential core values a couple must share to support a successful relationship.

4. How is gender a social phenomenon? Do you agree with Wood and Reich that our gender is the product of socialization? Or is it primarily, or at least partially, a biological phenomenon? Do you think male/female relations can be improved using the strategies that Wood and Reich suggests?

5. Why are non-disabled persons often so uncomfortable interacting with persons with disabilities?
    a. Ask students to consider this question by reflecting on their own experiences communicating with persons with disabilities. What made them uncomfortable? What was different about communicating with the person with a disability from communicating with non-disabled persons?
    b. Discuss the prevalence of uncertainty and unfamiliarity in intercultural communication. These feelings are very common and often account for much of our discomfort during intercultural interactions. What is often unfamiliar about communicating with persons with disabilities? What might we be uncertain about when we communicate with persons with disabilities?
    c. Using Braithwaite's suggestions as supporting material, ask students how they can go about becoming more comfortable with communication

between themselves and persons with disabilities. What can they do? How can they view the other persons?

6. Ask students to consider how media portrayals of lesbians and gays affect our perceptions of them. Ask students to list television shows or movies that they watch or have seen that portray gays or lesbians favorably/unfavorably. How did the show/movie affect their own perceptions of gays and/or lesbians.

Chapter Exercises

Exercise 4.1: Political Correctness or Necessary Changes?

This exercise incorporates themes from all the articles in chapter 4. It asks students to consider the popular phrase "political correctness" and determine for themselves whether it is a movement that suppresses free speech or whether it is, in part, really about changes in our language and perception of other cultures. Changes in how we talk about and refer to people often influence how we perceive those people. Take the evolution of the word *crippled* to refer to those individuals who use wheelchairs and walk with the aid of crutches. Over the past few decades, the word *crippled* went from *handicapped* to *disabled* to *physically challenged.* If you look at the progression of these terms and the more tolerant and inclusive social and legal changes that have affected physically challenged individuals, you can see a gradual positive development in how members of this group perceive themselves and are perceived by the able-bodied members of society. The same type of language evolution can be found in terms regarding women and gays and lesbian. As our language changes, attitudes and policies sometimes change with it. Although there may not be a direct causal link between language changes and policy and attitude changes, it is clear that language shapes our perception of the world and its people in different ways. With changes in perception come changes in how we act toward and interact with people. Guadalupe Friaz, assistant professor of ethnic studies at the University of Washington, describes language as political and always changing:

> When we talk about language we're talking about the relationships between people, and what people call each other reflects whatever tension and anxiety that society is going through.... Change is constant.... Group relationships always change, so of course terminology is going to change. (de Leon & Macdonald, 1992, p. A1)

Change inevitably brings about many different kinds of tension and disagreement in a society. Decisions must be made about whether to make changes, how to go about making changes, who will make the changes, who will be affected, etc. Changes in our language, school curricula, and teaching strategies are just a few examples of the transitions taking place in the United States today as a result of a heightened awareness of diversity.

The term "political correctness" is often used to describe this increased awareness and shift toward more inclusive and specific language. Those who have coined the phrase "political correctness" feel that these changes in language and thought have bred a climate of intolerance on university campuses. Some people have perceived enormous pressure to use the *right* terms when talking about certain cultural groups. Others even feel that their freedom of speech has been suppressed when they are chastised for espousing views that are not in step with the current climate of multiculturalism and diversity.

Engage students in a dialogue about "political correctness" and what it means to them. We would suggest that you have students discuss several of the questions below in small groups and then have each group report the results of their discussion to the class. You may also wish to have students write on the general question, "What is political correctness?" the day before having a class discussion. This kind of exercise can turn into a very spirited and even emotional debate on the merits and disadvantages of "political correctness." Encourage students to be honest about their own opinions yet respectful of their classmates' opinions as well.

Some questions to consider in small groups and as a larger class:

1. List some earlier terms used to identify women, gays, lesbians, and the disabled. Then list the more recent politically correct terms.
2. Define what you think the phrase "political correctness" means.
3. Offer an alternative definition of "political correctness," perhaps an opposing view from your own.
4. Why have there been such negative opinions expressed in the media about political correctness? What's wrong with advocating and using "politically correct" language?
5. What do you think about the linguistic and social changes that are currently taking place in our society?
6. Do you feel that there is pressure to be "politically correct"? Or is being "politically correct" really just about being sensitive to and respectful of all members of U.S. society?
7. What is there to be gained in our society by using language that refers more precisely to the cultural backgrounds of individuals? Conversely, what are the problems with using exact terms to refer to different groups of people? Consider this scenario.You are participating in a classroom discussion and use the word *black* to refer to U. S. citizens of African ancestry. A person in the class corrects you and explains that *African American* is the preferred term. What is your reaction to this correction?
8. How can we know how to refer to and address members of certain cultural groups?
9. Does it really matter what we call people? Can those people who are U.S. citizens just be called simply "Americans"? Why or why not?

Exercise 4.2: Privilege in U.S. Society

This exercise asks students to examine U. S. society and determine which groups enjoy certain privileges to which many other groups do not have access. It is common among those who have the "room at the top" to assume that other individuals have equal access to society's opportunities, rights, and services, not realizing that people's personal worlds are made up of experiences that can be very culture-specific and biased against other groups. The assumption that people are the same and share the same societal benefits can strain and even hinder the development of intercultural relationships because such an assumption is based on a lack of awareness and sensitivity to an acquaintance, friend, or romantic partner's experiences. By examining the societal privileges that several groups enjoy, we can increase the awareness of and sensitivity to others' experiences that can be so crucial in intercultural communication.

One way to introduce this exercise on privilege in U.S. society to students is to begin with an example of Euro-American privilege. "White privilege" is a phrase used to identify advantages that many European Americans have that are often not available to people of color. A serious and disturbing example of white privilege is the tendency for African American men to be stopped for questioning by the police in upscale neighborhoods where they may be perceived as suspicious or "out of place." Euro-American males usually do not suffer this kind of discrimination under these same circumstances. While some groups may enjoy more privileges than others, all groups have greater access to certain privileges than others. For example, women, in general, are probably stopped by police for questioning less frequently than men. Thus we might say that white males more so than black males, and women more so than men, have greater access to the "privilege" of not being unnecessarily harassed by the police.

The questions below focus on issues of privilege and culture. Some will be very difficult for students because they will require information regarding cultural groups about which they may know very little. Most likely, the more diverse your class is, the more varied and informative will be the discussion. Ask students to consider many of the different cultural characteristics of U.S. society when answering the questions, for example, laws, societal norms, traditions, stereotypes, prejudices, etc. Students should first discuss these questions in small groups. Afterward engage the class in a discussion by having each group report on its responses. Watch for assumptions being made as the discussion progresses. That is, are statements being made that assume students' experiences and perceptions are shared by other U.S. residents?

You may wish to give different questions to different groups so that all questions are covered. Add other questions not listed here and ask students to generate their own questions.

Questions for exercise 4.2

1. What societal privileges do you think European Americans have greater access to than other cultural groups? Are there any privileges that non-European Americans have that European Americans do not?
2. What societal privileges do you think heterosexuals enjoy that gay men and women do not?
3. What societal privileges do men enjoy that women do not?
4. What societal privileges do women enjoy that men do not?
5. What societal privileges do able-bodied individuals enjoy that disabled individuals do not?

6. What societal privileges do same-race couples enjoy that different race couples do not?
7. What societal privileges do opposite-sex couples enjoy that same sex couples do not?

Exercise 4.3: Stories to Live By

Every culture tells stories of creation, survival, ways to live, and so on. The Native Americans in the U.S. have an especially rich trove of stories that explain their traditional way of life. Have students read the following story, from the Sioux Indians of North Dakota and recorded by Mary McLaughlin in 1916, as an example of "walking in step" in harmony with nature. Ask them to reflect on how this story illustrates the concept of Harmony as explained by Garrett and Wilbur. Then ask students to come up with stories—the folklore of their own home or culture—used to illustrate right behavior.

The Little Mice

Once upon a time a prairie mouse busied herself all fall storing away a cache of beans. Every morning she was out early with her empty cast-off snake skin, which she filled with ground beans and dragged home with her teeth.

The little mouse had a cousin who was fond of dancing and talk, but who did not like to work. She was not careful to get her cache of beans and the season was already well gone before she thought to bestir herself. When she came to realize her need, she found she had no packing bag. So she went to her hardworking cousin and said:

"Cousin, I have no beans stored for winter and the season is nearly gone. But I have no snake skin to gather the beans in. Will you lend me one?"

"But why have you no packing bag? Where were you in the moon when the snakes cast off their skins?"

"I was here."

"What were you doing?"

"I was busy talking and dancing."

"And now you are punished," said the other. "It is always so with lazy, careless people. But I will let you have the snake skin. And now go, and by hard work and industry, try to recover your wasted time."—Mary L. McLaughlin. 1916. *Myths and Legends of the Sioux.*

Exercise 4.4: Sexual Harassment or Friendly Behavior?

Sexual harassment in professional environments has become a major and controversial issue in the past few years. It is an issue that has raised the consciousness of employers and employees, professors and students, and men and women in general. Sexual harassment is about many things: the abuse of power over subordinates and women, the definition of appropriate conduct in a working environment, and the right of all individuals to work in a non-threatening, non-coercive setting. At a more basic level, however, sexual harassment is often about how the same behavior can be perceived quite differently by the people involved. This exercise focuses on male/female differences in behavior perception and can be used in conjunction with the Wood and Reich article.

This case study asks students to consider the role of perception in sexual harassment. Why do men and women often perceive the same behavior quite differently? How do men define "appropriate behavior" in the workplace? How do women define it? Before asking students to read and discuss the case study below in small groups, have them answer the first question about sexual harassment. Choose from among questions two through ten for students to answer with their group members; ask students to consider the remaining questions as a large class. Although this is a topic that lends itself to a great deal of debate and even conflict, encourage students to be as honest in their responses as possible.

Case Study on Sexual Harassment

1. How would you define sexual harassment? (Please don't give a legal definition. Draw from your own opinions and experiences.) Now read the case study below and consider the questions that follow.

> Susan worked as a welder for a small, privately owned auto parts manufacturer. After only a few weeks on the job, she began to notice that centerfold pin-ups from men's magazines were prominently displayed at individual work sites around the shop. There were also pictures of nude women tacked to the company's community bulletin board. Susan asked her only female colleague, Joan, why these pictures were there but Joan just shrugged her shoulders and said, "I guess because they like to look at them while they're working." Joan seemed unconcerned about the pictures.
>
> But the pictures really bothered, even offended Susan. Susan felt that the pictures were pornographic and had no place in a work setting. She had to look at them whenever she went to talk to other employees or even pass their work stations, and she could not read the bulletin board without seeing the pictures there. After talking with her supervisor about her concern, he agreed to take down the pictures on the bulletin board but said that the men had a right to display the pictures at their individual work stations because that was their private space. Susan then asked individuals if they would display their centerfold pictures in less conspicuous places. All refused and said to "mellow out" because she was taking the issue too seriously. They felt the pictures were tasteful and anyway, "naked women are beautiful," they explained.
>
> Susan was not convinced. She continued to ask her supervisor for help but, getting nowhere, went to the director of the company. He also did nothing. Meanwhile, it appeared that even more pictures were being put up in plain sight of Susan's work station. While a few men did understand her outrage, they did not join her in her struggle to eliminate the pictures. Frustrated with the situation. she quit her job after only six months.

2. Compare your definitions of sexual harassment. Are there differences among group members?
3. Based on your definitions, was Susan experiencing sexual harassment? Why or why not?
4. How did most of Susan's coworkers and her supervisor perceive the display of centerfold pictures?
5. Why was Susan reacting so strongly to these displays?
6. Whose perceptions of this situation do you support (if anyone's) in this case study? Explain your answer.
7. Do you feel that Susan's coworkers had a right to display pictures of nude women at their own work stations? Explain your answer.
8. What rights did Susan have as an employee of the company?
9. Given each of your answers above, how would you have resolved this controversy if you had been Susan? A fellow coworker? Her supervisor? Director of the company? Have one group member take on the role of one of these people and be prepared to report to the class their individual perspectives.
10. Do you think that women and men perceive sexual harassment differently? If so, how can such differences be resolved in the work place? Were there differences among your group members? If so, were these differences along gender lines?

Exercise 4.5: Trading Places

This exercise is to be used in conjunction with the Wood and Reich article. Ask each student to consider the following scenario and answer the following questions.

> Imagine if you were to wake up tomorrow morning as a member of the opposite sex. Think about what that would be like. Answer the following questions anonymously on paper.
>
> 1. What would be different about your life?
> 2. What would be better about your life?
> 3. What would be worse about your life?

After all students have completed writing their responses, collect them and begin to read responses aloud. The responses written by both and men and women can be very insightful and provide valuable material for discussion. Some typical responses by males if they were to wake up as a female include: "I would have to spend more time on my physical appearance," and "I wouldn't walk alone late at night." Some typical responses by females if they were to wake up as a male include: "I would be more respected at work," and "I could use more profanity when speaking to friends." This exercise generates a lot of discussion and serves as a good supplement to the article about gender.

Exercise 4.6: Interactions Among the Disabled and Able-bodied

It is not uncommon for some people to feel uncomfortable around physically challenged individuals. Braithwaite and Braithwaite describe in their article the kind of communication that often occurs when an able-bodied and physically challenged person interact: greater physical distance, less eye contact, and shorter duration of talk. It is common for able-bodied, or "temporarily able-bodied," persons to focus on the disability instead of the person when interacting with disabled individuals. As a result, able-bodied individuals may be unsure of how to interact with less able-bodied people, and wonder nervously to themselves, "What can I say to this person *with a disability?*" They might do better to simply ask themselves, "What can I share with this person?"

Another feeling of uncertainty that might arise for an able-bodied person is how much assistance should they offer, or should they wait until a physically challenged person asks for assistance. When hearing people interact with members of the deaf culture, Jankowski (1991) says it is common for hearing people to believe that "they can explain things better because of the 'communication barrier' and will proceed with the conversation as though the deaf person were not there" (p. 149).

This exercise asks able-bodied students to consider their own feelings about and communicative behavior during interactions with disabled individuals. Ask students to read the following "Dear Abby" letter and answer the questions that follow in a small group. As with many of the exercises given in this manual, this exercise may be most effectively conducted by first having students consider in writing their perceptions of the disabled. Each group should have an opportunity to report the small group discussion findings in the larger class discussion.

> Dear Abby:
>
> You have championed many causes for the physically challenged, and I thank you for all you have done. Now, will you please do us one more favor? Please advise waiters, waitresses, flight attendants, and everyone else who serves the public, of the following:
>
> Because a person happens to be in a wheelchair with leg braces—or appears to be partially paralyzed due to polio, cerebral palsy, a stroke, or some unknown cause—please do not assume that he of she can neither think nor speak. I was badly clobbered by polio many years ago, but have been rehabilitated greatly, thanks to physical therapy, my own determination and a lot of hard work. However, I am in a wheelchair and somewhat physically impaired. When I am in a restaurant (or on a plane) and food orders are being taken, please speak directly to me. Do not turn to my companion and ask, "And what will SHE have?"
> CAN COMMUNICATE IN MARIETTA, OHIO. (*Dear Abby*, 1993, p. 8)

Some questions for discussion:

1. Why do people often communicate with disabled persons in the manner described by "Can Communicate in Marietta"?
2. What messages do they send to the disabled person when they communicate in this way?

3. Have you ever felt uncomfortable communicating with someone who was in a wheelchair or in some way physically disabled or challenged? Why do you think you felt this way?
4. What kept or keeps you from communicating, if at all, with a person who is disabled?
5. Describe your last communication encounter with a disabled person. How can you break the communication barriers between you and a disabled person?

Chapter Popular Film Suggestions

The following films lend themselves to a discussion of some of the issues explored by the essays in this chapter.

- ***Forrest Gump* (1994).** This film illustrates the triumph of life over adversity in both its portrayals of the lead character, Forrest Gump, whose "slowness" (low I.Q.) marks him as different, and of Lieutenant Dan Taylor whose life Gump saves in Vietnam—the lieutenant loses his legs and takes a while to appreciate the life he has been given.
  Web References:
  Berardinelli, J. *Forrest Gump*: A film review. 1/24/2005. http://movie-reviews.colossus.net/movies/f/forrest.html
  Maslin, J. Review of *Forrest Gump. The New York Times: Movies online*. 1/24/2005. http://movies2.nytimes.com/gst/movies/movie.html?v_id=131221

- ***The Boys in the Band* (1970).** Adnum describes this movie as a "two hour alcoholic talk-party - an overpopulated, gay *Who's Afraid Of Virginia Woolf* - it uncovers gay men at their sizzling emotional and intellectual cores – before suburbanality drove theatricality into the ground, and gym workouts and GI haircuts became the assimilative, cowardly norm."
  Web Reference:
  Mark A. "No camping." Review of *The Boys in the Band* (1970). Outrate.net. 1/24/2005. http://www.outrate.net/outratetheboysintheband.html

- ***Dreamkeeper*** (South Dakota, New Mexico, 2003; length: 2 hr 20 min). According to Shannon, this television miniseries tells the story of a young teen from the Lakota reservation who, while driving his grandfather to New Mexico, "gradually realizes that his grandfather's stories . . . are essential in preserving the fading cultures of the Lakota and the several other tribes whose folklore depends on unbroken generations of oral tradition."
  Web References:
  Shannon, J. Amazon.com Editorial review: *Dreamkeeper*. 1/24/2005. http://www.amazon.com/exec/obidos/tg/detail/-/B00019330O/ref=cm_rev_editorial_dp/103-5604910-7559814?v=glance&s=dvd&vi=reviews
  Hallmark Entertainment: *Dreamkeeper*. 1/24/2005. http://www.hallmarkent.com/property.php?propertyId=Dreamkeeper

Chapter Test Items

Multiple Choice

1. "Melting pot" and "color blind society" are metaphors for which of the following
   - a. interethnic communication message
   - b. assimilationism *
   - c. pluralism
   - d. reconciliation
   - e. extremism

2. The idea of sanctity of the group is a message of
   - a. assimilationism
   - b. pluralism *
   - c. reconciliation
   - d. extremism

3. Alan Wolfe (1998) describes the "vital center," the "middle," America as being the voices of
   - a. assimilationism
   - b. pluralism
   - c. reconciliation *
   - d. extremism

4. Those messages which express a preference for a maximum in-group/out-group separation are messages of
   - a. assimilationism
   - b. pluralism
   - c. reconciliation
   - d. extremism *

5. The messages of reconciliation reflect the struggle of Americans seeking which of the following?
   - a. moderation *
   - b. flexibility
   - c. separation
   - d. none of the above

6. Which of the following is not considered a Native American belief?
   - a. There is a single higher power known as Creator
   - b. The spirit world exists side by side with the physical world
   - c. The spirit will no longer be a part of the body after the body dies *
   - d. Illness affects the mind and spirit as well as the body

7. Which of the following four concepts to Native American spirituality emphasizes understanding the direction to one's path as a caretaker?
    a. Medicine
    b. Relation
    c. Vision *
    d. Harmony

8. Which of the following four concepts to Native American spirituality emphasizes the Circle of Life?
    a. Medicine
    b. Relation *
    c. Vision
    d. Harmony

9. Which of the following four concepts to Native American spirituality emphasizes acceptance?
    a. Medicine
    b. Relation
    c. Harmony *
    d. Vision

10. Terminal values are
    a. the final stages in coping with external pressures that a biracial couple may experience
    b. the goals or core value system each person has *
    c. the instrumental values
    d. the cultural norms of European Americans

11. In child-rearing practices, European American culture
    a. encourages independence and flexible rules *
    b. encourages dependence and rigid rules
    c. gives girls more flexibility than boys
    d. both a and c

12. For historical reasons, the African American culture
    a. tends toward more informality and weaker power distance
    b. tends toward more formality and power distance *
    c. tends toward more formality and weaker power distance
    d. tends toward more informality and power distance

13. Wood and Reich suggest that feedback and response cues such as "uh huh" and "hmm" from women can indicate which of the following to men?
    a. agreement *
    b. condescension
    c. desire
    d. weakness

14. Which of the following is NOT a severe consequence of stereotyping?
    a. The stereotyped group may engage in self-fulfilling behavior.
    b. Those who have preconceived notions may act upon their beliefs.
    c. The self-esteem and self-confidence of the stereotyped group may suffer.
    d. Interactions may improve only in a general sense. *

15. Which of the following is NOT a stereotype of gay males?
    a. gay males are effeminate
    b. gay males know how to dress
    c. gay males are homosexual *
    d. none of the above

16. In studies stereotypes about gay males,
    a. respondents who claimed to know at least one lesbian or gay person held more favorable attitudes toward gays and lesbians
    b. women held more favorable attitudes than men
    c. the largest number of people who said they knew no gay individuals were those who made under $20,000 annually
    d. all of the above *

17. How many people in the U.S. have some type of disability?
    a. one in five people *
    b. one in ten people
    c. one in twenty people
    d. one in thirty people

18. Which of the following was identified by Crewe and Athelstan (1985) as a "key life function" that may be affected by a disability?
    a. mobility
    b. employment
    c. self-care
    d. all of the above *

19. Which of the following forms of redefinition by the disabled describes the following comment made by one of Braithwaite's informants: "I am a person like anyone else."
    a. redefinition as members of a new culture
    b. redefinition of self *
    c. redefinition of disability
    d. redefinition of life

20. The label "handicapped person" is problematic and objectionable to people with disabilities because it emphasizes the disability instead of the
    a. culture
    b. relationship
    c. situation
    d. person *

21. Nonhandicapped or nondisabled persons are often referred to as _____ by members of the disabled culture.
    a. temporarily able-bodied *
    b. normal
    c. able-bodied
    d. futurely disabled

22. Of the three phases identified when adjusting to a disability, which includes an individual's focus on rehabilitation and all of the physical changes being experienced?
    a. stigma isolation *
    b. stigma recognition
    c. stigma incorporation
    d. stigma denial

23. Of the three phases identified when adjusting to a disability, which phase is identified as one where the individual has not yet noticed the changes in social relationships or communication with nondisabled others?
    a. stigma isolation *
    b. stigma recognition
    c. stigma incorporation
    d. stigma denial

True/False

T 1. Assimilationism is shaped by the three core principles of classical liberalism—individualism, universalism, and procedural equality.

F 2. Conformism is a type of interethnic communication message.

T 3. "Color-blind society" is a metaphor that projects the assimilationist message of the mainstreaming of ethnic minorities into the normative culture and institutions.

T 4. Pluralist messages have replaced the "melting pot" metaphor with newer metaphors such as "quilt" and "salad bowl."

F 5. The ideological circle encompasses three ideological positions.

F 6. Native Americans have been able to legally practice their spirituality and traditional ways in this country since 1998 when the American Indian Religious Freedom Act was passed.

T 7. According to Native American beliefs, illness affects the mind, body and spirit.

T 8. According to Native American beliefs there is medicine in every event, Memory, place, person, and movement.

F 9. According to Native American beliefs, there are "good experiences" and "bad experiences" in life.

T 10. According to Native American beliefs, the spirit world exists side by side with the physical world.

T 11. Native Americans believe that the spirit existed in the spirit world before it came into a physical body.

F 12. The Native American concept of medicine is similar to what medicine means in mainstream American society.

T 13. Race is socially constructed.

F 14. It has been well documented that there is more variation between groups than there is within a group.

T 15. Both African American and European American cultures tend to communicate in a more direct manner.

F 16. Women tend to be much less direct in communication style than men.

T 17. Samovar and Porter point out that up to 90% of the social content of a message is transmitted nonverbally.

F 18. Whites tend to look more while speaking; Blacks tend to look more while listening.

T 19. The monochromic person may perceive the polychronic partner as disorganized or scattered.

F 20. We are born with a gender.

T 21. Gender is socially constructed.

F 22. Gender and sex are synonymous.

T 23. We may choose to embody different genders in different situations.

T 24. No person is born with a particular gender.

F 25. *Feminine* and *masculine* are words that specify a person's sex.

T 26. Sex is innate.

F 27. The nonverbal communication of an able-bodied person usually signals acceptance more so than the verbal message.

T 28. Disability affects the behavioral, economic, and social aspects of a person's life.

T 29. Stigma incorporation represents "regaining wellness."

T 30. Disabled people sometimes refer to nondisabled people as TABs.

T 31. Scouting (Cub Scouts, Boy Scouts, Explorers) openly discriminates against boys who are or who might be gay.

F 32. You can always tell whether someone is gay or lesbian by the way she or he dresses.

T 33. Heterosexism assumes that the behavior of heterosexual individuals is "normal."

T 34. Independent estimates of the number of gays and lesbians in society today range from 10% to 15%.

F 35. "Gay-dar" is the intuitive ability used by heterosexuals in bars to sense that someone nearby might also be lesbian.

F 36. Most lesbians and gay men put a low premium on dating and forming intimate relationships.

Chapter Essay Questions

1. Discuss assimilationist messages. Provide examples of these types of messages in your response.
2. Discuss pluralist messages. Provide examples of these types of messages in your response.
3. Discuss reconciliation messages. Provide examples of these types of messages in your response. Discuss messages of extremism. Provide examples of these types of messages in your response.
4. Differentiate between messages of pluralism and messages of assimilation.
5. Explain the *ideological circle.*
6. Discuss the four concepts that are central to Native American Spirituality.
7. Explain the concept of Native American spirituality.
8. Explain the statement, "Medicine is everywhere" as it relates to Native American spirituality.
9. Why does Native American spirituality place great emphasis on the numbers four and seven?
10. Discuss the circle of life. How does it relate to the concept of relation?
11. How does the concept of harmony relate to purpose?
12. What is meant by the term terminal goal, and how do these goals affect relationships?
13. How do communication styles affect biracial relationships?
14. Differentiate between male and female sex and gender role stereotypes.
15. What is gender socialization?
16. How do the games of boys and girls differ and do such differences influence their communication patterns?
17. Using the examples provided by Wood and Reich, describe why men and women often have problems communicating?
18. How can men and women communicate more effectively?
19. What accounts for the rise in the number of persons with disabilities?
20. What's the difference between being *disabled* and *handicapped*?
21. What have been some problems with research on disabled persons' communication?
22. Describe the different ways that one becomes a member of the disabled culture?
23. What role does language play in the redefinition of disability for disabled and temporarily able-bodied persons?
24. What suggestions do Braithwaite and Braithwaite give for communicating with people with disabilities?
25. How do media portrayals of lesbians and gays perpetuate stereotypes? And how do the media foster positive images toward gays and lesbians?
26. What are the six interactive stages through which non-heterosexual individuals pass as they develop their identity?

Chapter References

Dear Abby. (1993, June 24). *The Seattle Times*, p. 8.

de Leon, F. M., & Macdonald, S. (1992, June 28). Name Power. *The Seattle Times-Seattle Post-Intelligencer*, p. A1.

Jankowski, K. (1992). On communicating with deaf people. In L. A. Samovar and R. E. Porter (Eds.), *Intercultural communication: A reader* (5th ed.) (pp. 142-150). Belmont, CA: Wadsworth.

McLaughlin, M.L., Ed. (1916). *Myths and legends of the Sioux* (Bismarck, ND: Bismarck Tribune Co., 1916, 1st ed.). University of Virginia Library Electronic Text Center, Electronic Text Center, University of Virginia Library. 1/24/2005. Available online: http://etext.lib.virginia.edu/toc/modeng/public/MclMyth.html.

Chapter 5 Intercultural Messages: Verbal and Nonverbal Communication

Chapter Synopsis

This chapter examines the interconnection between verbal messages and nonverbal messages, arguing that though there is an important connection between culture and language, successful intercultural communication requires more than an understanding of verbal interaction. While some may argue that the primary linguistic difference between cultures is located in grammatical structures, the contention of this chapter is that language is much more than a set of words and phrases. In order to understand a culture, it is important to understand not only the grammatical structure of the primary language of the culture, but the ways in which members of that culture learn and actually use language on a day-to-day basis. Understanding language as it occurs in a particular situation provides a window through which a variety of aspects of culture can be viewed.

Nonverbal behavior also provides important insight into cultural patterns of communication. In this chapter students will be introduced to the role and impact of movement, personal space, touch, time, gender, paralanguage, and silence in a variety of cultural contexts. As the editors note, nonverbal communication often serves as the frame for interpreting verbal communication, so learning about some of the patterns of communicating without words offers students of intercultural communication a broader understanding of communication among and between cultures.

Nonverbal behaviors are assumed for the most part to be unconscious behaviors. It is important for students to note that any portrayal of the nonverbal behaviors described as typical from one culture to the next are not characterizations of behaviors that are formally "taught" within each culture. Students who wish to communicate more effectively interculturally should not expect to "learn" appropriate nonverbal behaviors simply by reading about them in the text. Rather, what this text offers is a way of viewing behaviors that students might otherwise misinterpret for noncommunicative events.

After reading the articles in this chapter, students should be able to answer the following questions:

- What are some of the ways that different cultures use language?
- What is the link between language and culture?
- How do verbal messages interact with nonverbal behaviors to provide meaning?
- How are symbols directly tied to culture?
- What are some of the linguistic bases of cultural conflict?

Mary Fong, in "The Nexus of Language, Communication, and Culture" introduces the idea that the symbols we use, whether they are verbal or nonverbal, are directly related to our culture. She reviews the Sapir-Whorf hypothesis and traces later developments in the relationship between language and culture, then applies these techniques in two studies of Chinese language use.

In "German Language: Whose Language, Whose Culture?," Helen Kelly-Holmes both emphasizes the link between language and culture and illustrates how language can be used to talk about culture. She reminds us that meanings are not found in words but in the meanings that cultures attach to them. Though concentrating on the German language, her findings apply to nearly all cultures.

In "Dialogue and Cultural Communication Between Israeli Jews and Palestinians," Donald G. Ellis and Ifat Maoz review the different cultural communication codes that have emerged from the special circumstances of the Israeli Jews and Palestinians in order to establish dialogue between the opposing sides. Ellis and Maoz argue that these speech code differences are partially responsible for the failure of dialogue to resolve the conflict surrounding the two cultures.

In "Public Speaking Patterns in Kenya," Ann Neville Miller continues the argument that culture affects nearly every aspect of how people use language, asserting that culture even affects public speaking. Miller compares U.S. and Kenyan public speaking patterns. Successful speakers in the U.S. organize their speeches in a highly structured, logical, linear pattern. The Kenyan public speaker, in contrast, "gives illustrations, proverbs, and tells stories and then returns back to the thesis at the center, though not exactly at the place from which [he or she] departed." A Westerner hearing a Kenyan speech might find it aimless and disorganized.

Carolyn Roy's essay "Mexican *Dichos*: Lessons through Language" explores Mexican values through her review of *dichos* (popular proverbs, adages, and sayings that pass on values important to Mexicans). Several examples are provided to assist students with a better understanding of Mexican values.

Co-authors Peter A. Andersen and Hua Wang's essay "Unraveling Cultural Cues: Dimensions of Nonverbal Communication Across Cultures" make the point that nonverbal messages are culture bound. Andersen and Wang summarize briefly the basic codes of nonverbal communication, then analyze how these codes differ from one culture to another.

In "Japanese Nonverbal Communication: A Reflection of Cultural Themes," Erwin R. McDaniel uses the Japanese as a cultural model to illustrate how nonverbal communication practices function as a reflection, or representation of societal cultural themes. Students will learn how cultural influences can subtly shape a society's nonverbal communication behavior.

Chapter Outline

Nexus of Language, Communication, and Culture

Interrelationships of Language, Communication, and Culture

- Language is a symbolic system in which meaning is shared among people who identify with one another.
- Spoken language is a vehicle for people to communicate in social interaction by expressing their experience and creating experience.
- Words reflect the sender's attitude, beliefs, and points of view.
- Language expresses, symbolizes, and embodies cultural reality.
- Both language and communication reflect culture.
- Both written and oral languages are shaped by culture and, in turn, these languages shape culture.
- Language and communication both liberate—in enabling people to express themselves—and constrain them to conform to shared cultural standards.

Perspectives on Language and Culture

- Sapir-Whorf hypothesis
  - Language structure is necessary in order to produce thought
  - Language and its categories—grammar, syntax, and vocabulary—are the only categories by which we experience the world
  - Has dominated scholarly thinking for more than five decades
  - *Linguistic relativity*:
    - Holds that language and thought co-vary, i.e., people who speak different languages segment their world differently
    - A person not familiar with another person's cultural ways will be likely to misinterpret the person's actions
- Brown (1958) disagreed in part with the Sapir-Whorf hypothesis but supports idea of linguistic relativity
- Researchers no longer take seriously the deterministic view of the Sapir-Whorf hypothesis

Current Research Trends and Directions

- Current approaches to the study of language, communication, and culture are
- Developmental—the connection between language and cognitive processing in a culture
- Interactional—what people are doing with speech as they interact face-to-face
- Social psychological—the underlying factors that influence language choices in multilingual communication contexts
- Other approaches:
  - Sherzer (1987): analysis of discourse as the intersection where language and culture interrelate
  - Derives from *pragmatics* or *speech act theory*—the study of the connotative (inner) and denotative (outer) meanings of "expressions when used in a conversation or a written work" (217)
    - Pragmatics also entails cultural members applying their knowledge of the world to the interpretation of what is said and done in interaction

    - Ethnography of communication—describes and accounts for the interpretive systems and practices through which members construct actions and del with behaviors
- Aim is to discover not only linguistic structural regularities, but also regularities of usage that have motives, emotions, desires, knowledge, attitudes, and values attached to them

Language Studies

- Qualitative methods—discourse analysis, pragmatics, and ethnography of communication—jointly provide tools and perspectives to make possible in-depth examination of communicative phenomena

A Cultural Study

- Ethnographic study of the Chinese New Year celebration in Hong Kong (Fong, 2000)
- Chinese people engage in positive talk and avoid arguments and negative talk during Chinese New Year
- Avoid saying words that signify death, sickness, poverty, or anything else unlucky as this is supposed to be a happy occasion
- Should someone say an unlucky thing, accidentally, then the hearer uses expressions to reverse the bad luck (examples, page 218)
- Sequential rules statements provide formula:
  If … (context, condition, or situation, such as a speech event, speech act, or genre),
  then … (speaking and/or interaction pattern),
  because … (belief, value system, or cultural principle),
  meaning … (norm of interpretation of a symbol, speaking pattern, interaction pattern, particular speech act, speech event, etc.)

An Intercultural Study

- Study of compliment interactions between Chinese immigrants and European Americans from perspective of Chinese immigrants (Fong, 1998)
- Two cultural groups have differing ways of speaking in compliment interactions
    - European Americans on West Coast and in Midwest generally accept a compliment
    - Chinese have tendency to deny compliments in order to give an impression of modesty
- Yet, internal similarity between two groups—Chinese say "no" but internally accept compliment
- Four adaptations by Chinese immigrant participants (CIPs) to European American compliments found:
- Intercultural shock state
    - CIPs unfamiliar with European Americans' generosity in giving compliments, compliments containing strong positive adjectives, compliments intended to encourage a person after an unsatisfactory performance, compliments on a wide variety of topics
    - Unfamiliar with accepting compliments and face-to-face compliments in all types of relationships

- Intercultural resistance state
- Intercultural accommodation state
- Bicultural competence state
- Chinese immigrants value indirectness and modesty, so response may be denial or silence

German Language

- Language counts as part of culture and identity for the German-speaking world
- Language is constantly changing—it only lives through its speakers
- Words themselves have no meanings—meanings are attached to them by members of s speech community, a culture

Language and Culture

- Not a simple, one-way, cause-and-effect relationship
- Instead, two-way or circular or multilayered
- Through our use of a common language, we become a more coherent cultural group and reinforce our common identity as members of that group
- However, no such thing as a completely homogeneous linguistic and cultural group (because of age, gender, ethnic, educational, religious, political, class, linguistic differences)
- Membership in a nation or country does not preclude membership in other cultural, identity, or linguistic groups
- Language is not simply a code—language are inextricably linked to cultures, as reflected in their vocabulary, structures, rules about politeness, and so on
- Languages are the result of political, economic, historical, social, ideological, and cultural processes
- A country is governed and organized economically, politically, and administratively through processes that take place naturally through the language and inevitably mould and develop it

Linguistic Diversity, Cultural Diversity

- Regional varieties of English in Anglophone countries tend to manifest themselves mainly in terms of different accents
- German regional variation encompasses far more than simply phonological changes relating to pronunciation and accent—sentence structure, meanings, and vocabulary are all subject to change (termed a dialect)
- Difference between language and dialect:
    - Language has a flag and an army or navy (Dutch)
    - *Bayrisch* (Bavarian) and *Săchsisch* (Saxon)—both far removed from Standard or High German—are dialects
    - Dialects often defined sociologically, politically, or economically rather than linguistically
    - Dialects reflect and reinforce a strong regional culture and identity—a grammar of experiences and feelings
- Many Germans will refer first to their region, rather than to their country, when defining their culture and identity
- Knowledge of one's dialect—ability to speak it and switch to and from it—is fundamental to identity and culture in many parts of Germany

- In urban areas, use of dialect may be perceived as something older people do or seen as evidence of "low" culture ("vulgar" speech)
- In recent years, there's been a mini-revolution in using dialects in written texts and in contexts in which they were not previously seen (television news, politicians making speeches)
- Growing use of dialects reflects situation in which regional cultures and identities are intensifying—linguistic varieties seen as way of expressing a culture and identity specific to a particular part of Germany or a German-speaking country (Austria, Switzerland)
- Use of slang also an attempt to express an identity, usually tied up with membership in a group, defined by age or occupation, for example
- When using this language, such groups create their own mini-cultures, which include those who "speak the language" and exclude those who do not
- One group that has felt excluded by the German language is women—rendered invisible by its patriarchal grammar
- All the German-speaking countries are, in practice, multilingual to greater or lesser extent
- Large numbers of German immigrants collectively know as *Auslãnder*—"foreigner" or alien even though they may have been born in Germany or lived all their lives there
- Germany cannot be considered a linguistically or culturally homogeneous country
- Groups, localities, and regions all share various types of "German" and construct and reinforce a variety of complementary and competing cultures and subcultures, the sum of which equate to German language and culture

Whose German? Whose Culture?

- English an actual threat to Francophone and Germanophone cultures seen as real
- Attempts to control influence of English through institutions and groups concerned with defense and maintenance of their respective languages:
- Institutions that discuss how new concepts can be described and translated (usually from English) into acceptable forms
- Bodies concerned with domesticating foreign words, by giving them a gender, for instance, and deciding when a foreign word has become part of the German language
- Linguists and politicians concerned with the "purity" of the language and who decide on spelling
- Number of English words and phrases in German media is striking, especially in advertising
- May be symbol of globalism, of youth, of progress and modernity; may at the same time bear the properties of pan-Europeanness, Americanness, and internationalism
- Reason for preponderance of anglicisms or English words in German:
- Economic aid given to Germany by U.S. through Marshall Plan
- Omnipresence of American and Anglophone international culture
- Status of English as a global lingua franca

- Internet and its vocabulary appear to have consolidated position of English language in German linguistic culture and exemplify German language's easy access policy regarding foreign words

Language, Culture, and External Perceptions

- Negative perceptions of German language and culture may occur if one's introduction to the language occurs with viewing WWII film where "nasty-looking German soldiers are played by Anglophone actors with a German accent"
- Positive perceptions of German culture have resulted from technology associated with German products
- Important to remember that linking of language, culture, and identity is not inevitable; may be result of "manipulation by someone—politician, preacher, entrepreneur—who has manipulated this combination with some goal in sight"(229)
- "Language may not always be the cause, but instead, the effect of national culture" (229).

Dialogue and Cultural Communication Codes between Israeli Jews and Palestinians

Transformative Communication between Groups in Conflict

- Contact hypothesis: under certain conditions, contact between groups in conflict reduces prejudice and changes negative intergroup attitudes; optimal under following conditions:
  - Two groups should be of equal status
  - Contact should involve personal and sustained communication between individuals from two groups
  - Requires cooperative interdependence
  - Social norms favoring equality must be consensus among relevant authorities

Transformative Dialogues between Israelis and Palestinians

- Interactive problem-solving workshops developed by Herbert Kelman from Harvard University (1970s to present) brought together politically active and influential Israelis and Palestinians for private, direct communication facilitated by unofficial third-party mediators
- Concept of dialogue used that emphasizes interplay of different perspectives where something new and unique emerges
- Process of change and transformation during dialogue is difficult, complex, and slow
- Cultural communication codes typify interactions between Israeli Jews and Palestinians

Speech Codes

- "[Y]our use of language (word choice, slang, accents, syntax) and your tendencies to interpret and understand this language in a certain way depend on your cultural membership" (233).
- Two cultural communication codes known to characterize Israeli Jews (***dugri***) and Palestinians (***musayra***) make for difficult and uncoordinated communication

- Speech code of Arabs (Palestinians): ***Musayra*** ("to accommodate" or "go along with"):
  - Orients speaker toward a harmonious relationship with the other person
  - An Arab speaker engaging in *musayra* is being polite, indirect, courteous, and nonconfrontive to the other member of a conversation
  - *Musayra* has four communication features:
  - **Repetition**
    - Repetitive statements formulaic in nature
    - Used for complimenting and praising others
    - Also used as an argumentative style—repeated phrases used to influence beliefs (rather than Western-style logic)
  - **Indirectness**
    - Reflects cultural tendency to be interpersonally cautious and responsive to context
    - Facilitates politeness and face saving
  - **Elaboration**
    - An expressive and encompassing style
    - Leads to deeper connection between speakers and affirms relationships
  - **Affectiveness**
    - An intuitive and emotional style
    - Allows for identification with the other person and maintenance of an engaged relationship
- Speech code of Israeli Jews: ***Dugri*** ("straight talk")
  - Direct, pragmatic, assertive style
  - *Dugri* speech is "to the point"
  - Communication of understanding and information as the most important communicative goals
  - Emotional appeals and personal niceties of secondary importance
  - In *dugri*, speaker more concerned with maintaining his or her own image of clarity and directness (contrasts with *musayra*, in which it is important to maintain face of positive image of the other speaker)
- Philipsen (1997)—five main ideas that characterize cultural speech codes:
  - Speech codes are culturally distinctive
  - Speech codes result from a psychology and sociology unique to the culture
  - The meaning and significance of messages fundamentally depend on codes
  - Speech codes are located in the language and communication of native speakers
  - Speech codes can be used to understand, predict, and control communication

Argument between Israeli Jews and Palestinians

- Argument a persistent characteristic between these two groups, but an acceptable mechanism of conflict resolution
- Arguments between these two groups no consistent with their respective cultural speech codes

    - Palestinians more argumentative and used Western-style argumentation; more assertive than usual
    - Israeli Jews on defensive but also more hesitant and submissive in dialogues
- Dialogue context helps transform indigenous code of each group—suggest that speech codes are pliant and that situations and activities can be found that reduce cultural strength of these codes and makes change and growth possible

Public Speaking Patterns in Kenya

Kenyan Value Orientations

- Collectivism
    - Lifelong loyalty to one's ingroup
    - Responsibilities toward family extend far down the genealogical line and are financial as well as social
- High power distance
    - Family: respect and deference to parents & older relatives; power hierarchy clearly delineated: father supreme authority, then mother, then oldest child
    - School: teacher an authoritative figure
    - Workplace: lower-level worker approaches authority figure indirectly or through intermediary
- Polychronic time
    - Events and people more important than schedules and efficiency
    - Weddings and other social events may begin hours late
- High-context communication
    - Great amount of information is held in common among members, so less needs to be said explicitly
    - One of the marks of wisdom in the elderly is ability to convey messages indirectly through use of proverbs and analogies, in public and private settings

Public Speaking Patterns as Outgrowths of Kenyan Values

- Speaking Purposes
    - More ceremonial speeches than any other kind—speeches of greeting, introduction, tribute, thanks
    - Life events marked by ceremonies, which occasion multiple public speeches
    - For most Kenyans, public speaking an unavoidable responsibility
        - At "harambee," community fundraising event, guest of honor and various dignitaries make speeches
        - At weddings, anyone can dispense advice—doing so considered doing one's duty
        - At negotiations over bride price, many speeches are made; freely using proverbs and metaphors is expected
    - Hierarchy important: persons of prominence must not be left out and must be called on in hierarchical order to deliver speeches
- Supporting Material
    - Facts and figures not especially persuasive; rather, narrative and personal story more persuasive

    - Accomplished speaker will develop suspense, humor, and vivid characterizations in the telling
    - Use of proverbs and maxims are a sign of wisdom and experience
    - Speaker may use songs in the middle of a speech
    - Audience participation and response expected—speaker may leave sentence hanging and wait for audience to fill in the blank, or lead audience in chanting specific phrases
- Credibility
    - Wealth, family status, age, and ethnicity are of highest importance
    - Wealth mitigated by extent to which it's been used to help other members of the society
    - Unmarried man or married man with no sons or few children cannot speak with authority
    - Women's speech opportunities increasing
    - Age less venerated now than in past though young cannot address people in certain venues without permission
    - Kenya a nation of 40 distinct cultural groups, so ethnicity and language are important
    - Speeches may be divided into formal section in English and folksier section in a group's language, such as Swahili
    - Persons with particular status (due to age, wealth, or family) automatically assured of a hearing in public arena
    - Education also lends credibility to speaker
- Speech Structure
    - Web organizational pattern—speaker gives illustration, mentions proverb, or tells story, then returns back to thesis at center though usually not at place from which they departed originally
    - Speeches are not time limited

Mexican Dichos

- *Dichos* are popular sayings that include but are not limited to:
    - *Proverbios*/proverbs
    - *Adagios*/adages
    - *Refranes*/refrains
- *Dichos* reflect some of the values of the Mexican culture; such popular sayings transmit "what a culture deems significant"
- The Mexican language hybridizes the Spanish brought from Europe with the indigenous languages, predominately Nahuatl, of Mexico's native peoples
- *Dichos* may be pithy condensations of wisdom gained through centuries of experience; they are one form of transmitting folk wisdom.
- There is a Mexican tradition of playfulness with words or the use of double meaning, so not all sayings should be taken literally, but considered within the context of Mexican culture.

Some Mexican *dichos* (proverbs) that reflect values central to Mexican culture:

Acceptance of "God's Will"	Sparing Bestowal of Trust	Importance of Appearances	Respect for Privacy	Communalism	Family
No hay mal que por bien no venga. (There is no bad that good does not accompany.) *Mejor reír que llorar.* (Better to laugh than to cry.) *El hombre propone y Dios dispone.* (Man proposes and God disposes.) *No por mucho madrugar amanece mãs temprano.* (No matter how early one rises, the sun will not come up any sooner.) *Cuando el pobre tiene para carne sea vigilia.* (When the poor have [money] to buy meat, it must e lent.) *Quien canta su mal espanta.* (He who sings frightens away his grief.)	*En confianza está el peligro.* (There is danger in trust.) *La confianza también mata.* (Trust also kills.) *Ni te fies de amigo reconciliado, ni de manjar dos veces guisados.* (Do not trust a reconciled friend nor a dish twice cooked.) *Del dicho al hecho hay mucho trecho.* (From said to done, there is a great gap.) *Músico pagado foca mal son.* (The musician who has been paid plays bad music.)	*Dime con quien andas y te dire quien eres.* (Tell me with whom you associate [walk, travel], and I will tell you who you are.) *Quien anda con lobos a aullar se aprenda.* (One who goes around with wolves learns to howl.) *El que es buen gallo dondequiera canta.* (A good rooster can crow anywhere.)	*Agua que no has de beber, déjala correr.* (Water that you do not have to drink, leave it to flow.) *Bueno aconsejar, major remediar.* (It is good to give advice, but it is better to solve the problem.) *Si dices la verdad no pecas, pero no sabes los males que suscitas.* (If you tell the truth you do not sin, but you don't know the troubles you cause, so keep your own counsel.) *En boca cerrada no entran moscas.* (Flies do not enter a closed mouth.) *Un resbalón de langua es peor que el de los pies.* (A slip of the tongue is worse than a slip of the foot.) *Rezarle solo a su santo.* (Pray only to your saint.) *Major*	*Mucha ayuda, poco trabajo.* (Much help, little work.) *Vida sin amigos, muerte sin testigos.* (Life without friends; death without witnesses. Life without friends, no mourners when it ends.)	*¿A dónde vas que valgas más?* (Where are you going that you are worth more?) *Amor de padre o madre, lo demás es aire.* (The love of a mother or father, everything else is air.)

Acceptance of "God's Will"	Sparing Bestowal of Trust	Importance of Appearances	Respect for Privacy	Communalism	Family
			quedarse para vestir los santos que tener que desvestir un borracho. (It is better to remain single than to have to undress a drunk.) *Mãs vale solo que mal acompañado.* (It is better to remain single than to be disagreeably accompanied.) *A la mujer ni todo el amor ni todo el dinero.* (To a woman neither all your love nor all your money.) *Triste está la casa donde la gallina canta y el gallo calla.* (Sad is the house where the chicken crows and the rooster is quiet.)		

- Popular sayings
- Reflect basic cultural values
- Do not require literacy because they transmit values orally
- Metaphorically condense timeless lessons into readily recalled phrases

Unraveling Cultural Cues: Dimensions of Nonverbal Communication across Cultures

Nonverbal Codes

- Provide what verbal messages cannot express

- Generate more trust than verbal messages
- Physical Appearance
  - Factors having an impact upon initial encounter: Gender, height, weight, color of skin, & body shape, as well as clothes, jewelry, makeup, & accessories
  - Cultural attire can lead to steroptypes
- Proxemics
  - Generally examines communication via interpersonal space and distance
  - Cultures differ significantly
    - Mediterranean and Latin cultures maintain close distance
    - People from northern European and Northeast Asian cultures maintain greater distances
- Chronemics
  - Study of meanings, usage, & communication of time
  - Monochronic time—time used in linear way, with only one task undertaken at a time
  - Polychronic time—cultures tend to engage in multiple activities simultaneously
- Kinesics
  - Studies some aspects of people's facial expressions, body movements, gestures, & conversational regulators
  - Facial expressions can contain nonverbal messages that identify the person's nationality or culture
- Haptics
  - Tactile communication that also shows considerable intercultural variation
  - Vast differences shown in amount, location, type, & public or private manifestation
    - Italians & Greeks more "touchy" people than the English, French, & Dutch
    - Touching less common among Chinese & Japanese
    - Touching an Arab Muslim with the left hand is considered a social insult
- Oculesics
  - Study of messages sent by the eyes, including eye contact, blinks, eye movement, & pupil dilation
  - In North American & Western Europe direct eye contact communicates interest & respect
  - Japanese people may look away from another's eyes almost completely to be polite
- Vocalics, or paralanguage
  - Includes all nonverbal elements involved in using the voice
  - Culture affects the use of vocalics
    - African Americans & Jews tend to speak with more passion
    - Italians & Greeks talk much more & more loudly than Asians, who appreciate silence as a way of showing politeness
- Olfactics
  - Study of interpersonal communication via smell

- Americans are the most smell-aversive culture in the world

Dimensions of Intercultural Nonverbal Communication

- Cultures can be located along dimensions that help explain why people act in different ways
- Context

  The degree to which communication is explicit & verbal or implicit & nonverbal

  High-context (HC) message—most of the information is either in the physical context or internalized in the person; very little is in the coded, explicit, transmitted parts of the message; large emphasis on nonverbal codes (highest HC cultures found in Asia, especially China, Japan, & Korea)

  Low-context (LC) message—communicated through explicit code, usually via verbal communication; messages must be detailed & highly specific (lowest-context cultures are Swiss, German, North American, & Scandinavian
- Individualism-Collectivism
  - Individualistic cultures emphasize I-identity & value personal rights & freedom
  - Collectivistic cultures advocate 23-identity & are more group oriented
  - Determines how people live together—alone, in families, or in tribes
  - Hofstede (1980): 10 most individualistic nations: U.S., Australia, Great Britain, Canada, the Netherlands, New Zealand, Italy, Belgium, Denmark, & Sweden
  - Least individualistic nations: Venezuela, Columbia, Pakistan, Peru, Taiwan, Thailand, Singapore, Chile, & Hong Kong
  - Individuality is a primary value in Western cultures, of secondary importance in African cultures, & of little importance in Eastern & Muslim cultures
- Power Distance
  - Degree to which power, prestige, & wealth are unequally distributed in a culture; measured using Hofstede's (1980) Power Distance Index (PDI)
  - Cultures with a high PDI score have power concentrated in hands of a few rather than more equally distributed throughout the population (high PDI countries: Philippines, Mexico, Venezuela, India, Singapore, Brazil, Hong Kong, France, & Columbia)
  - Lowest PDI countries: Austria, Israel, Denmark, New Zealand, Ireland, Sweden, Norway, Finland, Switzerland,& Great Britain
  - United States slightly lower than medium in power distance
- Gender
  - Gender orientation of culture impacts many aspects of nonverbal behavior; gender, as used here, refers to rigidity of gender rules
  - In masculine cultures, gender rules are more rigid & traits such as strength, assertiveness, competitiveness, & ambitiousness are valued. Countries with 10 highest masculinity index scores: Japan, Austria, Venezuela, Italy, Switzerland, Mexico, Ireland, Great Britain, Germany, & the Philippines; U.S. tends to be a masculine country.
  - In more feminine or androgynous cultures, attributes such as affection, compassion, nurturance & emotionality are valued. Countries with lowest

masculinity index scores: Sweden, Norway, the Netherlands, Denmark, Finland, Chile, Portugal, Thailand, & Peru
    - Research suggests that androgynous patterns of behavior (including both masculine & feminine behaviors) result in more self-esteem, social competence, success, & intellectual development for both males & females.
- Uncertainty
    - Cultural predisposition to value risk & ambiguity (tolerance for ambiguity)
    - People intolerant of ambiguity have high levels of uncertainty avoidance & seek clear, black0and0white answers.
    - People tolerant of ambiguity have low levels of uncertainty avoidance and tend to be more tolerant, to accept ambiguous answers, & to see many shades of gray.
    - Countries high in uncertainty avoidance tend to display emotions more than do countries low in uncertainty avoidance.
    - Nonverbal behavior likely to be more codified & rule-governed in countries with high uncertainty avoidance; and tend to report more stylized & ritual behavior. (countries with highest levels of uncertainty avoidance: Greece, Portugal, Belgium, Japan, Peru, France, Chile, Spain, Argentina, & Turkey)
    - People from cultures that embrace uncertainty are more likely to treat strangers with positive nonverbal behaviors such as smiles. (countries with lowest levels of uncertainty avoidance: Singapore, Denmark, Sweden, Hong Kong, Ireland, Great Britain, India, the Philippines, The U.S., Canada, & New Zealand)
- Immediacy
    - Actions that signal closeness, intimacy, & availability for communication rather than avoidance and greater psychological distance; include smiling, touching, eye contact, closer distances, & more vocal animation
    - Cultures that display considerable interpersonal closeness or immediacy have been labeled contact cultures—people stand closer together & touch more
    - Low-contact cultures tend to stand apart & touch less
    - High-contact cultures generally located in warmer countries nearer the equator; low-contact cultures found in cooler climates farther from the equator.
    - High-contact cultures: most Arab countries, including North Africa; the Mediterranean region, including France, Greece, Italy, Portugal, & Spain; Jews from Europe and Middle East; Eastern Europeans & Russians; Latin America
    - Moderate-contact cultures: Australians, North Americans
    - Low-contact cultures: most of northern Europe; British Americans; white Anglo-Saxons (primary culture of U.S.); & virtually every Asian country (Asia is an extreme noncontact culture).

Japanese Nonverbal Communication: A Reflection of Cultural Themes

- Nonverbal communication practices function as a reflection, or representation, of societal cultural themes.
- More prevalent themes in Japanese culture:
    - Group affiliation (collectivism)
    - Hierarchy

- Social balance or harmony (*wa*)
- Empathy
- Mutual dependency
- Perseverance & sacrifice (*gaman*)
- Humility
- Formality (ritual, tradition, & protocol)

<u>Chapter Discussion Ideas</u>

1. Several researchers and scholars have abandoned the idea of linguistic relativity in order to focus on analysis of discourse. Do you feel that diversity in language categories and structure lead to cultural differences in thought and perceptions of the world? In what ways might linguistic relativity affect current analysis of discourse?

2. How do the Chinese immigrants and European Americans differ in their ways of compliment interactions?

3. What does Kelly-Holmes mean when she writes that "Words themselves have no inherent meanings. Meanings are instead attached to them by members of a speech community, a culture"?

4. What do Ellis and Maoz mean when they assert that the meaning and significance of messages fundamentally depend on speech codes?

5. How does the bicycle organization pattern used in Kenya differ from the linear method used in the U.S.? Why do Kenyans rely on the narrative for supporting material, whereas in the U.S. people rely on statistics and testimony to accomplish their speech purposes?

6. How do popular sayings reflect values in cultures? What popular sayings from your culture reflect values that you hold?

7. By reviewing Mexican *dichos* one can understand the Mexican culture's significant values. What are some of those values and how are they reflected in *dichos*?

8. According to Andersen and Wang, "culture is primarily a nonverbal phenomenon." To what extent do you agree or disagree with this conclusion?
    a. If we are to accept this claim that culture is not learned through explicit verbal instruction, what value is there in training people to be more interculturally aware?
    b. Encourage students to think about their own experiences with other cultures. If they say that they have never had any experience with a culture other than their own, suggest that they think about organizations, classrooms, and families as cultures. How have they learned how to behave appropriately in new cultures? Via explicit verbal instruction or by watching and learning through repeated observation of what people do?

9. Many people assume that we can learn to read a person's nonverbal communication like a book. There are even popular press books published on the subject. Andersen and Wang argue that we cannot read members of our own cultures let alone members of another culture. To what extent do you agree or disagree with this idea?

11. How might the homogeneity of the Japanese affect consistent themes in society? Compare the Japanese situation to that in the U.S.?

12. How are nonverbal factors of communication between and among cultures related to the verbal components of language?

13. Given the complexity of language, what advice would you have for someone who hopes to not only understand, but take part in the day-to-day life of another culture?

Chapter Exercises

Exercise 5.1: Words Are Outside, Meanings Are Inside

This activity can be used with Fong's article to explore different perceptions on the connection between language and culture. Because people come to an interaction with different perceptions about the world, they will not understand exactly the same thing when they hear or use a word. Even among culturally similar individuals, perceptions will differ and the meanings we ascribe to the words we use will not always be shared by those who are like us. The maxim "meanings are in people" refers to the notion that words do not hold meaning, people hold meaning. Words allow us to get our meanings across to others but they do not by themselves constitute meaning. We give words meaning based on our experiences, experiences that are often culture-specific. This exercise helps demonstrate the interconnection of language, meaning, experience, and culture.

This exercise asks students to reflect on what meanings they hold of certain words and how those meanings might differ from those held by people of other cultural groups. Ask students to characterize what they think the following words mean to them by using each in a complete, "illustrative" sentence: preacher, atheist, feminist, communism, Texan, capitalism, liberal, lesbian, sexist, and bigot. Add words that you feel would be especially suited for this exercise. By "illustrative," we mean a definition that illustrates or characterizes *to students* what these labels or concepts mean. For example, for the word *teenager* someone might write: "Someone who doesn't listen to her parents, doesn't trust anyone over thirty, and believes she is invincible." After students write a sentence for each word, ask them to share their responses with a group of their classmates.

Some questions to ask students during their small group or a class discussion: How did you arrive at your own meaning of each of the words? What differences and similarities were there among the sentences? What might account for such differences and similarities? Do you think your definitions are shared by most or few people in the U.S.? Who do you think would share your definitions? Have you ever had a conversation with someone from your own culture or another culture who had a very different meaning for a word than your own definition? How might the differences we ascribe to certain words and concepts affect our interactions with people who do not share our cultural background?

Exercise 5.2: Idiomatic Expressions

This activity can be used with Roy's article on *dichos* (popular sayings) or as a way to introduce the language unit to your students. This exercise demonstrates the difficulty in explaining and translating idioms to people who do not come from the same culture. Students will learn that idioms are *very* culture-bound and that knowing a language such as English does not ensure that one will understand all the idioms of the English language. This activity can be carried out in several ways. One way is to ask students to generate their own list of idioms and explain their definitions. Divide the class into groups of four to six students. Ask them to generate as many English idioms as they can think of from the U. S. This may be difficult at first because idioms are such a natural, unconscious part of conversation so it might be wise to give a few examples to get students started. Having international students in your classroom will enhance this exercise because many of them may not be familiar with all U.S. idioms. Students will discover that many idioms are difficult to define because native speakers of any language know the idioms of their culture intuitively through years of usage. Discuss the possible origins for the idioms that students generate.

A second way to carry out this activity is to use the handout that follows entitled "Idiomatic Expressions in English" that lists English idioms from three different cultures: the United States, Great Britain, and the Bahamas. Ask students to first explain what the U.S. idioms mean. International students may act as "judges" who determine whether the explanation of an idiom is adequate and whether understanding has been achieved. Then ask students to try to define the idioms in the other two lists. Which do they know, which can they accurately guess the meanings of, and which do they not understand? Give them the definitions to the British and Bahamian idioms and discuss possible reasons why these idioms were constructed the way they were.

Possible questions for discussion:

1. Why is it difficult to explain idioms from our own culture?
2. How do you think idioms are formed?
3. Why do they cause a great deal of trouble for normative speakers of any language?
4. Can you think of any idioms from the U.S. that you once did not understand but now do?
5. Could these idioms have been regionally based?
6. How did you come to understand each of these idioms? Did you ask for an explanation, or was the meaning clear contextually?

Exercise 5.2: Idiomatic Expressions in English

UNITED STATES

bite the dust
blow off steam
bone to pick
blow the whistle on
bored to tears
bread and butter
break the ice
brush off
beat around the bush
change one’s tune
chip on one’s shoulder
climb on the bandwagon

face the music
fair-weather friend
fed up
fine-tooth comb
get one’s feet wet
get through one’s head
feet on the ground
give up the ship
go against the grin
go to pot
in the family way
in the long run

keep your shirt on
land on ones feet
make no bones
neither here nor there
on the fence
on the whole
pay the piper
read between the lines
scratch the surface
save one's breath
miss the boat
take a back seat

GREAT BRITAIN

applaud to the echo
in bad odour
to be on (off) the beam
chop and change
as cold as charity
have a crow to pluck (pick)
die in harness
dree one’s weird
hang on a person's lips
come to heel

feel like a giant refreshed
of the first water
go to one’s account
not as green as he’s cabbage-looking
help a lame dog over a stile
a pretty pass
improve the occasion
have one’s knife in a person
late in the field

lose the day
merry as a cricket
with might and main
grasp the nettle
put in one's oar
shilly-shally
from pillar to post
pink of perfection
to stump up
lose caste

THE BAHAMAS

bitch up
butter for fat
clap somebody up
cut up with someone
what the diggins
don’t-care-‘f-I
fowled of doing something

in quest
lay on your chest/stomach
mix fool with sense
pick somebody’s mouth

broad-speaking
that’s chalk
cold in the arm, leg
cut your grass
dive up
draw hand
pick up gap seed

keep somebody hot
make him know
one mind tell me
pick up for somebody

get burned up
cheek somebody up
curry-favor someone
decide your mind
doggy after someone
eat off someone
grind somebody up in your heart
land somebody off
make your break
own something to somebody
pitch a stink

Exercise 5.2: Idiomatic Expressions in English

Key

GREAT BRITAIN (Collins, 1958)
Note: some of these may no longer be used in everyday conversation.

applaud to the echo: to acclaim and clap loudly, so that one rouses echoes
in bad odour: in disfavour, in disrepute
to be on/off the beam: to be on or off the point, to be relevant or irrelevant
chop and change: to be constantly changing, generally used derogatorily
come to keel: to show humble and complete obedience
feel like a giant refreshed: to feel physically or morally strong after something has happened
as cold as charity: lacking in signs of warm emotion
have a crow to pluck (pick): to have a complaint or criticism to make
die in harness: to die while still actively engaged in the course of one's regular work
dree one's weird: to endure with philosophic resignation what happens to one ("weird" is used here in place of fate)
hang on a person's lips: to listen closely to; similar to *hang on a person's every word*
of the first water: of the most excellent kind
go to one's account: to die
not as green as he's cabbage-looking: not so simple as one might think: not such a fool as he looks
help a lame dog over a stile: help a person deal with a difficulty with which he/she is incapable of coping
a pretty pass: a serious state of affairs
improve the occasion: to seize every advantage one can out of the circumstance
have one's knife in a person: to be constantly finding occasions for complaining about or blaming a person
late in the field: late on the scene
lose caste: to forfeit one social position by doing something that is regarded as socially discreditable
lose the day: to be defeated
merry as a cricket: extremely cheerful
with might and main: with all one's power
grasp the nettle: to tackle a difficulty or danger boldly
put in one's oar: to intervene in action or discussion
shilly-shally: to vacillate, waver, be undecided, hesitate
from pillar to post: to move from one place or resource to another
pink of perfection: the highest degree of what is perfect of its kind
to stump up: to pay money

Exercise 5.2: Idiomatic Expressions in English

Key

BAHAMAS (Holm, 1982)

bitch up: to ruin, spoil; to frustrate
broad-speaking: plain-speaking, outspoken
get burned up: to become exhausted through physical exertion
butter-for-fat: like for like; similar to *tit-for tat*
that's chalk: that's inevitable—a foregone conclusion; slang for *that's great*
cheek somebody up: to be impertinent to somebody
clap somebody up: to applaud somebody; similar to *applaud to the echo*
cold in the arm, leg: an inflammation of the arm or leg
curry-favor someone: give somebody an unfair advantage because of personal connections; curry somebody's favor
cut-up with someone: to flirt
cut your grass: to usurp someone else's prerogative or exclusive right or privilege
decide your mind: to make a decision
what the diggins: an exclamation of surprise
dive up: to dive into the water and bring something up
doggy after someone: to follow someone about constantly
don't-care-f-I: not caring, especially about social norms
draw hand: to make a leading or beckoning gesture
eat off someone: to eat at someone else's expense
fowled of doing something: engaged in doing something
pick up gap seed: to gather information for gossip
grind somebody up in your heart: to bear a grudge against somebody
in quest: to admit defeat in playing cards or marbles
keep somebody hot: to be at a person's heals, getting in his/her way
land somebody off: to drop someone off from a car or boat
lay on your chest/stomach: to cause indigestion or nightmares (of food eaten late at night)
make him know: to scold or punish
make your break: to seize an opportunity to do what one has been wanting to do
mix fool with sense: to attempt to deceive someone by interspersing lies with the truth
one mind tell me: I had a vague contradictory feeling (that something would happen, etc.)
own something to somebody: to confess something to somebody
pick somebody's mouth: to get information by engaging in seemingly casual conversation
pick up for somebody: to take somebody's side of the argument
pitch a stink: to object vehemently, cause a commotion

Exercise 5.3: Popular Sayings

This activity is designed to be used in conjunction with the Roy article on Mexican *dichos* (popular sayings). *Dichos* are one way that a culture teaches its members appropriate conduct, including effective ways of communication. Consider this cultural proverb well known to people in the United States: "You scratch my back, I'll scratch yours." This saying alludes to a rule of negotiation based on compromise and give and take. The Zairean proverb, "A little subtleness is better than a lot of force" suggests to members of this African culture that one should not be too pushy and overbearing when communicating. Proverbs are one way that our culture passes on wisdom. Roy discusses *dichos* that are specific to the Mexican culture. Have your students share some specific popular sayings that their families have taught them. For example, many Jewish children hear the proverb that "With money in your pocket, you are wise and you are handsome and you sing well too." Have students identify how these familial proverbs have impacted their lives. Be aware of any contrasting proverbs among the students. For example, "Honesty is the best policy" versus "Little white lies never hurt anyone." Contrasting proverbs can lead to a lively discussion when their implications are analyzed by the class.

Exercise 5.4: Case Studies on Language

The following activity is designed to illustrate for students how the same word or phrase can have very different meanings for individuals from different cultures. Students will understand that the simplest and taken-for-granted words and phrases in one culture can pose a problem in an intercultural interaction if different meanings are ascribed to the same verbal message. This activity can be done in groups or individually. Ask students to read the following case studies. Both case studies deal with a situation depicting a Kenyan and an individual from the U.S. interacting. Have them answer the questions that follow each case study.

<u>Case Study 1</u>

Joanna was a Peace Corps volunteer in Kenya who had just recently arrived at her site. She was anxious to meet many of the people of the community quickly and spent her first days riding her motorcycle through the hills near her house. While riding she stopped to talk with a Kenyan man named Kimani. They had a pleasant conversation and Kimani asked if they could talk again sometime because he was anxious to hear more about the United States. Joanna was eager to establish some friendships while in Kenya and told Kimani that she was glad to have found a friend. Kimani stopped by Joanna's house the next day and stayed for several hours. He visited Joanna regularly and brought her small gifts. Joanna realized quickly that Kimani wished to develop more than a friendship with her. She decided to discuss their relationship with him.

J: "Kimani, I think we need to talk about our friendship."
K: "Yes."
J: "I think you might want something more than I do, you know, something

more serious."

K: "You said you wanted us to be friends, right? That's what I want too."

J: "I guess I don't quite understand Kenyan customs yet. Do you bring gifts to your friends every time you visit them?"

K: "If I want to have a girlfriend, someone special, I do."

J: "But I thought you just wanted us to be friends."

K: "That's right, I do. I want us to be friends. That's why I am visiting you and bringing you gifts."

What word is the cause of Joanna and Kimani's confusion?
Explain why they are miscommunicating.
How would you continue this dialogue to solve this intercultural dilemma?

<u>Case Study 2</u>

Michael had just arrived at his school in Kenya. He was assigned to teach science at a rural high school outside of Kisumu. Charles, one of his students, visited him one Friday afternoon after school and they had a nice chat while drinking tea. As Charles was leaving, Michael waved to him and said, "See you later!" The following Monday, Charles approached Michael appearing confused.

C: "Mwalimu, I was waiting for you Friday evening but you never came."

M: "Was I supposed to meet you somewhere, Charles?"

C: "Well, I thought you were going to visit me at my home."

M: "Really? I don't remember telling you that Friday afternoon."

C: "You said that you would see me later so I thought that you would come visit me later that evening."

M: "Charles, I don't remember telling you that. Are you sure I said that?"

What phrase is the cause of Charles and Michael's confusion?
Explain why they are miscommunicating?
How would you continue this dialogue to solve this intercultural dilemma?

The first case study dealt with the word "friend" and the different meanings of "friend" being used by Joanna and Kimani. The word "friend" can have an additional meaning for Kenyans besides denoting an individual with whom one has a platonic relationship (the typical U.S. definition). For many Kenyans, to say someone of the opposite sex is your friend can also mean that you are having a romantic or intimate relationship with this person.

The second case study focused on the use of the common U.S. leave-taking phrase, "See you later!" Charles was probably not familiar with this idiomatic expression and took the phrase literally. Michael did not even remember having used this phrase because he said it almost unconsciously and was using it strictly to mean "good-bye" or "until we meet again."

Questions for discussion: Why do people attribute different meanings to the same word or phrase? Can any one word or phrase have one meaning? Or are there a number of definitions for every word and phrase? What role do experience and culture have in ascribing meaning to words and phrases? How do these case studies support the idea that language and experience are inextricably linked? What often happens when idioms are taken literally? Can you think of greetings, farewell phrases, and other small talk "niceties" that are used in your culture? Have you ever stopped to think what they might mean to someone who does not come from your culture? Have you ever heard an idiom that you didn't understand? Have you ever used a phrase or idiom that another person interpreted differently than you had intended?

Exercise 5.5: Nonverbal Greeting/Leave-Taking Behaviors

This activity is designed to heighten the students' awareness of how they take part in greeting and leave-taking behaviors and how these behaviors might be vastly different from other cultures of the world. This exercise will also make students aware of their own level of comfort in touching and being touched as well as their preferred space distance. Begin by dividing the class into two subgroups, X and Y, which represent groups of business professionals from two different cultures. Distinguish the two groups with something obvious such as colorful armbands, nametags, or ribbons. Ask Team Y to leave the room. You may give the teams written or verbal instructions.

Instruct Team X members that when Team Y comes back into the room they are to meet and greet their friends and business associates who are Team Y members. Inform Team X members that they come from a culture where close contact and warm embraces are the traditional style of saying "hello." Point out that when they shake hands on encountering Team Y members they must prolong the handshake for at least thirty seconds. Then they should make small talk for a few minutes (ask about family members, school, sports, etc., but do not engage in discussions of business; instead, redirect the conversation to other non-business topics), standing a little closer than is normally comfortable for them. A bell should ring after a few minutes and then Team X should say good-bye by giving their partner a warm embrace.

Instruct Team Y members that when they reenter the room they are to meet and greet members of Team X as friends and business associates in the traditional fashion of U.S. organizational culture by shaking hands. Team Y's objective is to begin a business transaction with Team X. They should say good-bye when the bell rings by shaking hands. The entire interaction should last for no more than three to four minutes.

Facilitate a **debriefing session** by asking for student comments about how they felt during the exercise. Discuss the awkwardness evident when different nonverbal rules were being used during the interaction. If you have a culturally diverse classroom, you will obviously get very different responses. These responses will undoubtedly enrich the discussion by lending first-hand insight into the touch and proxemic behavior of various cultural groups. Discuss with students the extent to which members of U.S. cultures engage in public touch behavior, when, and with whom. Also, talk with students about other cultures around the globe that engage in same-sex touching in public. For example, in Kenya and Nigeria men walk hand-in-hand frequently, yet mixed-sex handholding is rarely seen. In some African countries, handshakes are often extended, not the quick, firm grasps as is often the case in the U.S. Ask team Y if they felt frustrated at team X's refusal to talk about business. While U.S. business people are often in a "hurry" to get down to business, other cultures prefer to establish friendships before conducting business. This represents a different time orientation than is typical in the U.S.

Possible questions for further discussion: What happens when someone touches more than we are used to? How do we respond? Why? When do you feel comfortable hugging someone and whom do you feel comfortable hugging? Is such a greeting or goodbye appropriate for business associates? How does the amount of space between interactants impact a conversation? How much space do you like to have? What does standing closer to someone during a conversation indicate to you? How much of our nonverbal or affectionate behavior is culturally determined and how much is individually determined? How do you feel when you see two men and/or two women hugging? What happens when someone we are interacting with is on a different time orientation than our own? How do we respond? Why? What do these feelings tell us about the attitudes and behavior rules of our respective cultures? About our individual attitudes?

Exercise 5.6: When Another Is Silent

This activity deals with silence as a nonverbal behavior and is designed to be used with McDaniel's article on Japanese nonverbal communication as a reflection of Japanese culture. Most people have experienced a conversation where one person did most of the talking while the other took the "patient listener" role. Such experiences can lead to feelings of frustration and, sadly, sometimes to the end of developing relationships. On the other hand, it is also common to feel responsible for carrying the conversation with little assistance from a more silent friend or acquaintance. While both people in a conversation may have the responsibility of "monitoring" the extent to which they are sharing information and listening to the other share, striking a comfortable balance between the two is not always implicitly agreed upon by all individuals. The extent to which we speak and use silence in a conversation is often culturally determined.

As we grow up, we learn the cultural norms of interaction. Conversational competence in one culture may include asking many questions, while in another such communicative behavior would be deemed intrusive. This case study focuses on how different cultures perceive conversation competence during the first stages of a potential romantic relationship. Read the case and answer the questions that follow. As you read, consider your own experiences on first dates: what happened? How did you interpret the other person's communications?

Case Study

Jonathan and Noriko were out on their first date together. They had met in one of their classes and talked with each other several times at school. On the way over to the movie theater Jonathan noticed that Noriko was rather quiet, more quiet than when he had talked with her at school. After the movie, Jonathan suggested that they have coffee at a local cafe. Noriko still did not say very much as they sipped their coffee and Jonathan found himself filling in the silences with comments about school and questions about her family and growing up in Japan. He also talked a lot about his family since he was very close with them. Even though she answered his questions with short responses and didn't seem very willing to say much about her family, Noriko appeared to be in good spirits and when asked, said she was having a good time.

Jonathan dropped Noriko off at her apartment at about 11:00. They said goodnight at her door and as Jonathan got in his car, he was convinced Noriko had had a terrible time. He was worried that she hadn't said very much throughout the evening and wondered if he had offended her in some way. He talked with Noriko just before their class a few times the following week but they didn't make any plans to go out again. About a month later, after the school year had ended, Jonathan found out from a mutual friend that Noriko was disappointed that they never went out again. She said that she had really enjoyed his company and was hoping they could see each other again.

Questions for discussion: From the information above, describe the communication styles of Noriko and Jonathan. Why had Jonathan and Noriko perceived the success of their first date so differently? How might their relationship have developed differently? What could each have done to continue its development? What does quiet or silence communicate to you on a first date? Where did you get this interpretation(s)? Consider some alternative interpretations of silence. How does context and familiarity influence how we interpret their quietness or silence? Describe a time when a person you had just begun dating or had just met wasn't saying very much. How did you interpret this person's silence? Did you find out what this silence meant to this person?

Exercise 5.7: Time and Culture

The following case study demonstrates the difficulties people can encounter when learning and adapting to how individuals from other cultures perceive and orient to time. How time is viewed in some cultures is not a fixed orientation but can fluctuate depending on the context and the individual.

When people conceptualize time differently, their relationships may be affected. Ask students to read the case study below and answer the questions that follow. The narrator is a teacher from the United States teaching in the East African country of Uganda.

Case Study

I had arranged to meet Paul at 2:00 on Saturday in front of the post office. I had been invited by his mother for tea and he was meeting me to take me to their home in the hills surrounding the small town I called home for two years. Paul was an older student who started Form One (freshman) when he was 26. Being the oldest in the family, he had been needed at home and could not attend school until he was a young man. I was looking forward to meeting his family.

I arrived at the post office at 1:00. Because it was Saturday, there were not many people in town. The busiest days were Mondays and Thursdays—market days—and the weekends tended to bring fewer people into town during the day. As I waited for Paul, I watched the people come and go as they checked their mailboxes. 2:15 came and still no Paul. I was beginning to wonder whether I had heard 2:00 or 3:00 when Paul and I spoke the day before. I was sure it was 2:00. Well, 2:30 came and I was beginning to get frustrated; then 2:45 came, and now I was angry. Why did he say 2:00 and then not show up?

As my watch clicked to exactly 2:56, I saw Paul turn the corner by one of the several butchers in town. He approached the post office, smiled, and greeted me.

"It's a long walk to my home. I hope you're ready for a journey."

I said yes, half-waiting for an apology from him for being late. It never came.

"Paul, did you say you would meet me at 2:00 or 3:00?"

"I said 2:00. I hope you were not waiting long. Are you ready to go?"

Still no apology or explanation. After a very long walk we reached his home. The afternoon was wonderful and I thoroughly enjoyed meeting Paul's family. When I returned to school the following Monday, I asked one of the Kenyan teachers what she would have thought about Paul arriving almost an hour late.

"Oh, but he was not late. You said he came at 2:56. That's still 2:00."

"It's a lot closer to 3:00 than 2:00," I responded.

"Ah, perhaps in 'American time,' but remember here we are on 'African time.'"

Some questions for discussion in either small groups or as a class: How had the U.S. teacher understood "African time"? How would you describe African time? American time? Do you think the U.S. teacher should have been upset with Paul? Would you have left town? Would you have said something to Paul about arriving at 2:56? What might you have said? Can you identify and describe an event during a relationship that you have had, intercultural or intracultural, that was affected by differing conceptualizations of time? How did you respond to this difference and why did you respond this way? How might you respond now under similar circumstances? Any changes?

Exercise 5.8: Understanding Unfamiliar Cues

Just as with spoken language, we oftentimes cannot understand a nonverbal message that another person has sent us. Although these confusing nonverbal messages can take place during intracultural or intercultural communication situations, they can be especially confusing during intercultural interactions because there is often very little shared understanding among participants. For example, it is common among Kenyans to summon another person by making a forceful "tsss tsss" sound. To a culturally different visitor this can sound very much like calling an animal instead of a human being because it is similar to whistling when calling a dog in the U.S. In addition, this sound is made when getting the attention of both animals and people in Kenya. What is a visitor supposed to make of such a nonverbal message? Should offense be taken or understood as merely a pragmatic way of summoning a person with whom you wish to speak?

The following exercise asks students to consider nonverbal messages that they have found confusing during interactions with people from cultures different from their own. Ask students to answer each of the questions below in small groups. They should reflect on the nonverbal messages that they have experienced that left them feeling a bit confused or even offended. Each group should try to come up with at least two examples for questions one through three. Ask each group to share their responses with the class.

1. What are some nonverbal messages that can often cause confusion among people who are relatively culturally similar?
2. What are some nonverbal messages that can often cause confusion among people who do not share the same cultural background? Use your own experience to respond to this question.
3. Think about a conversation during which you did not completely understand some nonverbal messages that were being sent. Describe the conversation and the confusing nonverbal message(s).
4. At the time, what did you think this message meant? How did you arrive at this interpretation?
5. Could some kind of cultural difference account for your confusion? Why or why not?
6. How did the message and your confusion affect the outcome of the conversation or relationship?

Chapter Popular Film Suggestions

The following two films will help clarify the issues raised by the Helen Kelly-Holmes' essay, "German Language: Whose Language, Whose Culture?"

- ***Ali: Fear Eats the Soul*** (Germany, 1974; Rainer Werner Fassbinder, director; 93 minutes; German with English subtitles) Story of emotional trauma faced by an interracial couple in Germany—she a German widow and he an Arab worker. Close look at "racial tensions threatening German culture." Winner: International Critics Prize—Cannes Film Festival

  Web Reference:

  Ng, D. *Ali: Fear Eats the Soul*, DVD Review.
  http://www.imagesjournal.com/2003/reviews/ali/text.htm

- ***The All-round Reduced Personality***. (Germany,1977; Helke Sander, director; 98 min.; German with English subtitles)
  "A key work of the new German cinema, Helke Sander's film is a justly celebrated portrait of Edda, a free-lance photojournalist and a look at the divided city of Berlin -- a wryly funny but serious commentary on contemporary life. Sander, a leading figure of the women's movement in Germany, is the film's writer, director, and star. In the role of Edda, Sander has a hard time making ends meet to support herself and her daughter, and is forced to photograph boring functions while really wanting to take socially significant pictures, As she struggles to realize herself as an artist and a woman, Sander bravely portrays Edda as an individual straddling multiple worlds-- work, womanhood, motherhood, East, West, capitalism, and socialism." (http://web.utk.edu/~mfll/LRC/german.html)

  Web Reference:

  Modern Foreign Languages and Literatures.
  http://web.utk.edu/~mfll/LRC/german.html

The following film would lend itself very well to the consideration of cultural communication differences discussed by Donald G. Ellis and Ifat Maoz in "Dialogue and Cultural Communication Between Israeli Jews and Palestinians."

- ***Promises.*** (Israel, 2001; Justine Shapiro, B.Z. Goldberg, and Carlos Bolado, co-directors; 102 min.; Arabic, Hebrew & English with English subtitles) Documentary that travels from a Palestinian refugee camp to an Israeli settlement, where the filmmakers interview the children of these disparate cultures. "Seen through the eyes of these children … *Promises* offers a refreshing, human and sometimes humorous portrait of the Palestinian-Israeli conflict" (http://store.yahoo.com/olivefilms/promisesdvd.htm).

  Web References:

  Baltimore Citypaper Online, Review of *Promises* by Lee Gardner.
  http://www.citypaper.com/film/review.asp?id=2205

  Olive Films, Promises (DVD) synopsis
  http://store.yahoo.com/olivefilms/promisesdvd.htm

Chapter Test Items

Multiple Choice

1. Which of the following statements is true about culture?
   a. cultures comprise symbolic systems that create webs of meaning.
   b. cultures endure over long periods
   c. cultures are learned by humans through both explicit instruction and tacit acquisition
   d. all of the above *

2. Qualitative research methods examine the interrelationship of language and culture through
   a. ethnography
   b. pragmatics
   c. discourse analysis
   d. all of the above *

3. The unfortunate incident of breaking a glass object during Chinese New Year is transformed to a fortunate incident when
   a. the object is replaced
   b. the person breaking the object says a prayer
   c. the person orally uses a positive expression to describe the unfortunate act*
   d. by redescribing the incident as a purposeful gesture

4. Diversity in language categories and structure lead to cultural differences in thought is a concept known as
   a. linguistic relativity *
   b. linguistic subjectivity
   c. linguistic differences
   d. none of the above

5. Which of the following approaches focuses on the underlying factors that influence language choices in multilingual communication contexts?
   a. the developmental approach
   b. the interactional approach
   c. the social psychological approach *
   d. none of the above

6. Chinese immigrant participants are described as being in which state when they are unfamiliar with European Americans'generosity?
   a. intercultural shock state *
   b. intercultural resistance state
   c. intercultural accommodation state
   d. bicultural competence state

7. Language is
    a. the result of political, economic, historical, social, ideological, and cultural processes
    b. inextricably linked to culture
    c. not simply a code
    d. all of the above *

8. A dialect
    a. is the national language spoken in a region
    b. reflects a strong regional culture and identity *
    c. is related to pronunciation and accent
    d. none of the above

9. A group that has often felt excluded by the German language is
    a. gypsies
    b. Swiss
    c. women *
    d. *Auslander*

10. *Denglisch* refers to the
    a. omnipresence of American international culture
    b. hybrid of Deutsch and English *
    c. language of Bavarians
    d. none of the above

11. *Musayra*
    a. is the speech code commonly used by Arabs
    b. has to do with honor, hospitality, and collectivism
    c. emphasizes politeness, indirectness, being courteous, and nonconfrontive
    d. all of the above *

12. *Dugri*
    a. means "straight talk" *
    b. characterizes the speech code of Palestinians
    c. uses repetition, indirectness, elaboration, and affectiveness
    d. none of the above

13. Weddings in Kenya
    a. are generally brief ceremonies
    b. can last all day, as many guests can make speeches *
    c. last three days
    d. last three weeks

14. In contrast to Kenya, the U.S. culture relies on
    a. high-context communication and high power distance
    b. low-context communication and high power distance
    c. low-context communication and low power distance *
    d. high-context communication and low power distance

15. In contrast to the U.S., Kenyan culture has
    a. a polychronic view of time *
    b. a monochronic view of time
    c. a polymorphous view of time
    d. none of the above

16. The "harambee" is
    a. a wedding ceremony
    b. a political event
    c. a community fundraising event *
    d. none of the above

17. In negotiating a bride price, a speaker says the bride's family would require 20 goats as a major portion of the bride price; one way to interpret this is
    a. literally, as a request for 20 goats
    b. metaphorically, as a request for the sum of money that could purchase 20 goats *
    c. symbolically, as the groom being worth 20 goats
    d. an unrealistic way to haggle

18. Which of the following would NOT likely be used in a Kenyan speech:
    a. songs
    b. proverbs
    c. statistics *
    d. audience response

19. *Dichos*, popular sayings, have an impact on human behavior because
    a. they reflect many of the basic values of contemporary Mexican society
    b. they capture what a culture deems important
    c. they are handed down from one generation to the next
    d. all of the above *

20. "*No por mucho madrugar amancee más temprano*" (No matter how early one rises, the sun will not come up any sooner.) can be interpreted to mean that
    a. one must simply accept what one cannot change *
    b. if you don't rise early, you will miss out on a lot
    c. if you rise early, you will not miss out on anything
    d. one must simply accept what life brings

21. According to Roy's article about Mexican *dichos*, which of the following is NOT a significant value in Mexican culture?

a. cheerful acceptance of one's lot
b. the need to exercise caution when placing trust
c. the unimportance of appearances *
d. the sanctity of privacy

22. "*Cuando el pobre tiene para carne sea vigilia*" (When the poor have [money] to buy meat, it must be lent.) means that

a. The poor must accept that their luck will change when they have money.
b. The poor must eat beans and tortillas, not meat.
c. The poor must accept that they will not have good luck. *
d. none of the above

23. Nonverbal behaviors that consist of body movements, gestures, and facial expressions are categorized as

a. chronemics
b. proxemics
c. kinesics *
d. paralanguage

24. Differences between Arab cultures in which people tend to stand closely together when speaking and North American cultures in which people carry on conversation at a distance of eighteen to thirty-six inches are differences in

a. olfactics
b. vocalics
c. haptics
d. proxemics *

25. Nonverbal behaviors that communicate warmth and closeness are referred to as _______ behaviors.

a. contact
b. immediacy *
c. collective
d. internal

26. According to McDaniel, which cultural trait lessens Japanese reliance on verbal exchange?

a. vague statements
b. empathy *
c. ambiguity in conversations
d. None of the above

27. Hand gestures are never used in Japan in reference to a person who is present at the time; instead they are employed when referring to some absent party because
    a. it is against Confucian ethics
    b. the Japanese do not use any nonverbal gestures
    c. this reduces the opportunity for offending anyone present and helps sustain contextual harmony *
    d. none of the above

28. By avoiding eye contact, Japanese participants
    a. evince an air of humility and sustain situational *wa* *
    b. exercise power
    c. indicate disagreement
    d. none of the above

29. The Japanese attitude toward personal space is contradictory because
    a. they are passive about personal space but active about office space
    b. in uncrowded situations they maintain their personal space, but in crowded situations they do not resist contact with strangers *
    c. they strive to maintain greater personal space with Americans but less personal space with Hispanics
    d. none of the above

30. The Japanese proclivity for conservative dress styles and colors emphasizes their value of
    a. proper dress
    b. status
    c. collectivism *
    d. all of the above

True/False

T 1. All communication, whether verbal or nonverbal, occurs within cultural frameworks.

T 2. Cultures are dynamic rather than static.

F 3. Chinese immigrants value immodesty and have little problem accepting direct compliments from Americans.

T 4. Chinese employ language to reverse bad luck.

F 5. Developmental theorists are interested in identifying appropriate communication styles and norms in various cultures.

F 6. When Chinese immigrant participants were found to be in the intercultural shock state, they became very verbal participants.

F 7. Language automatically counts as part of culture and identity in the Anglophone world.

T 8. German regional variation encompasses changes to sentence structure, meanings, and vocabulary.

T 9. Dialects reflect and reinforce a strong regional culture and identity.

T 10. A diglossic situation is one where different and distinct varieties of languages are used for different and distinct purposes.

F 11. In urban areas of Germany, dialect is seen as the preserve of the young people.

T 12. Women have been excluded in the German language by its patriarchal grammar.

F 13. The term *Auslãnder*, which is usually translated "foreigner" or "alien," is a term often applied to Americans visiting Germany.

T 14. English is seen by French and German speakers as an actual threat to Francophone and Germanophone cultures.

T 15. *Musraya* means "to accommodate" or "go along with."

F 16. An Arab speaker who is engaging in the code of *musraya* is being impolite, direct, uncourteous, and confrontive.

T 17. *Dugri* is the opposite of *musayra.*

T 18. *Dugri* and *musayra* are excellent examples of speech codes.

T 19. Speech codes can be used to understand, predict, and control communication.

T 20. Israeli-Jews qualify their arguments, backtrack, and provide context.

F 21. The Israelis engage in something known as "tag-team" arguments.

T 22. The U.S. is oriented to low power distance; Kenya is oriented to high power distance.

T 23. High-context communication features pre-programmed information that is in the receiver and in the setting, with only minimal information in the transmitted message.

F 24. Low-context messages are prevalent in Kenya.

T 25. In Kenyan public speeches, the most convincing type of supporting material is a narrative.

F 26. Wealth and age are the two defining factors in establishing the credibility of a speaker in Kenya.

T 27. In Kenya, because the group is valued more highly than individual interests, it is necessary to give every relevant person the opportunity to be heard at a given occasion.

T 28. *Dichos* are a form of transmitting folk wisdom.

F 29. Through *dichos* we are reminded that our experiences are unique.

T 30. Nonverbal messages tell us how to interpret verbal messages.

T 31. The most externally obvious code of nonverbal behavior is physical appearance.

T 32. The nonverbal elements of the voice is known as paralanguage.

T 33. Smiling, touching, eye contact, closer distances, and more vocal animation are examples of immediacy behaviors.

F 34. People typically make conscious choices about their nonverbal behavior.

T 35. Nonverbal communication is subject to cultural variation.

F	36.	When confronted with out-group members, Japanese can be quite expressive and display considerable nonverbal affiliativeness.
T	37.	Self-restraint of body movement in out-group environments by the Japanese is designed to avoid attention and maintain situational harmony or balance.
F	38.	Japanese children experience little touch from their mothers and this non-touch standard continues into adulthood.
T	39.	For the Japanese, laughter can signal joy, disguise embarrassment, sadness, and anger.

Chapter Essay Questions

1. Discuss the Sapir-Whorf hypothesis with regard to the relationship between language and thought.
2. Explain the following formula "If ... then... because... meaning" when referring to the Chinese custom of reversing negative comments.
3. Explain how the Chinese deal with compliment interactions.
4. How do Chinese and Americans express themselves differently? Provide examples for support.
5. Explain how the Chinese language reflects the structure of the society.
6. Explain what Kelly-Holmes means when she writes that language counts as part of culture and identity "for the German-speaking world."
7. What is the difference between a dialect and a language?
8. Why in Germany do dialects often reflect status?
9. How does the German language exclude women through its grammar?
10. How do the German media contribute to the Anglicizing of the German language?
11. Explain the concept of two cultural communication codes termed *dugri* and *musayra* which are known to characterize the Israeli-Jews and Arabs.
12. Identify and explain the four communication features of *musraya.*
13. Discuss the well-documented code, *dugri,* used by the Israeli-Jews.
14. Explain *dugri* and *musraya* within the context of the five principles of speech codes.
15. Describe the Kenyan value orientation of collectivism, giving concrete examples drawn from family relationships.
16. What does it mean to say Kenyan culture has an orientation of high power distance? Contrast this with power distance in the U.S.
17. What are the differences between high- and low-context communication?
18. Contrast speech making in the U.S. with speech making in Kenya.
19. Explain the popular Mexican sayings "*Aqua que no has de beber, déjala correr* (Water that you do not have to drink, leave it to flow.) and *En boca cerrada no entran moscas*. (Flies do not enter a closed mouth.) What aspect of culture do these sayings reflect?
20. Explain the importance of family in the Mexican culture. Provide an example of one *dicho* that speaks to the importance of family.
21. What accounts for the finding that in individualistic countries like the United States, small talk, flirting, and dating are more important than in more collectivist cultures?
22. How does the degree to which a culture is individualistic or collectivistic affect the nonverbal behavior of that culture?
23. What is kinesic behavior? How does it vary from one culture to another? What types of communication problems can be caused by cultural differences in kinesic behavior?

24. Explain how social balance affects nearly all Japanese nonverbal behavior.
25. What does McDaniel mean by the "thematic consistency concept" in regard to culture?
26. How does culture influence personal appearance in Japanese and U.S. American culture?
27. Describe differences in the use of vocalics, or paralanguage, in Japan and the United States. How might these differences lead to misunderstandings during intercultural communication?

Chapter References

Collins, V. H. (1958). *A second book of English idioms.* London: Longmans, Green and Co.

Holm, J. A. (1982). *Dictionary of Bahamian English.* New York: Lexik House Publishers.

Chapter 6 Cultural Contexts: The Influence of the Setting

Chapter Synopsis

After reading this chapter, students will be more aware of the crucial link existing between context, culture, and communication. Three settings have been selected for examination in this chapter: business, education, and health care. Students should be able to make connections between their own experiences of communicating within each of the contexts discussed in the readings and compare their own cultural expectations with those articulated by the authors. This chapter offers students some practical application of the concepts presented in the previous chapter.

Sheryl Lindsley and Charles Braithwaite, in their essay "U.S. Americans and Mexicans Working Together: Five Core Concepts," provide a brief overview of the problems that have arisen from business practices between Mexicans and Americans over the last ten years. They then discuss five core concepts of Mexican culture in order to alleviate miscommunication between Mexicans and Americans doing business in Mexico.

In the second essay, "Application of American Management Theories and Practices to the Indian Business Environment," Suresh Gopalan and Angie Stahh focus on doing business in India by comparing and contrasting American and Indian values, the former from an individualistic cultural viewpoint, the latter from a collectivist cultural viewpoint.

Robert A. Friday, in "Contrasts in Discussion Behaviors of German and American Managers," traces the cultural expectations of both German and American managers across several dimensions, pointing out differences and how they may lead to misunderstandings and ineffective communication.

In "'Half-Truths' in Argentina, Brazil, and India," Nagesh Rao looks at the interaction between physicians and patients. A review of the literature is provided on the impact of culture on physician-patient communication. He presents data from interviews with physicians in Argentina, Brazil, and India.

Brian E. Mendyka, in his essay "Exploring Culture in Nursing," follows the case of a single Native American patient to reveal how differences in time, perceptions of illness, family relationships, and perceptions of self can create problems.

Geneva Gay, in "Culture and Communication in the Classroom," explores cultural diversity in university classrooms. Because most university students will take some of their courses from instructors from different countries, students need to be able to see the classroom as a multicultural, international environment. She offers insight and practical advice to students to assist them in navigating and learning in the diverse university classroom.

Johann Le Roux, in "Social Dynamics of the Multicultural Classroom," argues that the effective multicultural teacher must be sensitive to group and cultural affiliations. He looks at the problem of language, stereotyping, cultural expectations, self-concept, and conflict, and then offers detailed advice for overcoming these problems.

Chapter Outline

U.S. Americans and Mexicans Working Together: Five Core Concepts

- ***Confianza***

  Good working relationships come through:
  - Establishment of trust and confidence
  - Built through communicative behaviors that adhere to cultural norms for face saving, such as being indirect when appropriate
  - U.S. American managers should
    - Avoid displays of negative emotions, especially direct criticism
    - Convey their receptiveness to negative information, asking how they can help their employees
    - Pay close attention to nonverbal behaviors
- ***Simpatía***
  - Good communication is established through *simpatía* and is necessary for maintaining positive working relationships & for meeting productivity goals
  - Emphasizes emotional support and self-sacrifice for the good of the group
- ***Palanca***
  - Refers to leverage or power derived from affiliated connections, extensive networks of relationships among family members, relatives, former classmates, friends, and business associates
  - U.S. Americans tend to evaluate these relationships as "corrupt," but they have a long history in the development of Mexico from its colonial past
  - This must be distinguished from paying a bribe, *mordida*, which is illegal in both the U.S. and Mexico; *palanca* embodies a system of mutual obligation and reciprocated favors, not necessarily money or gifts
- ***Estabilidad***
  - Need for *estabilidad* or "stability" reinforces the value of personal relationships and permeates organizational behaviors
  - Some behaviors U.S. managers could take:
    - Ask questions about colleagues' families
    - Discuss personal matters before business (e.g., at the beginning of a meeting)
    - Take action to promote employees' personal well-being
    - Include family members in organizational activities
    - Take time off work to assist family members in need
    - Establish, develop, and maintain long-term interconnected networks of personal relationships

- ***Mañana***
  - Most Mexicans consider time to be more interpersonally negotiable (relationships guide activities), and what counts as "being on time" can be mediated by unexpected events beyond one's control
  - Organizational tasks do not get accomplished as quickly in Mexico as in the U.S. because of infrastructure and/or the bureaucratic process, which can slow things down
  - U.S. Americans need to
    - Adapt their behaviors to recognize that personal relationships are the foundation of good business in Mexico
    - Adjust their attitudes to recognize that Mexicans work very hard but have other priorities in life, too

Application of American Theories and Practices to the Indian Business Environment

To develop a cultural profile of any country requires understanding the fundamental assumptions and choices regarding the following:

- Human nature
- Natural and supernatural elements
- Time
- Work
- Relationships

Contrasting Profiles of American and Indian National Culture

American National Culture	Indian National Culture
Human Nature Orientation • Humans have a combination of good and evil qualities • Fundamental changes in human nature can be accomplished through combination of right training, education, and exposure • Focus is on helping the individual	**Human Nature Orientation** • An individual's situation in present life is largely a consequence of actions committed in a previous birth or births (life is predetermined) • Change is relatively difficult to accomplish • Widespread sense of fatalism
Relationship to Nature & Supernatural Elements • Natural resources and elements can and should be utilized for benefit of humankind • Americans believe they are in control of most of life's events & that their individual actions and effort will make a difference in their lives	**Relationship to Nature & Supernatural Elements** • People have a predisposition toward external locus of control—people basically helpless in affecting life's events
Time Orientation • Oriented to future; future will be better	**Time Orientation** • Time is an infinite loop—one that has

American National Culture	Indian National Culture
• Time is perishable and time is linear • Change is valued & embraced **Approach to Work** • Individual identity linked to occupation/career • Work considered an end in itself • Strong work ethic favors objectivity, competitiveness, and a need for achievement **Relationships in Society** • Americans tend to be highly individualistic, autonomous, and egalitarian (non-hierarchical) in nature • Independence stressed over dependency • Individual rights prized over group group goals	always been there and that will continue to exist • Focus on maintaining status quo **Approach to Work** • Work is a means to an end—to satisfy economic needs • Once primary needs are satisfied, focus shifts from work toward other pursuits **Relationships in Society** • Hierarchy and status valued • Age and seniority valued • Traditional notions of family

Management Practices in U.S. that Stem from American National Culture

- Organizations spend millions of dollars annually for training seminars and other HR development activities
- Companies actively involved in helping and interacting with the local community
- Intervene to ensure employee health, such as banning smoking inside offices
- Goal setting and motivational practices in organizations
- Time is compartmentalized—meeting deadlines, schedules, & appointments is emphasized
- Punctuality and promptness valued; strong disapproval toward tardiness and excessive delays
- Focus of corporate America is on achieving short-term goals based on quarterly targets
- U.S. laws require most qualified be hired for a job (anti-nepotism)
- Employees loyal to their profession, not to their organization
- Egalitarianism in the workplace

Management Practices in India

- Authors state that more research needed before American management values and style can be transferred to India

Contrasts in Discussion Behaviors of German and American Managers

American Managers' Expectations	German Managers' Expectations
Business is impersonal—Americans do not identify with their corporations	Business is not as impersonal—corporation closely related to German's own identity
Need to be liked is primary motivator	Need to be credible
Style embodies assertiveness, direct confrontation, and fair play—competition in business occurs within context of cooperation	Style embodies assertiveness, sophistication, and direct confrontation—no German sense of fair play

- Management style of German and American managers more likely to be influenced by their nationality than by corporate culture
- American managers'discussion style avoids *argumentum ad hominem,* focuses on arriving at consensus, and is based on the acceptance of value relativism
- German managers' discussion style, *Besprechung,* rejects value relativism in support of German values of fixed hierarchy and social order and focuses on arriving at truth or purer concepts
- In a discussion (or argument) between the American and German manager, who is often better educated and better versed in German-style debate misunderstanding can arise from these divergent management styles, for the American manager can feel attacked when the German manager strikes with vigor and enthusiasm at an error in the American manager's argument

"Half-Truths" in Argentina, Brazil, and India: An Intercultural Analysis of Physician-Patient Communication

Impact of Culture on Physician-Patient Communication

- Madeline Leininger's Theory of Culture Care and Diversity and Universality (1991)
  All cultures express care but attach different meanings to health-related practices
  Meaning is shaped by technology, religion, cultural norms, economics, and education
- Diversity also exists within cultural groups, influenced by ethnicity, religion, education, age, sex, and acculturation
- Health care provider needs to understand cultural variables affecting the patient's thinking and actions
- Health care provider also must be aware of how patient's cultural heritage intersects with the culture of the health care organization
- Some barriers to culturally appropriate care are language and jargon

Physician's Definition of Culture

- Physicians in Argentina, Brazil, and India saw their countries as heterogeneous
- Physicians in Argentina and Brazil focused mainly on socioeconomic status and education as main indicators of diversity
- Physicians in India saw diversity in terms of language, socioeconomic status, religion, and so on

"Half-Truths"

- In study of physicians in Argentina, Brazil, and India, 90% engaged in "half-truths" where physicians
  - Did not disclose the diagnosis immediately
  - Described the diagnosis in doses over several visits
  - Informed a family member of the diagnosis first before telling the patient
  - The type of half-truth used depended on the patient's psychological readiness to hear the diagnosis

Exploring Culture in Nursing: A Theory-Driven Practice

Essentializing Holistic Care: The Mind-Body-Spirit Axiom

- Essentialism is an ideology that emphasizes the meaning of human "parts" over the meaning of the "whole"
- By essentializing nursing care occurs when nurses reconfigure patient and family illness as nothing more than narrow technical issues, or "disease problems"
- Holistic approach is to affirm the patient's personal and cultural experience of illness as constituted by patient and family explanations and then use these explanations to cultivate therapeutic treatment
- Actively listening to patient's explanations of this cultural experience of illness
- Merging phenomenal fields of nurse and patient, leading the two to experience transpersonal caring
- Need to understand persons as phenomenal fields, " 'a person's frame of reference or subjective reality, composed of the totality of human experience'" (p. 320)

Interpersonal Aspects of Caring

- Include cognitive, behavioral, and affective domains and are important for providing holistic care
  - Cognitive domains are broad categories of intellectual, perceptual, and experiential nursing knowledge
  - Behavioral domains are technologic skills nurses learn to apply for promoting compassionate and effective nursing care
  - Affective domains include exercise and total expression or authenticity, congruence, empathy, genuineness, and non-possessive warmth

The Moral Work of Nursing and Holistic Care

- Helping patients find meaning in their illness experience
- To protect and foster patient agency
- Helping patients to have a life

Culture and Communication in the Classroom

Relationship among Culture, Communication, and Education

- Culture central to communication and communications central to education
- Sapir-Whorf Hypothesis—language is a way of defining experience, thinking, and knowing
- Vygotsky (1962): "thought development is determined by language … and the sociocultural experience of the child" (p. 328)

- Development of logic affected by a person's socialized speech, and intellectual growth contingent on mastery of social means of thought and language

Culturally Different Discourse Structures

Passive-receptive character of conventional classroom:

- Teacher speaks, students listen
- Take turn talking once permission granted
- Students expected to speak in complete sentences that include logical development of thought, precise information, appropriate vocabulary, and careful attention to grammar

Participatory-interactive discourse of some ethnic groups:

- Speakers expect listeners to engage them actively through vocalized motion and movement responses *as they are speaking*
- Speakers and listeners are action-provoking partners in construction of discourse
- This communication style observed among African Americans, Latinos, and Native Hawaiians

Ethnic Variations in Communication Styles

African Americans

- Call-response style of communicating—listeners give encouragement, commentary, compliments, and even criticism to speakers *as they talk*
- African Americans "gain the floor"—enter conversations—through personal assertiveness; don't wait for permission to speak
- Many teachers view these behaviors negatively and penalize students for them

Native Hawaiians

- Use a style similar to that of African Americans—called "talk-story" or "co-narrative"
- Involves several students working collaboratively, or talking together, to create an idea, tell a story, or complete a learning task

European American Females

- Some of the same traits of call-response and talk-story
- Occurs most often in situations where talk is casual and friendly—rapport-talk used to create community

Problem Solving and Task Engagement

- Many African American, Latino, Native American, and Asian American students use styles of inquiry and responding different from conventional classroom
- Most common practice is for teachers to ask convergent (single-answer) questions and use deductive approaches to solving problems
- Students of color, if strongly affiliated with their cultures, tend to be more inductive, interactive, and communal in solving problems
- Traditional African American and Latino cultures see problem solving as highly contextual—takes place on a stage or setting and is social in nature
- Latinos may begin tasks by asking colleagues about their families
- African Americans give a preamble to a talk, telling listeners where they are coming from—providing their underlying assumptions, ideology, and values
- Asian Americans use a process of collaborative and negotiated problem solving

Organizing Ideas in Discourse

- **Topic-centered discourse**—speakers focus on one issue at a time; arrange facts and ideas in logical, linear order; and make explicit relationships between facts and ideas
- **Topic-associative (topic-chaining) discourse**—episodic, anecdotal, thematic, and integrative; more than one issues addressed at once; related explanations unfold in overlapping, intersecting loops; relationships assumed or inferred rather than explicitly established; typical of Native Hawaiians and African Americans

Storytelling as Topic-Chaining Discourse

- African American speakers use a topic-chaining style to do many things at once: relate information; persuade others to support the speaker's point of view; network; counter opposition; exercise power; demonstrate one's verbal aestheticism
- Takes speaker a while to get to the point, so needs time to set up the discourse
- **Taking Positions and Presenting Self**
  - African American students relate differently to materials, issues, and topics discussed or analyzed
  - Value indirect and holistic communications, wisdom of the past, importance of the group

Personalizing or Objectifying Communications

- African Americans tend to take positions of advocacy and express personal points of view in discussions—facts, opinions, emotions, and reason are combined in presenting one's case
- African Americans more likely to challenge authority and expertise than students from other ethnic groups
- Asians and Asian Americans will sometimes interject laughter into conversations with the teacher about their performance to diffuse intensity of their confusion or give the impression that there is no problem
- European Americans' discourse almost the opposite of that of African Americans—they relate to issues and materials as spokespersons, not advocates, and consider the truth or merits of an idea to be intrinsic; believe emotions interfere with one's capacity to reason and quality of reasoning; try to avoid or minimize opposition in dialogue because they assume it will be confrontational

Playing with and on Words

- African Americans use repetition for emphasis and to create cadence in speech delivery
- Frequent use of verb pairs in writing of African American students

Ambivalence and Distancing in Communication

- Asian international and Asian American college students and professional colleagues tend not to declare either definitive advocacy or adversarial positions in either oral or written discourse
- Rather, they take moderate stances, seek out compromise positions, and look for ways to accommodate opposites

Gender Variations in Discourse Styles

- Females Communicate Differently from Males

- Gender Communication Patterns Established Early in Life
- Problems with "Gendered" Communication Styles—a plus for females to use male-style discourse, but a minus for males to use female-style discourse

Social Dynamics of the Multicultural Classroom

Language Issues in Multicultural Classrooms

- Children from ethnic groups can be penalized when they go to school for having little or no contact with the language medium of formal education
- Teacher perceptions of student ability often influenced by student's proficiency in terms of standard language varieties prevalent in school and society
- Differences in student vocabulary correlate directly with parental levels of education and with quality-of-life levels in general.
- Early achievement disparities tend to increase with age.

Social Judgment and Stereotyping in the Multicultural Classroom

- Research shows that:
- Teachers tend to award higher grades for same assignment when submitted by a student with a particular name
- Physically attractive persons are believed to have more desirable personalities, have higher status, enjoy more fulfilling lives, and are better parents and students
- Teachers' perceptions of students' speech leads to negative expectations about their personalities, social and cultural backgrounds, and academic abilities

Social Attraction, Repulsion, and Expectations in the Multicultural Classroom

- Students from minority cultures perform better in classrooms having a climate of acceptance
- Teacher serves pivotal role as initiator, manager, and demonstrator of intergroup acceptance and positive regard of others
- *Self-fulfilling prophecy* effect—students tend to see themselves and their abilities in accordance with the way the teacher conveys it to them

Self-Concept Formation in Multicultural Classrooms

- Effective teaching in the multicultural classroom is directed at positively influencing students' self-concepts.
- *Self-enhancement theorists*: Students' self-concepts influence their level of achievement.
- *Skills development model*: self-concept of ability is direct consequence of academic success

Dealing with Conflict in Multicultural Classrooms

- If managed properly, conflict can serve as purifying agent for strained relationships and is essential for a healthy climate in the classroom.
- Effective teacher deals with conflict constructively, integrating conflicting viewpoints into the problem-solving solution.

Discussion Ideas

1. Explain the Mexican notion of "face." How does the core concept of *confianza* relate to saving face? What about the concept of *sympatía*?
2. How would you define negotiation? Explain how direct confrontation is involved in negotiation. Explain how culture clash can occur during a negotiation. How can it be avoided?
3. What are some specific examples for each of Kluckhohn and Strodtbeck's five intercultural dimensions? List examples from the Indian culture using these five dimensions.
4. What is the influence of the American sense of "fair play" on decision making between German and American managers? If you were asked to help design a training program for a U.S. company that consistently engaged in business with Germany, what recommendations would you make after reading Friday's article?
5. Discuss how culture might impact physician-patient communication.
6. What is meant by the phrase "cultural experiences of illness"?
7. Discuss how culture plays a role in classroom communication. Ask students to draw upon their own experiences.
8. Do you believe that schools have an obligation to support and encourage a minority culture's language?
9. How can intercultural educators keep from stereotyping multicultural students?

Chapter Exercises

Exercise 6.1: Classroom Visitors

This activity is designed to give students an in-depth understanding of the role that culture plays in the business, health care, and classroom contexts and applies to all the articles in this chapter. It allows students to listen to and ask questions of business professionals, health care providers, and teachers. Students will acquire some "real life" understanding of the consequences of culture in the realm of business. Further, students will gain insight into how interaction between patients and health care workers can be affected by different perceptions of how illness should be prevented and treated. Students will also be able to talk with teachers about how culture has an impact on the school classroom in the United States.

This activity can be accomplished in two ways. First, students can interview someone in the business, health care, or educational context, ask the questions below, and then report their findings to the class. A second option is for you to invite members from at least three contexts to visit your classroom—invite two or three business professionals to your class. These visitors can be contacted via personal affiliations, local business communities, or through businesses that have a partnership with your college or university. Ask your visitors to address changes in the business environment due to culture. How have the personal cultural demographics of the organization changed over the last five/ten years? What cultural sensitivity training is being done? What adaptations/accommodations have been made due to increase cultural diversity in the workplace? Have office arrangements, space, time usage, uniforms, etc., been altered? Negotiations? Group dynamics? What difficulties arise in the multicultural organization?

Next, invite two or three health care workers (nurses, doctors, public health workers, counselors, etc.) to your class. These visitors can be contacted on your college or university campus or from the surrounding community. Such health care facilities as Planned Parenthood, women's health care and community clinics, hospices, local hospitals, and the health department in your city are excellent possible resources. Ask your visitors to address the role of culture and cultural sensitivity in their jobs and to share some of their experiences with students about those clients and patients who come from different cultures. What are some of the difficulties that they have had to face? How are their intercultural interactions enjoyable and stimulating? What strategies do they use to help their clients? How successful are they? What suggestions do they have for improving relations between culturally different patients and health care workers?

Finally, invite two or three K-12 teachers to your class. These visitors can be contacted at local schools throughout your community. Invite teachers who teach in a multicultural school and who are culturally diverse among themselves. Other resources are the local school districts in your community. They may be able to direct you to individuals in charge of multicultural programs and multicultural specialists at certain schools. Ask your visitors to address the influence that culture has in the classroom and share some of the experiences they have had with their students. Ask them to describe the cultural backgrounds of their students and the different learning styles to which their students are accustomed. What are the specific needs of students who come from different cultures? What difficulties arise in a multicultural classroom? What aspects do they particularly enjoy and find rewarding? What strategies do they use to teach children from different cultures? How are non-English speaking students assisted in their school and classroom?

Invite students to ask the speakers questions. This activity can also be done with visitors from the business, health care, and education professions sharing the same class period. A debriefing session during the class session after the visits would be helpful to allow students to discuss some of their own thoughts about the visitors and the impact of culture on context.

Possible questions for discussion:
What are your own cross-cultural experiences in the business, health care, or educational environment? Do you think our society addresses the issue of cultural differences in the business, healthcare, or classroom environment(s) enough? Give examples of how U.S. society has conceptualized and administered business, health care, and education from a mono-cultural perspective. Give examples of how U.S. society has attempted to adapt to cultural diversity in the business, health care, and educational settings. What type of training could you suggest for business professionals, health care providers, and educators to make them more aware of cultural differences and the need to be sensitive to these differences?

Exercise 6.2: Cultural Views of Job Satisfaction

Different people want different things from their intimate relationships with others. Some are looking for only basic companionship, others want someone who will listen and empathize, and still others are searching for a person who will primarily satisfy their physical needs for affection and sex. We can't assume that our partners want what we want from our relationship. The same notion holds true when we try to determine what people look for in their jobs and careers. While some people may be looking for stable, high-paying employment, others are primarily interested in working with co-workers who are supportive and friendly. And just as in our romantic relationships, if we assume that the people we work with seek the same kind of working conditions and environment that we do, our assumptions may result in crossed-signals and miscommunication.

This exercise asks students to identify the components of job satisfaction for themselves and then to ask someone who has a different cultural background to assess his or her needs as an employee. Because different cultures value and conceive of work differently, students may come up with some interesting contrasts. Ask students to rank the following items from 1 to 10 according to how important they feel each is in contributing to their morale as an employee. Then have them ask an acquaintance or friend who is from a different country or ethnic group to do the same for the second set of items. If you class is very diverse, students may wish to simply exchange and compare their responses with a member of the class. What differences do they see between the two sets of rankings? How might such differences affect working relationships?

Your Description of Job Satisfaction		Friend's Description of Job Satisfaction
________	Interesting work	________
________	Personal loyalty of supervisors	________
________	Full appreciation of work done	________
________	Help on personal problems	________
________	High wages	________
________	Job Security	________
________	Tactful discipline	________
________	Feeling of being in on things	________
________	Good working conditions	________
________	Promotion in the company	________

Questions for class discussion:
What differences do you see between the item you ranked as number one and the item your friend ranked as number one? What do you think accounts for these differences? What differences do you see between the item you ranked as number ten and the item your friend ranked as number ten? What do you think accounts for these differences? Consider your ranking of the job satisfaction items. What do you feel has influenced this ranking? How might your culture, upbringing, experiences, beliefs, and values have affected your needs as an employee? Ask the friend who ranked the second list of items to consider how his or her culture, upbringing, experiences, beliefs, and values influenced his or her job needs. Consider the differences you found between the two sets of job satisfaction rankings. How might such differences affect the working relationship between two co-workers? How would each approach his or her job? How can we adapt to the different needs of our co-workers? As supervisors, how can we adapt to the different notions of job satisfaction of our employees?

Exercise 6.3: Cultural Notions of Health and Illness

This exercise asks students to consider the following questions:

- How do health care workers perceive the communication process with their clients?
- Do they adapt their typical way of communicating when interacting with a client who is of the opposite sex, from a different country, or of a different ethnic group?

The goal of this exercise is to find out how doctors, nurses, and health care professionals perceive and respond to the influence of culture in their interpersonal relationships with patients and clients. Ask students to contact two or three professionals in the health care field and talk with them for approximately thirty minutes about their interactions with patients who are in some way culturally dissimilar to themselves. These people can be contacted through medical school, nursing, and public health programs on most college or university campuses. Students can also contact health care professionals in their communities. Planned Parenthood, women's and community clinics, hospices, local hospitals, and the city health department are excellent resources.

Below is a list of questions for students to use to conduct their interviews. Add questions of your own to this list. Encourage students to send a copy of the questions they will be asking to the people they will interview before the day of the interview. This will give them an opportunity to reflect on their interactions with patients. After students have completed their interviews, ask them to respond to the six questions listed under "Post Interview Questions." Ask students to share their responses with their classmates by participating in small group discussions. They should pool their "data" and answer the following general questions:

- How does culture affect the health care setting and relationships between health care professionals and their clients?
- How does culture affect communication in these relationships?

Interview Questions

- Describe some of the patients/clients that you see in your work.
- Describe the cultural backgrounds of some of your patients.
- How would you describe the relationship between a client or patient and a health care professional?
- How does communication play a role in your treatment of a patient?
- How is communication more challenging when the patient is from a different cultural background as your own?
- What do you do to adapt to the patient's way of communicating?
- Would you describe a situation where you found communication with a patient from a different cultural particularly challenging?
- How has a patient's cultural beliefs about doctors and illness affected your communication with and subsequent treatment of this person?

Post Interview Questions

- What health care professional did you interview and how many years' experience does he or she have?
- What is this person's cultural background?
- How does this person describe the client-health care professional relationship?
- What role does communication have in his or her treatment of a patient?
- How do the cultural backgrounds of his or her patients affect interactions with them?
- Have the particular cultural values and beliefs of a patient ever affected this health care professional's communication with or treatment of a patient?

Exercise 6.4: Diversity and Discussion in the Classroom

The classroom can be an excellent environment to engage in intercultural communication with people from a variety of backgrounds. Some of the most fruitful and compelling learning takes place in classes where students from all walks of life engage in discussions about issues that affect our world. Without such diversity, students would have only like-minded individuals to share their ideas with; debate and critical thinking are often stifled in such environments. The danger of fervent discussion among diverse peoples, however, is that such conversations can result in the breakdown of communication because views may be so different that no common ground appears to exist. How can diverse students engage in meaningful discussion and debate while building and maintaining interpersonal relationships that can survive beyond the classroom?

This exercise asks students to consider two classroom scenarios where university students are debating the often controversial issues of affirmative action and women's rights. In each hypothetical scenario, students from different cultural, ethnic, religious, and political backgrounds are gathered to discuss each of these issues. Ask students to read each scenario and respond to questions that follow from the viewpoint of a student who is also taking part in the discussion. As members of this class, students should consider what they can do to encourage the development of a comprehensive, thought-provoking discussion. What interpersonal dynamics must be considered when opposing opinions may be couched in an antagonistic tone or based on strongly held cultural values?

Discussion 1: Affirmative Action

Students in "Policy Making in the United States" settle into their seats. The instructor begins the discussion on affirmative action by giving some historical background on what it is and why it was initially implemented. After this introduction, she asks students to express their views on the goals of affirmative action and whether they feel it is a policy that should continue. Jennifer, a Caucasian woman in her mid 20s, is the first to speak.

> J: "I just don't think affirmative action is necessary anymore. At one point in time, like in the 60s, it was important to enable women and people of color to have equal access to all jobs and careers. But those opportunities are now available to all people, not just white males."

After Jennifer finishes, George, a Mexican American man of about 20, immediately responds to her comment.

> G: "Things are not that different today. People of color don't have access to all jobs and careers because they must still face the racism and discrimination that often go on when they apply for a job."
>
> J: "But why should you discriminate against whites in order not to discriminate against blacks? It doesn't make sense."
>
> G: "Affirmative action is not about discrimination against whites. It's about making sure that people who have previously been left out of the game get a chance to play."
>
> J: "Whatever you want to call it, it really is discrimination—reverse discrimination."
>
> G: "You can only see it for what it isn't doing for whites instead of seeing what it is doing to help nonwhites."

There is a momentary pause as George finishes. You raise your hand to make a comment. The teacher calls on you.

Question: Write out how you would respond to Jennifer and George's short dialogue. Consider not only your own opinions about affirmative action but perhaps more importantly, think about how you as a fellow discussant can contribute to the primary goal of the discussion: to exchange disparate opinions while encouraging positive interpersonal dynamics among diverse class members.

Discussion 2: Women's Rights

You are in an Anthropology 101 discussion section and the topic of the present unit is women's lives in developing countries. The teaching assistant in your class has begun a discussion on marriage customs in Islamic cultures of Africa. Hanan, a Muslim woman from Ethiopia, offers a comment.

> H: "In some countries, it is common for Islamic children to be betrothed when they are very young, especially girls. Sometimes girls of eight or nine are betrothed to men in their twenties but they live with their parents until puberty."

Kathy, a woman born and raised in the U.S., immediately responds to Hanan. They begin a dialogue.

> K: "O.K.., so it's real common. But is it fair? I mean, the girls don't even have a say in who they will spend their lives with, who their husbands will be. That seems to take away the rights of the girl."

> H: "It's the kind of life that some Muslims understand and accept. It's just a different way of looking at marriage. And Islam isn't the only religion that practices this kind of arrangement."

> K: "I understand. But it just seems to force women to do something that they have no say in, no voice."

There is a momentary pause as Kathy finishes. You raise your hand to make a comment. The teacher calls on you.

Question: Write out how you would respond to Hanan and Kathy's short dialogue. Consider not only your own opinions about Islamic marriage customs but perhaps more importantly, think about how you as a fellow discussant can contribute to the primary goal of the discussion: to exchange disparate opinions while encouraging positive interpersonal dynamics among diverse class members.

Chapter Popular Film Suggestions

Few films about the specific issues covered in this chapter are available. However, the films listed below cover some aspects of cultural practices in an intercultural corporate world and would make for fruitful discussions of the norms observed.

- ***Working Girl*** (New York,1988; director Mike Nichols; 115 min.) A film about a young woman's struggle for success in the corporate world of advertising. The film illustrates class struggles between the wealthy and well-educated in America and the working class woman who has had to go to night school to get ahead.

Online Review:
Possibly Mike Nichols' most purely enjoyable film since The Graduate, this witty, vibrant take on females in the work force boasts an exceptional cast (including Harrison Ford in a rare romantic leading role) and a savvy screenplay (by Kevin Wade) that effectively deconstructs the battle of the sexes in corporate America. A romantic comedy that is both romantic and comic in equal measure, the movie has fun satirizing the everyday lives of the working class, but retains a core of recognition so the viewer can always find the film relatable and believable. A Cinderella-type story to be sure, but winning and bitingly funny. The film received Oscar nominations for all three principal female roles, including a great Sigourney Weaver as Melanie Griffith's boss from hell, and Best Picture. It also picked up a trophy for Best Original Song, honoring Carly Simon's wonderfully uplifting theme, "Let the River Run." ~ Jason Clark, All Movie Guide, http://movies.msn.com/movies/movie.aspx?mp=v&m=144891

Web References

All Watchers.com: Working Girl Movie Review, http://www.allwatchers.com/Topics/Info_3548.asp.

All Movie Guide, Review of *Working Girl*, http://movies.msn.com/movies/movie.aspx?mp=v&m=144891.

- ***Finding Forrester*** (2000; director, Gus Van Sant; 2 hr 15 min)
  An interesting drama/comedy about the education of an African American male who is a gifted writer.

  Excerpt from an online review:
  Finding Forrester follows a sixteen-year-old African American kid from Harlem (newcomer Robert Brown), who is a well-read budding writer. . . . Jamal's demons are mostly external. Because he goes to school in Harlem, his talent has small chance of being recognized, especially because he avoids performing any better than necessary. To do so would mean rejection by his peers, so he keeps a low academic profile and spends his afternoons playing basketball–something he also does extremely well. But when he performs outstandingly on a standardized test, a downtown private school comes calling. Their scholarship offer is strictly on an academic basis, they claim, but they "won't be disappointed" if he chooses to play basketball. Obviously, issues of race and economic disadvantage make Jamal uncomfortable at his new school, but it's his only chance at a real education. (http://www.aboutfilm.com/movies/f/findingforrester.htm)

  Web Reference

  Finding Forrester. http://www.aboutfilm.com/movies/f/findingforrester.htm

Chapter Test Items

Multiple Choice

1. Which of the following concepts for doing business in Mexico focuses on "trust"?
   a. *confianza* *
   b. *simpatía*
   c. *palanca*
   d. *estabilidad*

2. Which of the following core concepts for doing business in Mexico refers to the power derived from affiliated connections?
   a. *confianza*
   b. *simpatía*
   c. *palanca* *
   d. *estabilidad*

3. Which of the following core concepts for doing business in Mexico reinforces the value of personal relationships?
   a. *confianza*
   b. *simpatía*
   c. *palanca*
   d. *estabilidad* *

4. The value Mexicans place on stability or *estabilidad* is centered in
   a. the Catholic church
   b. corporate affiliations
   c. the government
   d. the family *

5. For Americans, "tomorrow" refers specifically to the following day, whereas for Mexicans, *mañana* means which of the following?
   a. some time in the near future
   b. some time in the future that is always deferred
   c. some time in the future that may be deferred *
   d. both a and c

6. During financial hardships an employee might continue to work for his or her manager without a paycheck. Which core concept does this demonstrate?
   a. *confianza*
   b. *simpatía*
   c. *palanca*
   d. *establidad* *

7. Americans tend to believe that humans
   a. are inherently good
   b. have a combination of good and evil qualities *
   c. cannot change their innate natures
   d. cannot improve their lives by their individual actions

8. Gopalan and Stahl contend that poverty in India is tolerated to a greater extent than in other cultures because
   a. many Indians believe life is predetermined
   b. there is a widespread sense of fatalism in the Indian psyche
   c. a and b *
   d. neither a nor b

9. Organizations in the U.S that ban smoking in the workplace are operating on the assumption that
   a. intervention can result in an improved society *
   b. laws cannot be broken
   c. a and b
   d. neither a nor b

10. Two key assumptions that are building blocks for strategic management practices in American organizations are
    a. Time is linear and time is a commodity with a perishable value *
    b. Time and money
    c. Human nature and time
    d. Exploitation of nature and time

11. According to Friday, the American manager's expectation or need to be liked is in direct contrast with the German manager's need to be
    a. educated
    b. credible *
    c. confrontational
    d. fair

12. Unlike the German manager's orientation to his or her corporation, the American manager's orientation
    a. is long term
    b. is typically formal
    c. often consists of on-the-job training *
    d. teaches specific rules and procedures

13. One indication given by Friday that Germans tend to focus on the past more than their American counterparts is evidenced in the fact that
   a. German architecture is older than American architecture
   b. Americans engaged in space exploration before the Germans
   c. Germans tend to begin discussions with historical background information*
   d. Americans have lower standards for higher education than their German counterparts.

14. A "half-truth" can be defined as
   a. physicians who did not disclose a diagnosis immediately
   b. physicians who described the diagnosis in doses over several visits
   c. physicians who informed a family member of the diagnosis before telling the patient
   d. all of the above can be defined as "half-truths" *

15. Which of the following is an individualistic culture?
   a. Argentina
   b. Brazil
   c. India
   d. United States *

16. Essentialism refers to
   a. the axiom mind-body-spirit
   b. an ideology that emphasizes the meaning of humans "parts" over the "whole" *
   c. the patient's personal and cultural experience of illness
   d. the risk for illness

17. A holistic approach to nursing care can best be described as
   a. affirming the patient's personal and cultural experience of illness and using this construct to cultivate therapeutic treatment *
   b. a term used by native Americans to describe treatment by a medicine man
   c. encompassing the use of natural herbs, sweat lodges, and meditation
   d. the reconfiguration of patient illness as technical issues

18. According to Watson, confusion or ambiguity can be lessened and even avoided by understanding persons as phenomenal fields; by phenomenal fields, he means:
   a. a person's frame of reference or subjective reality, composed of the totality of human experience
   b. respect for a person's culture, cultural meanings, and an appreciation of humans as individuals who experience life
   c. a person's view of "context," shaped by culture—the meaning of what we see, touch, taste, smell, or hear
   d. all of the above *

19. The broad categories of intellectual, perceptual, and experiential nursing knowledge are known as:
    a. cognitive domains *
    b. behavioral domains
    c. affective domains
    d. none of the above

20. The technologic skills that nurses learn to apply for promoting compassionate and effective nursing care are known as:
    a. cognitive domains
    b. behavioral domains *
    c. affective domains
    d. none of the above

21. The exercise and total expression of authenticity, congruence, empathy, genuineness, and non-possessive warmth are known as:
    a. cognitive domains
    b. behavioral domains
    c. affective domains *
    d. none of the above

22. Participatory-interactive communication style has been observed among
    a. African Americans
    b. Latinos
    c. Native Hawaiians
    d. all of the above *

23. Which of the following uses "talk story" to create an idea, tell a story, or complete a learning task?
    a. Native Hawaiian students *
    b. Asian students
    c. European American students
    d. African American students

24. Who employs "topic-chaining" discourse as a way to communicate in the classroom?
    a. African American students *
    b. Asian students
    c. Native American students
    d. none of the above

25. Through which of the following ways do African Americans "gain the floor" or get participatory entry into conversations?
    a. personal assertiveness
    b. the strength of the impulse to be involved
    c. the persuasive power of the point they wish to make
    d. all of the above *

26. The *self-fulfilling prophecy* effect
    a. leads to stereotyping in the classroom
    b. occurs when students see themselves and their abilities in accordance with the way the teacher conveys it to them *
    c. shows teachers are not prejudiced in their classroom teaching styles
    d. demonstrates the axiom of mindfulness

True/False

F 1. NAFTA has helped small businesses in the U.S., Canada, and Mexico.

F 2. U.S. plants located south of the border have been praised for providing a good wage, keeping their workers healthy and safe, and respecting and following environmental policy.

T 3. *Mordida* refers to paying a bribe.

T 4. Americans have a tendency to think about *mañana* as referring to some specific time period.

T 5. The majority of Americans believe that fundamental changes in human nature can be accomplished through a combination of right training, education, and exposure.

T 6. Most (not all) Indians believe that an individual's situation in life is a consequence of actions committed in a previous birth or births.

F 7. Indians have a linear concept of time.

T 8. Americans link individual identity with their professions.

T 9. When Germans and Americans come together in discussion, the German's drive is to establish hierarchy, the American's is to dissolve it.

T 10. According to Friday, American managers approach the business relationship more impersonally than German managers.

F 11. German managers are more likely to be selected and promoted based on personal accomplishments than their education and credentials.

F 12. Traditionally, German managers share the American sense of "fair play."

T 13. American managers being trained to work with their German counterparts will best learn through interactive role playing when the focus is on debriefing.

F 14. Western medical training programs are actively integrating intercultural communication training in their curriculum.

T 15. The task of understanding and diagnosing medical conditions is often complicated by cultural differences.

T 16. Interaction between a physician and patient is inherently an intercultural encounter even when the two parties perceive they are from the same culture.

F 17. "Yes" always means yes across cultural boundaries.

T 18. Most Argentinean physicians focused primarily on education and socioeconomic status to describe the diversity in their country.

T 19. Physicians in Argentina, Brazil, and India saw their countries as hetereogeneous.

F 20. Empathy is a human quality that evidences a commitment to sustaining human integrity.

T 21. Congruence is a human quality that supports accurate, consistent, and faithful devotion to patient- and family-centered goals.

T 22. The most common practice among teachers is to ask convergent questions and use deductive approaches to solving problems.

F 23. The gender of a person communicating may be more problematic than the "gendered" style of communication.

T 24. Students of color who are strongly affiliated with their traditional cultures tend to be more inductive, interactive, and communal in task performance.

F 25. In traditional African American and Latino cultures, problem solving is not contextual.

Chapter Essay Questions

1. Briefly describe the difference between how Americans and Mexicans begin a business meeting. What is the cultural significance of these different approaches?
2. Explain Mexican core concept of *simpatía*. How might an American misunderstand this concept? What is it about American cultural values that would make for such misunderstandings?
3. Americans often find the practices surrounding palanca to be corrupt without reflecting on similar practices common in the U.S. What are some of the American business practices that are comparable? Use concrete examples and explain your answer.
4. Discuss the concept of time in Mexican business. Include in your discussion the meaning of *mañana* in Mexico versus how Americans view this concept. Provide examples to support your response.
5. Discuss the concept of *estabilidad* in the Mexican work environment.
6. Discuss *compradrazgo* and *comadrazgo* systems as a way for managers to demonstrate responsibility for employees' well-being.
7. How would Americans and Indians differ in their view of company loyalty?
8. Can behavioral models of management be transferred from culture to culture?
9. Compare and contrast the German and American manager's focus with regard to their orientation to cooperation and relationship to business.
10. Indicate how differences in education, learning styles, and problem solving between German and American managers may influence their learning styles.
11. What does Friday mean by the term "guidance system" and of what importance is it to his discussion of German and American managers?

12. Define the German term *Besprechung.*
13. What difference might it make that American managers are more oriented toward the future than German managers who are grounded in their past tradition?
14. If you were asked to help design a training program for a U.S. company that consistently engaged in business with Germany, what recommendations would you make after reading Friday's article?
15. Explain the concept of half-truths in physician-patient communication. How does this concept relate to collectivism?
16. Explain how physicians' perceptions of cultural diversity in Argentina and Brazil differ from those in India.
17. How do physicians define success in terms of their interaction with patients?
18. Describe Mendyka's view of "holistic nursing."
19. Why does Mendyka advance the positive effects of "holistic nursing"?
20. How can culturally determined rules dictating what is appropriate content for communication influence teaching and learning in university classrooms?
21. Differentiate between passive-receptive and participatory-interactive styles of discourse.
22. Discuss some of the reasons why Asian Americans perform so well in high-level mathematics classes. Could these same reasons be adapted to other ethnic groups, e.g., African Americans? If so, why? If not, why not?
23. Discuss some traditional women's ways of communicating and how they can be problematic for classroom teachers.
24. Discuss topic-centered and topic-associated or topic-chaining techniques as forms of discourse in a classroom.
25. What are some of the specific problems of cultural stereotyping as it applies to the multicultural classroom?

Chapter References

Powell, B. (1995, November 6). "Keep your profits." *Newsweek*, p.98.

Mullavey-O'Byrne, C. (1994). *Intercultural communication for health care professionals*. In R. W. Brislin & T. Yoshida, (Eds.), *Improving intercultural interaction: Modules for cross-cultural training programs*. London: Sage Publications.

Chapter 7 Communicating Interculturally: Becoming Competent

Chapter Synopsis

Articles in this chapter address both problems and solutions in a variety of intercultural contexts. Descriptions of and suggestions for competent communication interculturally are offered. After reading this chapter, students should be more prepared to actually engage in intercultural communication rather than simply talk about it.

In their essay "Intercultural Awareness," Guo-Ming Chen and William J. Starosta stress the importance of intercultural awareness. Three levels of intercultural awareness are addressed along with two approaches for the study of intercultural awareness.

Stella Ting-Toomey, in "Managing Intercultural Conflicts Effectively," focuses on the specific context of intercultural conflict. Her essay offers students a framework within which to understand cultural differences in the event of interpersonal conflict, but she also suggests a series of skills that can be helpful in managing conflict when it occurs in the intercultural encounter.

Abhik Roy and Bayo Oludaja's essay, "The Role of Dialogue in managing Intergroup Conflict," contend that a dialogue method can best overcome intergroup conflict. The best way to do so, they suggest, is by striving for openness, mutuality, respect, fairness, equality, directness, honesty, and truth. It also requires us to be flexible and confront our own prejudices.

In "Sojourner Adaptation," Polly Begley examines the phenomenon of cultural adaptation by providing answers to the following question: "What does one face when one crosses cultural boundaries?" She helps us not only understand the phenomenon of *culture shock*, but provides us with ideas for adapting successfully to a new cultural environment.

Chapter Outline

Intercultural Awareness

- Among six most common intercultural training programs, only three are directly concerned with intercultural awareness: cognitive, cultural awareness, and self-awareness training
- Cognitive training promotes understanding of cultural differences and similarities
- Cultural awareness training requires participants to understand the aspects of culture that are universal and specific
- Self-awareness training helps participants identify attitudes, opinions, and biases embedded in their own culture that influence the way they communicate
- Intercultural awareness emphasizes changing personal thinking about the environment through understanding one's own and others' cultures

- Cultural awareness requires understanding the "cultural map"

Levels of Intercultural Awareness

- Awareness of superficial cultural traits—information gleaned from media, tourism books, or first impression
- Awareness of significant and subtle cultural traits that contrast markedly with another's—two phases:
  - First phase, experienced through cultural conflict may lead to depression, helplessness, hostility, anxiety, withdrawal, or disorientation resembling culture shock
  - Second phase, experienced through rational and intellectual analysis, differences in cultural traits begin to make sense
- Awareness of how another culture feels from the insider's perspective—requires ability to see the culture from an insider's perspective through empathy
  - Empathy can be activated through "transspection," an understanding gained by practice in estimating behaviors or internal states of others, trying to learn their beliefs, assumptions, perspectives, feelings, and consequences of those feelings in the other's context
  - Empathy is ability to project feelings to others with a shared epistemology

Approaches to the Study of Intercultural Awareness

- Culture-general approach aims to understand culture's global influence on human behavior
- Common techniques used in intercultural training programs are assimilators and baFa baFa simulation
- Culture-specific approach aims to impart information about a specific culture and cultural guidelines for interacting with people in a specified culture
- Role plays and area studies are commonly used in training

Models for the Study of Intercultural Awareness

- Fact learning—profiling the culture
  - *Culturegram* uses four categories to develop this profile: customs and courtesies, the people, the lifestyle, and the nation
  - Harris and Moran (1989) use a coordinated systems approach with eight systems: kinship, education, economic, political, religious, association, health, and recreational
- Deep structure of a culture more difficult to obtain
- Cultural values communicated through verbal and nonverbal symbols
- Cultural values determine our communication patterns
- Parsons' (1951) model uses five categories of examining a culture's values: gratification-discipline dilemma; private vs. collective interest dilemma; universalism vs. particularism; achievement vs. ascription; specificity vs. diffuseness
- Kluckhohn and Strodtbeck's (1961) model looks at five universal problems faced by cultures; human nature, human-nature relationship, sense of time, activity, and social relations
- Condon and Yousef (1975) extended the categories of Kluckhohn and Studtbeck's model to cover six basic spheres of human societies—the self, family, society,

humanity, nature, and supernatural—and attached four or five universal problems to each sphere
- Hall's (1976) model classifies culture into high-context and low-context
- Hofstede's (1983, 1984) model looks at five dimensions of cultural values from the organizational perspective: individualism-collectivism, power distance, uncertainty avoidance, masculinity-femininity, and Confucian dynamism
- The study of cultural values the most important gateway to reach intercultural awareness

Assessment of Intercultural Awareness
- Measurements have been developed to assess our understanding of the basic factual information of the culture and cultural values
- Measurements of basic factual information:
- Saville-Troik's Questions to Ask about Culture (1978)—20 categories for learning about the basic factual information of a culture; 128 questions
- Kitao's Test of American Culture (1981)—100 multiple-choice questions about 49 different areas of American culture
- Kohl's Fifty Questions about Culture (1984)—50 open-ended questions to help sojourners better know their host country and culture
- Harris and Moran's Pre-deployment Area Questionnaire (1989)-92 "yes" or "no" questions used to reflect different aspects to the business interaction

Managing Intercultural Conflicts Effectively

A Cultural Variability Perspective
- Individualism-Collectivism Value Tendencies
  - Core building block is relative emphasis on the "autonomous self" or the "connected self"
  - If we follow an independent construal of self orientation, communicative action will tend to be more self-focused, more ego-based, and more self-expressive
  - If we follow an interdependent construal of self orientation, tend to use group norms, group interests, and group responsibilities to interpret and evaluate others' conflict behaviors
- Low Context and High Context
  - Low-context (LC) communication refers to communication patterns of linear logic interaction approach, direct verbal interaction style, overt intention expressions, and sender-oriented value
  - For individualistic, LC communicators, bargaining resources in conflict typically revolve around individual pride and self-esteem, individual ego-based emotions, and individual sense of autonomy and power
  - High-context (HC) communication refers to communication patterns of spiral logic interaction approach, indirect verbal negotiation mode, subtle nonverbal nuances, responsive intention inference, and interpreter-sensitive value
  - For collectivistic, HC communicators, negotiation resources typically revolve around relational "face" maintenance and group harmony, face-related emotions, and a reciprocal sense of favors and obligations

- M-Time and P-Time
- Monochronic time schedule (M-time)—usually compartmentalize time schedules to serve individualistic-based needs and tend to separate task-oriented time from socioemotional time; also more future conscious of time than centered in past or present
- Polychronic time (P-time) schedule stresses involvement of people and completion of transactions rather than adherence to preset schedules; predominate in group-based, high-context cultures

Violations of Conflict Expectations

- Cultural Conflict Assumptions
  - For individualistic, LC communicators, conflict typically follows a problem-solving model; conflict viewed as potentially functional
  - For collectivistic, HC interactants, conflict follows a face-maintenance model; conflict viewed as dysfunctional
- Conflict Issues and Process Violations
  - In individualistic cultures, conflict issues typically arise through the violation of autonomous space, privacy, individual power, and sense of individual fairness and equity.
  - For individualistic, M-time people, conflict resolution processes should follow a clear agenda of opening, expressing conflicting interests, negotiating, and closing sequences.
  - In collectivistic cultures, conflict issues typically revolve around the violation of in-group or out-group boundaries, norms of group loyalty and commitment, and reciprocal obligations and trust.
  - For collectivistic, P-time people, conflict facework processes have no clear beginning and no clear end.
- Cross-Cultural Conflict Interaction Styles

  In individualistic cultures, the conflict management process relies heavily on verbal offense and defense to justify one's position, to articulate one's emotions, and to raise objections.

  In collectivistic conflict situations, ambiguous, indirect verbal messages are used, as are subtle nonverbal gestures or nonverbal silence.

Effective Conflict Management

To deal with conflict in collectivistic culture, ***individualists*** need to:

- Be mindful of face maintenance assumptions
- Be proactive in dealing with low-grade conflict situations by using informal consultation or the "go-between" method
- "Give face" and try not to push opponent's back against the wall without any room for maneuvering face loss or face recovery
- Be sensitive to importance of quiet, mindful observation
- Practice attentive listening skills and feel co-presence of other person
- Discard Western-based model of effective communication skills; learn not to use blunt word "no"
- Let go of a conflict situation if the conflict party does not want to deal with it directly; have a cooling period.

In a conflict situation in an individualistic, LC culture, ***collectivists*** need to:

- Be mindful of the problem-solving assumptions
- Focus on resolving the substantive issues of the conflict and learn to openly express opinions or points of view
- Engage in an assertive, leveling style of conflict behavior
- Own individual responsibility for the conflict decision-making process; use "I" statements to describe feelings
- Provide verbal feedback and engage in active listening skills
- Use direct, integrative verbal messages that clearly convey concern over both the relational and substantive issues
- Commit to working out the conflict situation with the conflict party.

The Role of Dialogue in Managing Intergroup Conflict

Martin Buber's Philosophy of Dialogue

- Dialogue is the unity of contraries because an individual must stand her/his ground and at the same time remain open to the other.
- **I-It versus I-Thou**
- In I-It relation, a person uses and experiences the other person as an object for his/her profit or self-interest
- In the I-Thou relation, an individual is appreciated in all her/his uniqueness and is not objectified
- For Buber the dialogic relationship of I-Thou helps humans attain their completeness by understanding one another in a spirit of authenticity
- **Confirming the Other**
- Dialogue calls for genuine acceptance of the other, even in conflict
- **Unfolding versus Imposing**
- During dialogical encounter, interactants help to see each other's perspective without any kind of manipulation
- **Being versus Seeming**
- One should remain true, honest, and authenticate with others, even in conflict situation
- **Confronting the Truth**
- One has to strive for the truth even when it causes pain and discomfort

Karl Jasper's Philosophy of Limitless Communication

- Humans can discover unity in truth through authentic esistential comunication
- **The Encompassing**
- Conception of the absolute unity of Being
- Modes of encompassing:
  Individual derives sensations from the empirical world
  Individual experiences consciousness-as-such—realm of cognition
  Spirit, sum total of individual's Idea—mode by which individual reflects on things within and without
- **Reason**
- The "glue" that holds different modes of Encompassing together

- **Communication**
- The origin of self-being
- Requires a willingness to risk oneself totally in a communication—a process that occurs only with another
- **Truth**
- Truth and communication are inseparable
- Communication fundamental to human nature
- Truth is relative and changing
- Seeking truth requires compromise

Hans-Georg Gadamer's Perspective of Dialogical Communication

- Dialogue does not simply involve understanding what the other person says and how she/he feels, but coming to grips with one another.
- **I-Thou Relationship**
- A relation based on:
- Open-mindedness and mutuality
- A willingness to listen to the claims of the other with an eye to their possible validity
- To allow oneself to be open to the possibility that the other person's viewpoint Is right while mine is wrong
- **Socratic Question and Answer**
- An appropriate question opens up the subject matter so that a dialogue can emerge
- An inappropriate question is a rhetorical one
- **The Role of Prejudice in Understanding**
- View that human prejudice is the basis of all understanding
- Prejudice means "prejudgment" and can be either positive or negative
- In order to gain an understanding every individual undergoes a process of projecting her/his prejudices
- Communication requires the suspension of one's prejudices
- **Understanding**
- In genuine dialogue, participants will be able to weigh counterarguments while holding onto their own viewpoints.

Jürgen Habermas, Communicative Ethics, and Ideal Speech Situation

- Dialogical communication as teleologically oriented toward a state of mutual recognition and respect for persons
- Every communicative utterance can be divided into three general categories: truth, rightness, and claims to truthfulness
- Consensus theory of truth
- Cogency of arguments, soundness, deductive or inductive strength will enable parties to accept a truth claim or a claim to appropriateness
- "Ideal Speech Situation"
  Speakers cannot contradict themselves
  Speakers are required to assert only what they believe
  Every person who is competent to speak must be given opportunity to do so
  Everyone permitted to question any assertion
  Everyone allowed to introduce any assertion into the discourse

Everyone allowed to express his/her attitudes, desires, and needs

There should be no internal or external coercion that prevents speakers from exercising their rights

Implications for Conflict Management

- Learn to acknowledge other participants in the encounter as equals.
- Approach the conflict with openness.
- Confront your prejudices.
- Affirm the other party.
- Use questioning as a means of dialogical exploration of the issues rather than make dogmatic assertions.
- Be flexible.

Sojourner Adaptation

Sojourners, Culture, and Adaptation

- Sojourners—people who cross cultural boundaries; includes immigrants, refugees, business executives, students, or tourists
- Culture shock (Oberg 1960)—term negatively received
- Cross-cultural adaptation refers to how a sojourner chooses to cope with cultural changes
- Adaptation an umbrella term that encompasses culture shock, assimilation, adjustment, acculturation, integration, and coping
- Coping can include seeking out specific cultural knowledge, adopting a different style of communication, reserving judgment on unfamiliar cultural practices, or withdrawing from intercultural interactions

Challenges

- Ethnocentrism—bias leading people to judge another culture's habits and practices as right or wrong, good or bad according to their own cultural attitudes
- Language Barriers—language skills are linked with adaptation effectiveness; sojourners without learning the language of others will experience more difficulty adapting
- Disequilibrium—anxiety resulting from confusion and uncertainty in a new culture; adaptation process typically characterized by "ups" and "downs"
- Length of Stay—influences adaptation process; individuals who seek long-term business relations, work, travel, or residence are motivated to make significant changes in their communicative styles, whereas tourists need only a few phrases and less knowledge to get along for short periods
- Level of Knowledge—incorrect information, broad cultural generalizations, or stereotypes are destructive and may lead to misunderstandings

Strategies

- Preparation—culture-general approach is best as it teaches us to reject false generalizations and to recognize unique and exceptional characteristics of each person; also some language phrases should be learned
- Personality Characteristics—openness and strength of personality are influential determinants of cross-cultural adaptation effectiveness
- Personal Determination—can stem from external factors or internal factors

    - External factors refer to length of stay, purpose of visit, or attitude of local culture
    - Internal factors include ability to think across cultures and a value of multiculturalism
- Amount of Time Spent Communicating—most important factor predicting adaptation is the frequency of host communication participation; practical wisdom can only be gained through conversations with people from other cultures

Discussion Ideas

1. What are the six components of intercultural sensitivity according to Chen and Starosta? How does each of these relate to intercultural sensitivity as they define it?
2. What is the relationship between low- and high-context cultures and cultures that are primarily individualistic or collectivistic with regard to approaches to conflict?
3. Differentiate between the role of third-party intervention in individualistic, low-context cultures and collectivistic high-context cultures. Why would it be important in a high-context culture to have an impartial mediator?
4. Is dialogue, as discussed by Roy and Oludaja, possible in today's world?
5. Begley suggests that cross-cultural adaptation encompasses such experiences as culture shock, assimilation, adjustment, acculturation, integration, and coping. How do these terms differ? Begley also identifies several challenges to cross-cultural adaptation, such as ethnocentrism, differences in language, disequilibrium, and length of stay. Of course, not all cross-cultural situations offer the same level of adaptation difficulties to sojourners. Consider the adaptation challenges that the refugees from Kosovo faced when they were forced from their homes in April, 1999, compared to those challenges faced by U.S. Peace Corps volunteers. How do the challenges described by Begley change when one *chooses* to cross over into another society versus people who are *forced* from their homes? What other challenges would you add to Begley's list to encompass forced cross-cultural adaptation?

Chapter Exercises

Exercise 7.1: Improving Ourselves

This activity incorporates all of the articles in Chapter 7 and focuses on the communicative behavior of students and, specifically, those aspects of their behavior that they would like to change. This activity uses the concepts in the articles in Chapter 7 as a backdrop (competence, conflict, work force diversity, acculturation, and intercultural sensitivity) for improving intercultural communication. Using the articles in Chapter 7 as a starting point, students will be given an opportunity to verbalize and develop strategies for a particular characteristic of their communicative behavior that they view as a weakness or "problem area." Begin by asking students to come prepared for the next class period with one aspect of their communicative behavior that they see as problematic or that needs "fixing." Encourage them to talk to their friends or family and solicit their opinions. But the students must agree with the opinions of their friends and family because there is a tendency for people not to make an effort to change if they don't see a problem. Have students answer the following questions:

1. Describe this communicative behavior that you would like to change.
2. Give one example when you communicated in this way. Include the other interactant's response to your behavior.
3. What strategy can you think of that will remedy this behavior?

When students come to the following class period, ask them to break into small groups. Each group member should share what he or she has written, ask the group for feedback about the strategy developed, and solicit other possible strategies. Each student should walk away from his or her group with a list of strategies. Regroup as a class and have students share some of their areas for change. The instructor should act as a probing questioner: What can you do to improve your communication with others? What will you do? How will you know if you have been successful? What effect will this improvement have on your relationships with other people?

Engage the class in a discussion on how their specific communication problems might affect their ability to be competent intercultural communicators. How might their behavior be perceived by individuals from other cultures? How would working on this one communicative behavior enhance their effectiveness as intercultural communicators? The discussion should begin to address the issue of becoming interculturally competent through improving one's own communication with others. Encourage students to use some of the strategies offered. An assignment could even be given that asks them to document their attempts at actively applying one or more strategies.

Exercise 7.2: Developing Intercultural Relationships

This exercise accompanies the article by Chen and Starosta. At times the unfamiliar can excite us. If we knew everything about the people we formed relationships with, there would be no surprises, nothing to uncover and explore. But too much unfamiliarity can be unsettling. We like to have something we can be certain of in our relationships. At least in the initial stages, intercultural relationships may be characterized by more uncertainty than intracultural relationships. This increased uncertainty about who another is might be one reason why people are sometimes hesitant to form relationships with culturally dissimilar individuals.

This exercise focuses on how we develop intercultural relationships and the attributes necessary for the development of such relationships. It asks students to consider their own network of friends and the extent to which they have developed relationships with people who are culturally dissimilar. First, ask students to respond to questions one and two below by themselves. Then have them get into small groups and respond to questions three through seven. As students answer each of the questions, they should consider their own intercultural relationships that they have developed. Have each group report some of their findings to the class.

Questions to Answer Individually

1. How many relationships (romantic partners and people you consider to be friends) with culturally different people do you have? (Remember to consider relationships with people from different ethnicities, religions, sexual orientations, degree of able-bodiedness, sex (male or female), etc.) What types of relationships are these (i.e., friends, romantic partners, relatives, acquaintances, etc.)? Discuss some possible reasons for the network of friends you have developed.
2. Describe an intercultural relationship that you have with someone that you find to be very satisfying. What makes it so satisfying?

Questions to Answer in Small Groups

3. List five positive and unique aspects of intercultural relationships.
4. List five reasons why people are hesitant to develop relationships (platonic or romantic) with people from other cultures.
5. Which one of the above reasons pertains (if at all) most directly to you? Please explain your answer.
6. Many intercultural communication specialists mention open-mindedness as one attribute necessary for the development of successful intercultural relationships. What are some other attributes or ways of thinking that a person should have in order to develop relationships with culturally different people?
7. Which of the above do you feel you might need to develop further? Why did you choose these attributes to work on?

Exercise 7.3: Individualism, Collectivism, Reward Distribution and Conflict

This activity can be used with Ting-Toomey's article on managing intercultural conflicts effectively. One area that may result in intercultural conflict is the area of reward distribution particularly when both collectivistic and individualist cultures are involved. Ting-Toomey notes:

> In terms of the relationship between the norm of fairness and cross-cultural conflict interaction style, results from past research indicate that individualists typically prefer to use the equity norm (self-deservingness norm) in dealing with reward allocation in group conflict interaction. In comparison, collectivists oftentimes prefer to use the equality norm (the equal distribution norm) to deal with in-group members and thus avoid group disharmony. (p. 379-380)

The following exercise was developed by R. W. Brislin (1994) and can be found in *Improving Intercultural Interactions: Modules for Cross-cultural Training*. Consult this excellent reference book for other appropriate exercises. Divide the students into two groups (one group will represent collectivists and the other will represent individualists) and have the students read the case study on the next page. After reading the case study, have each group draft a distribution of money based on either their collectivist or individualist tendencies. Then have the groups role-play a negotiation to resolve their distribution differences utilizing the conflict management strategies offered by Ting-Toomey.

For discussion, Brislin (1994) provides the following explanation to accompany the exercise (handout next page):

> ***Individualists*** generally prefer an equity distribution, that is, rewards based on contributions. If Person A contributed 40% of the work, he should receive approximately 40% of the rewards. Other people should also receive rewards based on their contributions. Person E is not likely to get much special attention from individualists in monetary terms. Instead, the team might name the road after this high status person. Person F, despite his special circumstances, would likely receive a share equal to his contributions. These distributions are based on the idea that it is necessary to reward individual accomplishment or the person will see little reason to work hard on the next project.
>
> In comparison, ***collectivists*** prefer an equality distribution in which all people receive the same level of rewards. If there were five people who contributed to the project, each would receive approximately 20% of the rewards. This will keep the group functioning smoothly. The idea is that if one person gets more, it will disrupt the group; besides, the lesser contributors may contribute more on the next project. Collectivists are also more likely to give special attention to person E whose status was instrumental in acquiring the project. They are likely to vote a solid $10,000 to person E in recognition of his effort even though he does not need the money. For person F with special circumstances, they are likely to give him more than the others in the group, or to assume that person F's special needs have already been taken care of by the company separately from the distribution of the $100,000. (pp. 80-81; emphasis added)

Exercise 7.3: Rewards Case Study (Brislin, 1994, pp. 80-81)

Assume that you are employed in a company (for profit) that contracts to do construction work (e.g., roads, sewage treatment facilities) in rural areas of the community where you live. The company recently received a contract for $800,000 (U.S.) to build a road. Given a number of fortunate circumstances, such as good weather, the project was completed for $700,000. It is now the end of the fiscal year and the board of directors has decided that the extra $100,000 can be distributed the way people (who were involved in the road construction project) decide. The following people are somehow involved. All have been in the company for at least five years and get along well together

Person A was the hardest worker and was clearly responsible for supervising a great deal of the actual day-to-day work on the project. At least 40% of the day-to-day work on the project was done by him

Persons B, C, and D were solid but not spectacular contributors. They were competent workers but not outstanding. Each contributed about 15% of the actual day-to-day work on the project

Person E is a very high status and wealthy person in the organization and in the community. Although he did not engage in any of day-to-day work on the road construction project and did not write the proposal for funding, it is known within the organization that he called upon his connections and used his influence so that the original $800,000 contract would go to the company.

Person F is a contributor much like B, C, and D. His contribution was about 15% of the work needed for the project's completion. F's father died recently, however, and person F has considerable expenses associated with the funeral, nursing care for his mother, and the education of his much younger brothers (his father left no estate).

Your group is unassociated with the project but has been asked to help in the decision making concerning the distribution of the $100,000. How would you distribute the money?

	Amount	Explanation (Why?)
Person A		
Person B		
Person C		
Person D		
Person E		
Person F		
Total =	$100,000	

Exercise 7.4: Acculturation

This activity is related to Begley's article on sojourner adaptation and will allow students to experience vicariously the process of acculturation. Using the information provided by Begley, students are to interview someone who has crossed cultural boundaries by entering the U.S. Depending on the diversity of the class, some students may be in the midst of the adaptation/acculturation process themselves. If so, these students may share their own personal experiences or they may choose to interview someone else. The idea is to make real for the students the dramatic and all-encompassing challenges of having to construct a new life in an unfamiliar place. Some of the following questions may be helpful when conducting the interview.

1. What things have you done to help deal with the high level of uncertainty and anxiety in moving to a new culture?
2. What cross-cultural challenges have you faced since moving to the U.S.?
3. Do you feel that your adaptation has been slow?
4. What do you miss most about your original culture?
5. Do you participate in a variety of social functions in the U.S.?
6. Are you in close contact with members of your own ethnicity here in the U.S.? How large is this group?
7. Do you maintain ties with your original culture? How often?
8. Do you feel the U.S. culture has been receptive and welcoming?
9. Do you feel pressure to conform to U.S. values, attitudes, and beliefs?
10. Do you speak English? Has this influenced your adaptation to the culture?
11. What changes have occurred in you as a person as a result of your moving here?
12. Do you feel these are positive changes?

Exercise 7.5: Intercultural Talk Journals

In order to understand how people from other cultures communicate interpersonally, it is useful to actually engage in conversations with them. But talking is only the first step. Having students actively reflecting on their experiences with culturally different people can help them make sense of what happened, allow them to assess what they have learned, and make changes in their communication. This activity is designed to give students more intercultural experiences and familiarity with other cultures.

Ask students to start a "talk" journal during the first weeks of the term. In this journal, they should describe the interactions they have with people from different cultures and record some of their perceptions and feelings experienced during these encounters. Students should be reminded that although people may share their ethnic background, they may also be members of other cultures. Women, gays and lesbians, people who are deaf or blind, physically challenged individuals, Jews, Mormons, and the elderly are just a sampling of individuals who belong to cultures that have their own distinct way of living and orientation to the world. Writing in their talk journals about conversations with members of these cultures would be appropriate (if they are members of any of these cultures, the journal may give them insight into their own cultural practices as well).

Encourage students to write in their journals at the end of every week. Their comments and observations should focus on some of the topics listed below. You may wish to collect the journals and respond to some of the students' comments. Be aware, however, that knowing you will be reading their journals may alter students' entries; some students may not even wish you to read their entries. After students have made several entries in their talk journals, ask them to answer the questions entitled "Post Talk Journal Questions." Have students share (if they wish) their talk journal entrees and what they learned from them in a small group or class discussion towards the end of the term.

Suggested Topics for Talk Journal Entries

1. The number of interpersonal contacts with people from cultures different from your own.
2. Where did you encounter people from different cultures?
3. Descriptions of the encounters.
4. How do the people you spoke with communicate? What is important in their lives?
5. How is their culture manifested in their behavior or communication?
6. Were your interpersonal contacts marked by any misunderstandings due to cultural differences? What were those misunderstandings?
7. What were some of the highlights of your conversations?
8. What were your personal reactions to being around people from different cultures?
9. How would you do things differently next time you talked with this person or another person from the same cultural background?

Post-Talk Journal Questions

1. What did you learn about how people from other cultures communicate and interact interpersonally?
2. What did you learn about yourself as an interpersonal communicator during intercultural interactions? What kinds of feelings arose for you as you talked with these people?
3. Describe one strength that you have as an intercultural communicator and one area for improvement.

Exercise 7.6: Metamessages and Intercultural Communication

This exercise is meant to be used with the articles by Begley and Chen & Starosta. Unless we tape record our conversations, it is almost impossible to hear how others hear us. We probably have more knowledge about the content of our speech than about our ways of speaking. It is possible to offend another person by the tone, volume, or even rate of our speech—and be oblivious to what we are communicating. While we traditionally think of conflicts between people as disagreements over ideology and perspective, conflicts can just as easily arise over how ideas are communicated. Such conflicts are based on the metamessages—messages about one's own communication—people send when they use a certain tone or way of speaking to communicate. Metamessages provide a frame or context for understanding the messages we send (Stewart & D'Angelo, 1988). Metamessages during intercultural communication can be easily misunderstood because interactants do not have the same frame or context with which to interpret the communication.

This case study focuses on how conflicts can arise between culturally different people because of how metamessages are communicated. Have students read Carmina's story below. As they are reading, ask them to think about times when others have communicated with them in similar ways and situations when they have sent metamessages that might have been perceived as offensive or condescending, or were misinterpreted by people who are from different cultural or ethnic backgrounds.

Case Study

Carmina works in an office with five other people. Ever since her supervisor hired her, Carmina has noticed that she talks much more slowly to her than to the native English speakers in the office. Carmina's first language is Spanish and she speaks flawless, accented English. Yet her supervisor still speaks to her using simple language at a markedly slow rate. No other person in the office speaks to Carmina in this way and two co-workers have even commented on the supervisor's annoying habit of speaking "special" English to her. It has become increasingly uncomfortable and offensive to talk with her supervisor, but Carmina isn't sure how to bring up the subject. After all, she is new to the office and doesn't want to cause any problems—especially between her supervisor and herself.

Questions for students to consider:

1. Write down some reasons why the supervisor was using "special" English with Carmina. What was she thinking? What might have been her intentions?
2. Why might speaking in this way be offensive to people? When would it be appropriate?
3. How might Carmina go about talking with her supervisor about this issue?
4. How could Carmina's co-workers help?
5. As a non-native speaker of another language, have you ever faced the situation that Carmina is experiencing? Have you ever communicated with a non-native speaker the way Carmina's supervisor did with her? Describe what happened in either situation.
6. Describe a situation when someone sent metamessages that you found condescending or disrespectful. What happened and how did you handle the situation?

7. How can we let someone know that we find the way they are speaking to us offensive? Write down a few strategies.

Chapter Popular Film Suggestions

- ***My Big Fat Greek Wedding*** (U.S., 2002; director: Joel Zwick; screenplay: Nia Vardalos; length: 1 hr 34 min). This film follows the blossoming of Toula, a Greek American, as she attempts to change her limited outlook on life as a waitress in her family's Greek restaurant. This film also deals with intergenerational conflicts brought about by the assimilation/acculturation of the children of Greek immigrants, this time in the U.S., whose Westernization culminates in the daughter falling in love with and marrying a young American male of European descent. Each side, including the respective families, has to learn to appreciate cultural differences and accommodate them in order for the happy ending to occur.
  Web Reference:
  My Big Fat Greek Wedding: A Film Review by James Berardinelli. http://movie-reviews.collossus.net/movies/m/my_big_fat.html

- ***Lost in Translation*** (2003; director and screenplay, Sofia Coppola; 1 hr 42 min) A great film showing the difficulty experienced by U.S. American sojourners to Japan; nicely illustrates many of the difficulties outlined in this chapter, especially Begley's article. Kenneth Tynan writes in The Los Angeles Times review of the movie that "As the title indicates, 'Lost in Translation' is a film about dislocations and disorientations. Informed by Coppola's own experiences in Tokyo (and magically shot by cinematographer Lance Acord), the film is very smart about national differences, about the strangeness of being in a place where you don't know the cultural markers. But that's only part of its success" (http://www.lost-in-translation.com/home.html).
  Web References:
  Lost in Translation, Offical Web Site. http://www.lost-in-translation.com/

Chapter Test Items

Multiple Choice

1. Which of the following is not a component of intercultural sensitivity?
   a. judgment *
   b. self-esteem
   c. self-monitoring
   d. interaction involvement

2. Intercultural awareness refers to which of the following?
   a. the cognitive aspect of intercultural communication
   b. understanding cultural conventions and how they affect behavior
   c. understanding cultural conventions and how they affect thought
   d. all of the above *

3. Which of the following is an advantage of role-based training in groups?
   a. it serves as a method of diagnosis
   b. it provides opportunities for observing a variety of ways to deal with problems
   c. it enables trainees to gain new insights that are important for cultural and self-understanding
   d. all of the above *

4. Individualistic conflict negotiators are more likely to attend to which of the following issues?
   a. objective, substantive issues *
   b. relational issues
   c. socioemotional issues
   d. issues of interpretation

5. In collectivistic, high-context cultures, third party mediators are likely to be
   a. impartial parties
   b. of lower status than the primary negotiators
   c. a professional mediator
   d. a person related to both parties of the dispute *

6. Which of the following statements is most accurate?
   a. Individualistic cultures are more likely than collectivistic cultures to operate on M-time. *
   b. Individualistic cultures are less likely than collectivistic cultures to operate on M-time.
   c. Individualistic cultures are more likely than collectivistic cultures to operate on P-time.
   d. There is no relationship between individualistic and collectivistic cultures and M- or P-time.

7. Individualistic, low-context cultures are more likely to value a conflict style that
   a. is indirect
   b. uses the equality norm
   c. uses the equity norm *
   d. reflects the salience of a "we" identity

8. Which of the following is necessary to engage in a "mindfulness" state in intercultural interaction?
   a. being open to old information
   b. awareness of multiple perspectives *
   c. reinforcing existing categories
   d. thinking before speaking

9. In Martin Buber's philosophy of dialogue, it is unacceptable for one person in a conflict to
   a. show acceptance of the other's point of view
   b. try to influence the other *
   c. let the other realize his/her potential
   d. a and c

10. Cipher-language, one of Karl Jasper's original achievements, refers to the idea that ciphers are a
   a. means of organizing ideas we want to keep from others in a conflict
   b. means of selecting symbols to represent issues in a conflict
   c. means of apprehending transcendent truth either by direct expression or through symbols *
   d. means of deconstructing an argument

11. In Hans-Georg Gadamer's view, prejudice
   a. means "prejudgment"
   b. can be positive or negative
   c. must be suspended in a communication
   d. all of the above *

12. In Jürgen Habermas' "Ideal Speech Situation," which of the following would not be allowed:
   a. everyone is allowed to introduce any assertion into the discourse
   b. a speaker cannot contradict herself *
   c. everyone can question any assertion
   d. a speaker can only assert what he believes

13. Which one of the following is NOT one of the challenges of cross-cultural adaptation mentioned by Begley?
   a. ethnocentrism
   b. loneliness *
   c. disequalibrium
   d. level of knowledge

14. Experiencing emotional "lows" of uncertainty when one has crossed into another culture is identified by Begley as
   a. ethnocentrism
   b. cross-cultural depression
   c. disequilibrium *
   d. stagnation

15. Two words that capture the antithesis of ethnocentrism are:
   a. kindness and patience
   b. liberal and receptive
   c. tolerant and progressive
   d. openness and flexibility *

16. Which of the following is NOT one of the suggestions provided by Begley for successful cross-cultural adaptation?
   a. frequency of time spent communicating
   b. cultural background *
   c. personal determination
   d. personality characteristics

True/False

T 1. Intercultural awareness is the cognitive perspective of intercultural communication.

T 2. Intercultural awareness requires individuals to understand that they are cultural beings.

T 3. Intercultural awareness and sensitivity are the prerequisites for intercultural competence.

T 4. Reciprocal determinism means that person variables, situation variables, and behavior continuously interact with one another.

T 5. No one culture exists exclusively at one extreme of the communication context continuum.

F 6. M-time cultures tend to view time as more contextually based and relationally oriented.

T 7. Every intercultural conflict consists of both substantive and relational issues.

T	8.	The higher a person is in positional power in a collectivist culture, the more likely he or she will use silence as a deliberate, cautionary conflict strategy.
F	9.	Listening is synonymous with hearing.
T	10.	Avoiding conflict does not always mean that collectivists do not care about conflict.
F	11.	Admitting bias means perpetuating bias.
F	12.	One's personality is not a factor in whether or not one is able to successfully adapt to another culture.
F	13.	Language is usually not a major challenge in cross-cultural adaptation as long as the individual really wants to adapt.
T	14.	External factors influencing one's personal determination to successfully adapt to another culture include the length of stay in the host culture.
F	15.	Acquiring a broad base of knowledge about cultural differences is less effective for cross-cultural adaptation than to learn specific details about a culture one is about to visit.

Chapter Essay Questions

1. Chen and Starosta claim that intercultural sensitivity enhances intercultural effectiveness. What do they mean by this? What would effectiveness include? Does it refer solely to overt success in the business world? To what else might it apply?
2. Define and explain the relationships between each of the following: intercultural awareness, sensitivity, and competence.
3. What do they mean when Chen and Starosta say that intercultural awareness necessitates that people understand themselves (not just others) as cultural beings? What are the implications of understanding oneself as a cultural being as opposed to a being that just appeared out of nowhere? What is the relationship between cultural awareness and a sense of history?
4. How does Ting-Toomey define intercultural conflict?
5. Differentiate between "independent construal of self" and "interdependent construal of self."
6. Compare and contrast the value tendencies of individualism and collectivism.
7. What is the relationship between "in-groups" and "out-groups" and the individualism-collectivism dimension of value tendencies?
8. What is the relationship between low- and high-context cultures and cultures that are primarily individualistic or collectivistic with regard to approaches to conflict?
9. Describe the concept of "face" and its importance to understanding and engaging in intercultural conflict.
10. Identify three central issues for conflict in both individualistic, low-context cultures and collectivistic, high-context cultures.
11. Differentiate between the role of third party intervention in individualistic, low-context cultures and collectivistic, high-context cultures.
12. Describe the concept of "mindfulness" and its relevance to managing intercultural conflicts.

13. According to Gadamer, what is the major distinction between appropriate questions and rhetorical questions?
14. Choose two of Begley's suggestions for successful cross-cultural adaptation and use your own cross-cultural experience to support them. Demonstrate how you applied these suggestions in a cross-cultural environment.
15. Using Begley's article, respond to the following statement: Learning a culture's language is only one step in the cross-cultural adaptation process.
16. Describe what Begley refers to as the *external* and *internal* factors involved in one's personal determination to successfully adapt to another culture.

Chapter References

Brislin, R. W. (1994). *Individualism and collectivism as the source of many specific cultural differences.* In R. W. Brislin & T. Yoshida (Eds.), *Improving intercultural interactions: Modules for cross-cultural training.* London: Sage Publications.

Stewart, J., & D'Angelo, G. (1988). *Together: Communication interpersonally.* (3rd ed.). New York: Random House.

Chapter 8 Ethical Considerations: Prospects for the Future

Chapter Synopsis

This chapter explores the issue of ethics and intercultural communication. The five essays in this chapter touch on ethical and philosophical considerations when members of diverse cultures must live together. This chapter offers various perspectives on developing and improving intercultural communication so that diverse cultures can live together without destroying each other.

Thomas Sowell, in "Cultural Diversity: A World View," discusses the strong sociopolitical resistance to accepting the reality of different levels and kinds of skills, interests, habits, and orientations among different groups of people. He supports his position by examining immigration patterns of adaptation in the U.S.

In "The Limits of Cultural Diversity," Harlan Cleveland introduces students to the ethics and philosophical assumptions surrounding intercultural communication. Instead of fear and tribal loyalties, he advocates "civilization" as universal values, ideas, and practices that are accepted as useful everywhere in order to form a global civil society.

Young Yun Kim, in "Intercultural Personhood: An Integration of Eastern and Western Perspectives," proposes that becoming intercultural persons with intercultural personhood is essential in order for different cultures and countries to get along.

Sam Dragga's essay, "Ethical Intercultural Technical Communication: Looking through the Lens of Confucian Ethics," looks at the problems ensuing when technical communicators find themselves in a multicultural, intercultural situation where there is little guidance to identify ethical practices in intercultural technical communication.

In "Business Ethics and Intercultural Communication: Exploring the Overlap Between Two Academic Fields," Johannes Brinkmann introduces basic ethical definitions through classic case examples. He concludes with a list of ten theses that summarize the use of ethical communications in intercultural business communication.

Chapter Outline

Cultural Diversity: A World View

- Two ways of talking about diversity for Sowell: the stultifying and, in his view harmful, idea of preserving a culture through ideological and political practices, and the way her prefers—diversity as the historic sharing of cultural advances to improve the human race
- Sowell argues that different is, in many cases, *better* and that is why people have, through exposure of ideas and inventions from other cultures, dropped their own

methods in favor of the cultural advanced methods of doing things; examples include:

- Paper and printing, vital to Western civilization (using books is *better* than using scrolls), originated in China, as did the magnetic compass, which enabled the great ages of Western exploration
- Mathematical concepts migrated from other cultures—trigonometry from ancient Egypt
- Our whole numbering system from the Hindus of India (mistakenly called Arabic numerals because obtained first through Arab intermediaries though origin in India)—using numerals is *better* than using old system of Roman numerals
- Chess from India, gunpowder from China, mathematical concepts from Islamic world

- For Sowell, "Cultural competition is not a zero-sum game. It is what advances the human race" (399).
- Sowell argues that groups, or cultures, excel in their own special occupations and industries, regardless of where they live; examples:
  - Germans have been prominent piano makers (in America, Russia, Australia, France, and England)
  - Chinese immigrants have run more than half the grocery stores in Kingston, Jamaica, and Panama City and conducted more than half of all retail trade in Malaysia, the Philippines, Vietnam, and Cambodia
- Sowell contends that "Nothing has been more common than for particular groups—often a minority—to dominate particular occupations or industries" (400). Many examples are given.
- Sowell supports his argument about diversity by discussing how persistent cultural differences can be seen in immigration patterns:
  - Jewish immigrants from Eastern Europe and Italian immigrants arrived at same time, lived in same neighborhoods, attended schools, yet, despite virtually identical environment, have very different social histories
  - Same patterns seen in Argentina, Australia, Canada, or Western Europe
  - His point: "They were different before they got on the boats to cross the ocean, and those differences crossed the ocean with them" (401).
- Sowell raises questions: What is the purpose of culture?
  - Why cultures exist: To serve the vital, practical requirements of human life
  - To structure a society so as to perpetuate the species
  - To pass on hard-learned knowledge and experience of past generations
  - Sowell: "Cultures are not bumper stickers. They are living, changing ways of doing all the things that have to be done in life" (404).

The Limits to Cultural Diversity

An Excess of Cultural Identity

- Societies based on fear of outsiders tend toward "totalitarian" governance

- When fear drives people to hold onto to their traditional culture, it is harder for them to learn to be tolerant of others who may be guided by different faiths and loyalties
- Cultures keep redefining themselves by mixing with other cultures
- Cleveland argues that the problem is cultural overenthusiasm—what's needed is counterforce of wider views, global perspectives, and more universal ideas

Culture and Civilization

- Fuzzy concept that culture is synonym of civilization
- New concept: civilization is what is universal—values, ideas, and practices that are in general currency everywhere
- Thus culture is the substance and symbols of the community; it meets the basic human need for a sense of belonging

Lessons from American Experience

- "Diversity cannot be governed by drowning it in 'integration'" (407).
- Waves of new Americans learned to tolerate one another, first as groups, then as individuals
- They learned that all men are brothers and that all brothers are different—that "equality is not the product of similarity; it is the cheerful acknowledgment of difference" (407).
- Cleveland posits this "cheerful acknowledgment of difference" as the alternative to a global spread of ethnic cleansing and religious rivalry

Intercultural Personhood: An Integration of Eastern and Western Perspectives

- Kim proposes the concept of *intercultural personhood*—a kind of self-other orientation that is open to growth
- His conception based on readings about an international cultural ideal drawn from differing Eastern and Western cultural ideals

Eastern and Western Cultural Traditions

- Universe and Nature—notion of impermanence of all forms and the appreciation of the aliveness of the universe in the Eastern worldview contrasts with the Western emphasis on the definitive forms of physical reality and their improvement through social and material progress
- Knowledge—Eastern cultural drive for human development is aimed at spiritual attainment of oneness with the universe; the Western cultural drive finds its expression in its drive for material and social progress
- Time—Eastern polychronic time orientation is rooted in synchronization of human behavior with the rhythms of nature; the Western tie prientation is driven by the synchronization of human behavior with the rhythms of the clock or machine
- Communication—Hall depicted Asian cultures as high-context and Western cultures as low-context

Beyond Cultural Differences

Potential benefits of incorporating Eastern views into the West:

- Heightened sense of freedom

- Greater awareness of the aliveness and wholeness of the universe
- Increased sensitivity to rhythms of nature
- A way to bridge the gap between groups and individuals

Emergence of Intercultural Personhood

Identity Transformation—direct function of dramatically increasing intercultural communication activities

Ethical Intercultural Technical Communication: Looking Through the Lens of Confucian Ethics

Americans and Chinese come to the subject of ethics from different perspectives

Unless we develop a comprehensive understanding of such differences, effective and ethical communication is unlikely to occur

The Chinese Philosophical Tradition

- Primarily Confucian or Neo-Confucian
- Chinese philosophy is almost always a practical vehicle for self-realization or self-cultivation
- Human beings considered capable of attaining perfection without divine intervention within a process that proceeds from perfection of the individual to perfection of the world, from personal improvement to social and political efficacy

The Ethics of Confucius

- **Goodness**
- Most important of the virtues; ethical individuals desire for others that which they desire for themselves, treating others as they would like others to treat them
- To do business in China, requires the ethical positioning of oneself as a friend instead of a stranger; initial attention focused on establishing a personal relationship
- Goodness inextricably linked to food in China
- Negative effect of goodness on Chinese: ethical obligations to parents and grandparents lead to respect for age and seniority over intelligence, initiative, and ingenuity, creating more conservative society
- **Righteousness**
- Refers to consistently doing the right thing, choosing morality over profit or success
- Inspires the rituals, the 300 major rules and 3,000 minor rules regarding appropriate behavior
- According to Confucius, superior human beings are motivated by righteousness and inferior people by profit—encourages a denigration of business people and a veneration of the political and academic professions
- Greed, self-promotion seen as unethical; compliments met with denial
- Negative impact of righteousness on Chinese: possibility of blind obedience; denigration of business has potential of driving ethical people from business and leaving it to the unscrupulous
- **Wisdom**
- Key to self-improvement

- Achieved through learning, with schooling considered superior to experience
- Formal education and degrees thus offer higher level of authority and credibility
- Education has more to do with cultivation of morality than with acquisition of knowledge
- Most critical wisdom is knowledge of people, i.e., being a good judge of character
- Humanities favored over science and engineering
- Negative side: equating education and moral superiority, and privileging of humanities has potential to divert creativity and ingenuity to artistic purposes and thus slow scientific and technological progress
- **Faithfulness**
- Matching one's words with one's deeds, thus establishing both credibility and reliability
- In business negotiations, Chinese will ordinarily resist making promises or commitments, especially in absence of previous or existing relationship
- Eloquence distrusted
- Risk to Chinese society: passivity
- **Reverence**
- Moral alertness or awareness of one's social responsibilities and a sincere devotion to discharging them
- Self-cultivation through schooling is individual's necessary contribution to his or her community
- Service to family, friends, supervisors, and officials inspires highest levels of dedication and diligence
- Negative impact: devotion to social duties could lead to deleterious single-mindedness and servility
- **Courage**
- Self-sacrifice in the pursuit of goodness; only a virtue if the individual is also guided by righteousness
- Allows Chinese to shield family and friends from dangerous foreigners and inhibits aggressive international exploits, but also has potential to reinforce parochial and isolationist attitudes and policies

Ethical Analysis of Intercultural Communication

- Based on case study of Kellogg's Coco Pops, looks at persuasion, instruction, and education

The Lens of Ethics

- Provides vital perspective for technical communicators

Business Ethics and Intercultural Communication: Exploring the Overlap Between Two Academic Fields

Cross-Cultural Business Ethics: Classic Cases and Important Issues

- The Nestlé Infant Formula marketing case
- The Union Carbide incident in Bhopal, India
- Participation of ITT and other U.S. companies in overthrow of Allende government in Chile
- Companies doing business in South Africa during the apartheid period

- Issue of birth control
- Human rights violations in a country wherein a multinational company is doing business
- Child labor
- Gift giving
- Respect for faith and beliefs and principles of free expression in marketing such works as Rushdie's *Satanic Verses*
- Northern Norwegian tradition of minke whaling

Issue Categories for Cases

- Health, environment, and safety (local versus global standards)
- International marketing issues, including bribery
- Multinational company size, power, and responsibility
- Code of conduct development
- Outsourcing, slave, and child labor
- Arms trade
- Co-responsibility for human rights violation
- Interference with political stability and self-determination
- Non-ethnocentric handling of norm and value diversity

Cultural and Ethical Relativism

- Cultural relativism is a worldview and standpoint that no culture is superior to any other one
- Ethical relativism is a worldview and standpoint that claims that there is no culture-free, universal morality and therefore no way of ranking moral views and practices as more or less right, at least across cultures
- Both positions have been criticized as extreme positions, but at the same time widely used as basic labels of theoretical orientation
- What is needed is an intercultural moral consensus about an ethical minimum

The Individual-Level Ideal: Open-Mindedness and Moral Integrity

- In education or recruitment situations, cultural and ethical relativism turns into a question of individual attitudes and capabilities and how such qualities can be assessed. Three examples of assessment models:
- Koester and Olebe's Behavioral Scale for Intercultural Competence (BASIC) focuses on intercultural open-mindedness using eight categories
- Bennett's Developmental Model of Intercultural Sensitivity (DMIS) suggests there is a learning process assumption from lower to higher stages
- Kohlberg's model is concerned with individual moral maturity development and assessment—a continuum of cultural-moral opportunism

Dialectics of Cultural and Ethical Relativism

- Cultural and ethical relativism are different but interdependent—one can accept a culture on its own premises without accepting it, and one can accept it without understanding it

Chapter Discussion Ideas

1. How does Sowell's treatment of the notion of diversity differ from the general usage in the U.S. today?
2. What role does geography play in developing diversity among groups?
3. Explain Cleveland's concept of civilization. Are universal laws and rules possible? Why or why not?
4. How do we adopt Kim's notion of intercultural personhood? What characteristics do we include in this concept? Which do we exclude?
5. Why does Dragga believe if necessary to unite the fields of business ethics and intercultural communication? Why is it important to include education in an intercultural marketing campaign?
6. Explain why Dragga believed Confucian ethics would be a proper model for intercultural ethics. How does the Confucian principle of faithfulness relate to intercultural business negotiations?
7. In the classic case of the Nestlé Infant Formula, what do you believe should have been the proper intercultural message to send to mothers about the risks involved in using the product?
8. How do you feel about U.S. companies doing business in other cultures engaging in gift giving or bribery if that is the custom of that culture?

Chapter Exercises

Exercise 8.1: Cultural Universals

This activity can be used with Cleveland's article on cultural diversity and asks the students to think seriously about the growing diversity in the United States as well as the idea of "wholeness incorporating diversity." Divide students into small groups and have them reread the following excerpt from Cleveland's article:

> ... *civilization* is what's universal—values, ideas, and practices that are in general currency everywhere, either because they are viewed as objectively "true" or because they are accepted pragmatically as useful in the existing circumstances. These accepted "truths" offer the promise of weaving together a *civitas* of universal laws and rules, becoming the basis for a global civil society. (p. 406)

After reading the excerpt, have students make a list of laws, rules, or practices that are generally accepted on a universal basis. (Cleveland offers, as one example, the international exchange of money). Groups must be prepared to defend the universality of these items. Additionally, have the groups create a list of laws, rules, and practices that they believe would contribute to pluralism if they were universal. Again, groups must support and defend their answers. When the groups have completed their lists, write on the board those laws, rules, and practices that were common among all groups. Have the students discuss the reality of these ideas being enacted and their effect on individual communities, the U.S., and the world.

Exercise 8.2: The East-West Game

This activity is an accompaniment for Kim's article on intercultural personhood or combining key attributes of the East and West. The East-West Game was originally entitled "The Emperor's Pot" and first developed by Donald Batchelder of Experiment in International Living (Hoopes & Ventura, 1979). It simulates a negotiation session between two very different cultures. By taking part in this intercultural negotiation session, students will be able to test their ability to communicate with a culture that thinks and behaves in very different ways. The problems that often occur during intercultural communication will also be illustrated.

This activity is most useful when conducted over two or three class sessions. The exercise has been adapted to accommodate the university classroom and allow all participants to either watch or take part in the entire process. There are four phases in the activity:

Phase I:	Students are divided into two groups and given time to "adopt" their new culture and plan their negotiation session.
Phase II:	The class regroups and the negotiations begin.
Phase III:	East and West meet in their own groups to discuss what happened.
Phase IV:	class discussion. (Phase III can be left out if there is a time constraint.)

The negotiations center on a highly coveted cultural artifact that the East has and the West wants. The West has come to the East to negotiate for the artifact. The handouts on the next two pages provide each team with instructions for the activity.

Questions to stimulate discussion during the debriefing afterward:

1. What cultural traits characterized your culture?
2. What traits did you notice in the other culture?
3. How difficult was it to put on another culture?
4. How did your own individual and cultural traits prevent you from fully adopting the East or West culture?
5. How did you plan your approach to the negotiations?
6. Did you attempt to determine how the other side might behave?
7. Were your assumptions correct?
8. Did you notice any differences in nonverbal behavior between the two groups? The use of verbal language?
9. During the negotiations, when did you first notice that there might be a problem?
10. What barriers caused this problem?
11. Was this barrier broken and productive negotiations allowed to continue?
12. What strategies were used to be culturally sensitive?
13. What strategies were used to get the artifact or keep it from the other team?
14. How could the negotiations have been more successful?

Exercise 8.2: The East-West Game (Hoopes & Ventura, 1979)

Instructions for the East

Your group represents an ancient Eastern culture that, although poor, is very proud of its long history and heritage.You have a highly treasured artifact that is as old as 400 AD. It is *the* national treasure and culturally you cannot give it up. The West wants this artifact and has been strongly pressured to return with it. (You may wish to identify a single behavior demonstrated by the West that will win them the artifact.)

What complicates these negotiations is that you come from a culture that is very agreeable, polite, and always seeking to answer in the affirmative whether you mean "yes" or not. You never state anything as flatly negative during negotiation sessions. You never tell your opposing team that they will never get the artifact. Sometimes you may stop the negotiations to talk amongst yourselves. You always seem to agree and go along with the other team because offending another party might result in the other losing face

You do not use strong, direct eye contact. You occasionally look them in the eye but never for prolonged periods of time nor with any degree of intensity. Using mediation is common in your culture. For example, although the Chief Spokesman may do a lot of the talking, he will very often ask his team members what they think. He will often allow other members to speak and carry on the negotiations with the other side.

Before meeting the other team, look at the following list of roles and cultural traits. Decide who will have each role, adopt the cultural traits that govern your culture, and choose an approach you will take in the negotiations.

Roles:

Chief Spokesman, Minister of Education and Culture, Security Officer, Political Officer, Protocol Officer, Information Officer, Recorder (to list all the assumptions, values, etc., of other side), Time-keeper (to keep each phase exactly on schedule), GOD (Group Organizational Director—the overall organizer of the East Team), Most Honored Grandmother, Spokesman (most honored), Advisors, and all others.

Cultural Traits:

"We": the group is most highly valued, not the individual; individual always in social role; cannot do anything to conflict with group.

Form: Outward form is most important. Manners extremely important, must participate in activities considered important by group, even if one disagrees.

Nature: Conformity to the rules of nature is best.

Progress: Change is both negative and positive. Technical change necessary; social change bad.

Efficiency: Considered less important than higher values such as form, saving face, conformity to custom.

Time: Not precisely measured, not primary consideration. Present, not future, given priority.

Humility: Related to one's social status. One never takes advantage of one's rank. One must always defer to one of higher social rank, must always try to appear humble.

Money: Saving for the sake of saving is seldom considered a virtue. Price is regarded as an index of quality.

Age: Great reverence for age. Age means wisdom and certain privileges. Honorific titles are always used when addressing an elder. Person of higher rank must attempt to defer to and honor special inferiors.

Education: Highly valued. Means of raising whole family's status.

Authority: Obedience to authority; individual rights mean little.

Moral Superiority: A moral smugness that stems from a conviction that East people are a special people with a set of values and conditions that make them unique.

Exercise 8.2: The East-West Game (Hoopes & Ventura, 1979)

Instructions for the West

Your group represents a Western culture that is rich and powerful. There is a highly treasured artifact in the possession of the East that is a highly valued part of their heritage. They are a poor country but will be very reluctant to give up the artifact. Your national museum and your government have strongly urged you to get the artifact at any cost. Money is no problem. You cannot come out and say that you will get the artifact at any cost because the East is world renowned as shrewd traders. But you believe that every person has his/her price.

Culturally, you feel it is important to try to figure out the strategies acceptable to the other side so that you can enter and progress through the negotiations smoothly. But you should always try to stay within the cultural traits listed below. You are success-oriented, hard-working, efficient, future-oriented, and you use time productively. You like to move things along.

Before meeting the other team, look at the following list of roles and cultural traits. Decide who will have each role, adopt the cultural traits that govern your culture, and choose an approach you will take in the negotiations.

Roles:

Curator of National Museum (expert on Oriental Art); Millionaire (major donator of museum); Diplomatic Officer; Public Relations man or woman; CIA agent posing as an Area Studies Specialist; Journalist; Chief of your task-group (forceful administrator); Recorder—to list all assumptions, values, etc., of other side; Time-keeper—to keep each phase of exercise exactly on schedule; GOD (Group Organizational Director)—the overall organizer of the West team; Advisors; all others.

Cultural Traits:

"I": Ego-centric.

Individualism: Self-reliance and initiative expected from other side. Status achieved from own efforts. Achievement is good and requires competitiveness. Competition is expected.

Social Conformity: Outward conformity to opinions of others has certain value.

Activism: Being active and "on top of things," especially when uncertain, is a virtue. Achievement and goal-oriented activities stressed.

Pragmatism: Practical ingenuity applied to social and materialistic problems.

Progress: Change in itself is good. Humans must work to control nature.

Efficiency: Social organizations and individuals must be efficient.

Time: Precisely measured and must be used productively and efficiently.

Aggressiveness: Ambition, competition, and self-assertiveness to achieve success are emphasized.

Money: An economic tool and yardstick for social status, influence, power, satisfaction.

Youth: Highly valued. Old people wish they were young again.

Education: Means to an end. Reflection on family prestige. Means to attain skill, money, status.

Authority: Rules/laws generally obeyed, but don't like to be ordered to obey. Authority must not infringe on individual rights.

Moral Superiority: A moral smugness that stems from a conviction that West people are a special people with a set of values and conditions that make them unique.

Exercise 8.3: What if ...

We know that how we react to people is based on how we perceive them and their actions. Our world is based on our perceptions of others and their perceptions of us. Oftentimes, these perceptions are not based on personal information about others as individuals but on cultural information gleaned from the media, family, and friends. That is, we use previously gathered information from a variety of sources to perceive and understand new people that we meet.

Ask students to imagine developing a relationship (platonic or romantic) with individuals who hold each given perception of the world below. This exercise can be conducted in small groups or as an individual in-class or out-of-class assignment. Some questions to ask students during a large class discussion are: How might a certain belief affect your relationship with this imaginary person? Does your perception of the world fit or complement your friend's or partner's? Or are your perceptions diametrically at odds? How can we communicate and develop intercultural relationships when our worldviews can oftentimes be so different? What must we consider as you attempt to communicate with people who do not share your worldview?

HOW MIGHT YOUR RELATIONSHIP BE AFFECTED IF . . .

1. . . . your spouse believed in reincarnation and karma?
2. . . . your friend believed that all events in the world are determined by Fate?
3. . . . your friend believed that certain ethnic or racial groups are intellectually inferior?
4. . . . your significant other believed that women are superior to men? That men were superior to women?
5. . . . your roommates believed that the rights of groups are more important than those of the individual? The rights of the individual are more important than those of the group?
6. . . . a new friend believed adamantly that homosexuality is immoral and should not be accepted by society as normal? That homosexuality is moral and should be accepted?
7. . . . your neighbor believed in using only traditional medicine and spiritual healing whenever she or her family became ill?

Exercise 8.4: "Mom and Dad, Guess What....?"

Students may experience or have experienced forming an intimate relationship with someone of whom their family and friends disapproved, or may have a friend or relative who has had this experience. Such situations often occur because our family and friends have certain expectations about who is an appropriate dating or marriage partner. These expectations are firmly entrenched in our perceptions of people who are different from us and in cultural norms of relationship development and sexual behavior. Our families can have a profound impact on the development and success of our romantic relationships.

The following exercise asks students to imagine that they have developed certain relationships of which their parents may not approve and that they are coming home to talk with them about their decision. The goal of this exercise is threefold. First, it will allow students to consider how their parents might react to the news that they are about to marry someone of a different political belief, religion, or ethnicity, or of the same sex. In addition, this exercise will allow them to think about how they might react as a parent to their own child's news of such a marriage. Finally, we have designed this exercise to offer valuable insight into how attitudes toward nontraditional marriages have changed in the past three decades.

Ask students to role-play with another classmate the following scenes. They are to take on the role of their parents and the role of themselves as parents.

Your Parents

Think about your parents' attitudes about marriage, relationships, and cultural differences. How would they react if you told them you were going to marry someone who:

1. had a disability?
2. was of a different religion?
3. was of a different ethnicity?
4. was of the same sex?

We realize that you cannot truly know how your parents would react (unless you have seen their reactions to one or more of these situations) but try to imagine how they would respond given your understanding of who they are and their belief systems.

You as a Parent

Now take on the role of the parent. How would you react if your child told you he or she was going to marry someone . . . .

1. who had a disability? Why would you react this way?
2. was of a different religion? Why would you react this way?
3. was of a different ethnicity? Why would you react this way?
4. was of the same sex? Why would you react this way?

We realize that unless you are a parent, you probably do not know how you would react to your child given these circumstances. Again, try to imagine given your present belief and value systems.

Analysis of Your Responses

1. What differences do you see between your responses and what you believe would be your parents' responses?
2. What is acceptable today that was not in the 1970s, 1980s, or 1990s? What attitudes have largely not changed very much at all?
3. How might a family be affected by nontraditional and intercultural marriages?
4. Have you or a member of your family ever entered into a marriage with someone who was culturally different or different from what was "expected"? If so, describe how people reacted to this new family member.

Chapter Popular Film Suggestions

The following films look at conflicting cultures in ways that illustrate the principles outlined in this chapter of what it takes for different cultures to live and work together peacefully through intercultural understanding.

- ***Wedding in Galilee*** (Israel, 1985; director, Michel Khleifi; 113 min.; Arabic and Hebrew with English subtitles)
  Story of marriage, tradition, and national identity told from an Arab point of view. "The elder of a Palestinian village under Israeli military rule wants permission to hold a traditional wedding for his son that will go past the imposed curfew. The Army commander agrees on the condition that he and his officers be invited as guests of honor at the ceremony. . . . [an] often compelling meditation on two conflicting cultures who attempt to put aside their differences for one long day of celebration" (http://store.yahoo.com/ollivefilms/weingrad.html).
  Web References
  Olive Films. *Wedding in Galilee.* http://store.yahoo.com/ollivefilms/weingrad.html
  Aufderheide, P. *Wedding in Galilee.* (1992) Cross-Cultural Film Guide. http://www.library.american.edu/subject/media/aufderheide/wedding.html

- ***James' Journey to Jerusalem*** (2003; director, Ra'anan Alexandrowicz; 87 min.; English, Zulu & Hebrew w/ English subtitles)
  "A cannily droll mix of social commentary and modern fairy tale, Israeli filmmaker Ra'anan Alexandrowicz's debut feature follows the adventures of James, a devout Christian making a pilgrimage from his African village to the Holy Land. He becomes part of the migrant labor workforce in Tel Aviv and pursues his religious quest—until he gets a little taste of fortune by turning the tables on his employers. With a moving and charismatic performance by South African actor Siyabonga Melongisi Shibe, James' Journey to Jerusalem is an astute exploration of the economic, moral and spiritual hypocrisies of Western society filtered through an evocative portrait of modern Israel's cultural and generational divisions" (http://store.yahoo.com/olivefilms/jajotojed.html).

Web References

Olive Films. *James' Journey to Jerusalem.* http://store.yahoo.com/olivefilms/jajotojed.html

James' Journey to Jerusalem—Film Review. http://www.james-journey.com/press281003.asp

Chapter Test Items

Multiple Choice

1. According to Sowell, cultures adopt the inventions or practices of other cultures when they are
   a. better than their own *
   b. forced by their governments to adopt them
   c. destitute
   d. indecisive about what to do

2. The game of chess was invented in
   a. China
   b. Russia
   c. India *
   d. Spain

3. Our numbering system originated among
   a. the Arabs
   b. the Chinese
   c. the Greeks
   d. the Hindus *

4. German immigrants, regardless of where in the world they have settled, have been renowned for their
   a. wine making
   b. beer brewing *
   c. candy making
   d. cloth making

5. During World War II, the Japanese who had immigrated to Brazil were loyal to
   a. America
   b. Japan *
   c. Brazil
   d. none of the above

6. Sowell argues that the continent of Africa is less urbanized than Western Europe because it lacks
   a. waterways *
   b. long rainy seasons
   c. a homogeneous culture
   d. a shared language

7. What factor does Cleveland identify as a primary incentive for people to develop multiple personalities with plural group loyalties?
   a. This is a more mobile world as evidenced by the fact that in 1994 more people moved than ever before in world history. *
   b. Fear has caused people to become loyal to only one group.
   c. Political structures are being questioned.
   d. None of the above.

8. According to Cleveland, two major impediments to better standards of life and freedom for all are
   a. technology and class differences
   b. human rights and poverty
   c. culture and diversity *
   d. diversity and human rights

9. In the East, according to Cleveland, a concept understood through ____ is one of complete meaning and immediately experienced, apprehended, and contemplated.
   a. analysis
   b. emotion
   c. spiritualism
   d. intuition *

10. What does the term "undifferentiated" mean in terms of Eastern philosophy and consciousness?
   a. wholeness *
   b. uniqueness
   c. distinctness
   d. serenity

11. The relationship of the views of East and West can best be described as
   a. competing
   b. antagonistic
   c. complementary *
   d. dualistic

12. Western thought tends to equate logic with

   a. necessity
   b. truth *
   c. progress
   d. correctness

13. Which of the following is/are considered path(s) to enlightenment in Hindu thought?

   a. emotion *
   b. reason
   c. pragmatic connections
   d. both a and c

14. In Confucian ethics, the most important of the virtues is

   a. righteousness
   b. goodness *
   c. reverence
   d. faithfulness

15. In Confucian ethics, righteousness inspires

   a. morality over profit
   b. the 300 major rules and 3,000 minor rules regarding appropriate behavior
   c. the denial of compliments
   d. all of the above *

16. In Confucian ethics, it is considered courageous

   a. for employees to criticize their employer if motivation is to benefit the company
   b. to dare to establish new relationships
   c. to shield family and friends from dangerous foreigners
   d. a and c *

17. Cultural relativism is a worldview that holds that

   a. obvious empirical differences of moral beliefs and practices do not prove that they are all right
   b. no culture is superior to any other one *
   c. disagreement about judgments does not necessarily prove disagreement about the principles on which such judgments are based
   d. there is no culture-free, universal morality

18. Ethical relativism holds that
    a. there is no culture-free, universal morality *
    b. ethics should be based upon theory
    c. no culture is superior to any other one
    d. there are no valid moral beliefs

True/False

T 1. Trigonometry came from ancient Egypt.

F 2. Paper and printing came from India.

T 3. By the early 16th century, the sultan of the Ottoman Empire had on his palace medical staff 42 Jewish physicians and 21 Muslim physicians.

F 4. In the U.S., Japanese immigrants were interned because they were loyal to Japan.

T 5. The Japanese who immigrated to Brazil own approximately three-quarters as much land in Brazil as there is in Japan.

T 6. According to Cleveland, the "civilization" construct will work because nobody is in charge of practices that are generally accepted.

F 7. Traditions of separateness and discrimination are always permanent and immutable.

F 8. In earlier times, the waves of new Americans learned to tolerate each other as individuals and then as groups.

T 9 According to Kim, the Western view of the world is characteristically dualistic, materialistic, and lifeless.

T 10. In the East, a virtuous person is not one who only strives for the "good" and eliminates the "bad" but one who strives for a balance between the two.

F 11. The Western perception of time is best represented as a wheel that is continually turning.

F 12. Explicit and clear verbalization best characterizes the Eastern way of communicating.

T 13. The West is concerned more than the East with building greater ego strength.

T 14. In China, red is the color of good luck.

F 15. In marketing its cereal to the Chinese, Kellogg is making an ethical claim when it instructs the Chinese on its cereal box to add milk to the Coco Pops before eating them.

T 16. Individuals with whom Chinese people have an existing relationship will usually be preferred to those who are strangers.

F 17. In Confucian ethics, it is considered moral to put oneself before the obligations of family and friends.

Chapter Essay Questions

1. How does Sowell's treatment of the notion of diversity differ from the general usage in the United States today?
2. What role does geography play in developing diversity among groups?
3. Identify some of the reasons Cleveland believes the U.S. is moving toward pluralism.
4. How do Eastern and Western peoples view the relationship of nature and humans?
5. What is the differentiated aesthetic continuum?
6. How do Western and Eastern peoples traditionally conceptualize knowledge?
7. How do the East and West perceive time differently?
8. How do Eastern and Western views of relationships, groups, and the self differ?
9. How does one communicate one's feelings in Eastern and Western culture.
10. Describe how our lives demand both scientific and aesthetic modes of apprehension.
11. What are the benefits of incorporating an Eastern aesthetic orientation into Western life?
12. What is "intercultural personhood" and how and why should we strive to attain it?
13. What is the Confucian concept of goodness and how does it apply to intercultural communication?
14. How did Kellogg Company use "persuasion" as a tool in marketing Coco Pops to a Chinese consumer base?
15. What does Brinkmann mean by the term *cultural and ethical relativism*?
16. How does Brinkmann distinguish between ethics and morality?

Chapter References

Hoopes, D. S., and Ventura, P. (Eds.). (1979). *Intercultural sourcebook: Cross-cultural training methodologies*. LaGrange Park, IL: Intercultural Network.